REVELATION

REVELATION

$\blacklozenge$

H. A. IRONSIDE

Revised Edition

Introductory Notes by
John Phillips

LOIZEAUX
Neptune, New Jersey

First Edition, 1920
Revised Edition, 1996

REVELATION
© 1996 by Loizeaux Brothers

A Publication of Loizeaux Brothers, Inc.
*A Nonprofit Organization Devoted to the Lord's Work
and to the Spread of His Truth*

Unless otherwise indicated, Scriptures quotations are
taken from the King James version of the Bible.

Profile taken from *Exploring the Scriptures*
© 1965, 1970, 1989 by John Phillips.

Library of Congress Cataloging-in-Publication Data

Ironside, H. A. (Henry Allan), 1876-1951.
Revelation / H. A. Ironside: introductory notes by John Phillips.
—Rev. ed.
Rev. ed. of: Lectures on the book of Revelation.
ISBN 0-87213-407-5 (pbk.: alk. paper)
1. Bible. N.T. Revelation—Commentaries. I. Ironside, H. A.
(Henry Allan), 1876-1951. Lectures on the book of Revelation.
II. Title.
BS2825.3.I76 1996
228'.07—dc20 96-1068

Printed in the United States of America
10 9 8 7 6 5 4 3 2 1

CONTENTS

A PROFILE

REVELATION
THE FUTURE UNVEILED

BY JOHN PHILLIPS

The book of Revelation is given its divine title in the first verse: "The Revelation of Jesus Christ." The language of the book is Greek, but its thought and idioms are Hebrew and it is saturated with Old Testament language. There are some 550 references to Old Testament passages in the book. Revelation is closely related to the book of Daniel, to which it forms a sequel. Also many interesting comparisons and contrasts can be made between Genesis and Revelation. Genesis tells of paradise lost, Revelation speaks of paradise regained. The garden of Eden in Genesis gives way in Revelation to the city of God. The tree of life in Genesis is seen again in Revelation. The serpent appears in Genesis and meets his doom in Revelation. Sin, sorrow, tears, the curse—all began in Genesis and all vanish in Revelation. The book of Revelation naturally completes the circle of revealed truth begun in Genesis.

There are four main schools of interpretation of this book. The *preterists* maintain that the greatest part of the book has already been fulfilled in the early history of the church. The *historicists* claim that the book of Revelation covers the whole period of history from the apostolic period to the present time. The *idealists* spiritualize the teaching of the book and say that it does not set forth actual events at all but that its symbols depict spiritual realities. The *futurists* believe that the major part of the book has to do with what is still future.

The book of Revelation presents visions of grace, visions of government, and visions of glory.

I. INTRODUCTION (1:1-3)
II. VISIONS OF GRACE (1:4–3:22)
   A. The Vision John Had of the Christ (1:4-20)
      1. His Position (1:4-6)
      2. His Purpose (1:7-8)
      3. His Providence (1:9-11)
      4. His Person (1:12-16)
      5. His Power (1:17-20)
   B. The Views Jesus Has of the Church (2:1–3:22)
      1. The Practical View
         a. Conditions That Were Present Then
         b. Conditions That Are Persistent Still
      2. The Prophetical View
III. VISIONS OF GOVERNMENT (4–20)
   A. The Beginning of Sorrows (4–11)
      1. The Throne of Power in Heaven (4–5)
      2. The Throes of Power on Earth (6–11)
         a. The Breaking of the Seals (6–8)
            (1) Details Given Particularly
            (2) Design Given Parenthetically
         b. The Blowing of the Trumpets (9–11)
            (1) Details Given Particularly
            (2) Design Given Parenthetically
   B. The Beasts of Earth (12–18)
      1. A Preview of Their Kingdom (12)
      (The maturity of the plan)
         a. The Extermination of Saints
         b. The Exaltation of Satan
      2. An Overview of Their Kingdom (13–16)
      (the malignity of the period)
         a. The Demands of the Beast
         b. The Designs of the Beast
         c. The Doom of the Beast

I. INTRODUCTION

The basic underlying structure of Revelation is that of chronology interrupted by commentary. There are numerous commentary sections in the book, some brief, some embracing several chapters. This constant fluctuation can be very confusing. The chronology of the book is carried in the major portion of the book by the seals, trumpets, and vials. Once we are through with the vials, the recurring expression "and I saw" marks the onward march of events. The following figure shows how some of the chapters are chronologically related.

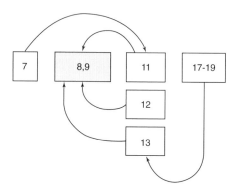

The more vital parenthetical sections in the book are those describing the sealing of the 144,000 (chapter 7); the incidents of the little book and the two witnesses (chapters 10 and 11); the preliminary description of the great tribulation (chapter 12); the description of the two beasts (chapter 13); the anticipatory events that lead up to the final judgments (chapter 14); the description of the two Babylons (chapters 17 and 18).

The scenes in the book of Revelation alternate between Heaven and earth with a precise regularity. We are given a scene in Heaven in which God's will is declared, and that is followed by a scene on earth wherein God's will is done. Thus this book shows us the full and final answer to that petition the Lord taught the disciples to make: "Thy will be done in earth as it is in heaven."

II. VISIONS OF GRACE

The Glorified Lord

The first of John's visions was of the glorified Lord Himself. John saw Him in a threefold aspect; Godward, as the one "which is, and which was, and which is to come" (1:4); selfward, as "the faithful witness, and the first-begotten of the dead, and the prince of the kings of the earth" (1:5); manward, as the one "that loved us, and washed us from our sins in his own blood, And hath made us kings and priests unto God" (1:5-6). John described Him: His garment, His hair, His eyes, His feet, His voice, His hand, His mouth, and

His countenance. So terrific was the vision that John fell at His feet as dead (17). There is an interesting progression to be observed in this vision. John said, "I heard" (10), "I turned" (12), "I saw" (12), and "I fell" (17). It was the same beloved Lord upon whose breast he had leaned in former times, but now He was glorified and awesome. Yet, in grace, He ministered to the fears of His servant. John said, "And he laid his right hand upon me, saying unto me, Fear not" (17).

The Seven Churches

The vision of the glorified Lord was followed by a presentation of the views the Lord Jesus had of the churches. There are at least three different ways of studying the seven letters to the churches of Asia. We can see in them admonitions to seven literal churches in Asia Minor that existed in John's day. We can see in them practical injunctions to churches in all ages of the church era, the seven churches addressed typifying conditions which constantly reappear in various local gatherings of God's people. We can take the seven churches as being prophetical and symbolizing the entire history of the church on earth. According to this view Ephesus depicts the postapostolic era with the gradual falling away of the church from its first love. Smyrna sets forth the era of the persecuting Caesars. Pergamos focuses attention on the day when Christianity became the state religion of the Roman empire. Thyatira covers the papal era. Sardis deals with the growth of Protestantism. Philadelphia draws attention to the religious revivals and the new emphasis on missions that would come toward the end. And Laodicea brings down the curtain on the worldliness of the church at last.

III. VISIONS OF GOVERNMENT

The greater part of the book of Revelation deals with the judgments of God which harden the hearts of men, making possible the coming the beast, the antichrist, the man of sin. After showing us that God is still on the throne (chapters 4–5), John showed how the seals and trumpets usher in appalling conditions on earth. Under the seals man is seen bringing trouble on the earth but under the trumpets it is Satan who is the prime actor. The last three trumpet judgments have additional horror in the form of woes (8:13; 12:12).

When the trumpet judgments have run their course, the scene is set for the appearing of the devil's false messiah. This person is called the beast in Revelation 13 and is given his power by Satan. Chapter 17, which looks back upon the coming of this beast, tells us he will be a resurrected man and will be hand in glove with a worldwide apostate religious system. The beast will be ably seconded in his schemes by a second beast (the false prophet) who will persuade the peoples of the earth to worship the first beast's image. Signs and lying wonders will be performed by this pair to awe the world and bring all people under their influence. Those who refuse to wear the beast's "mark" will be slain. Two prophets, appearing in the spirit and power of Moses and Elijah, will spearhead the resistance of the faithful, but eventually the two prophets will be slain in Jerusalem and their death will become the occasion for universal jubilation.

This Satan-inspired joy will be short-lived because the slain prophets will be publicly restored to life by God. To consolidate his power, the antichrist will use his allies to overthrow the apostate religious system that had helped him in the early days of his rise to dominion. The beast's kingdom will at first give every promise of prosperity, as chapter 18 depicts, but when he shows his true colors and insists that all men wear his mark, God will intervene. As the beast's tyranny increases God will begin to pour out His vials of wrath against him. The final act in the drama will take place when the armies of the world are summoned to Armageddon to fight against the Lord Himself. The Lord will descend from Heaven on a white horse and sweep the field. The two beasts will be cast into the lake of fire, and the devil will be chained for a thousand years. At the end of the millennium period Satan will again be loosed and lead the last rebellion against the Lord. Fiery judgment will sweep the globe, and then all the dead of all the ages (all those who have had no share in the first resurrection) will be summoned to appear before the great white throne. At this last dread trial men will be judged by their works and doomed accordingly.

IV. VISIONS OF GLORY

Only eight verses (21:1-8) are devoted to a description of the new creation—we could wish it were eight volumes! The Holy Spirit, for the most part, remains silent about what we will be doing in eternity, but we can be sure God has marvelous plans to make eternity an exciting experience for His own.

We have a detailed description, however, of the new capital, the heavenly Jerusalem. It seems best to view this as a real place (John 14:1-3). It would seem that this celestial city will be brought into a meaningful relation to the earth during the millennium—probably by being placed in stationary orbit over the earthly Jerusalem.

The millennial age will end in rebellion, as we have seen. Before God detonates the universe, the celestial city will, seemingly, become another "Noah's ark" for those of earth's people who love the Lord. They will probably be transported to the celestial city, which will then be taken back out of time and eternity, from whence it came. Then flaming fires will embrace the earth, the solar system, and all of space. The new heaven and the new earth, which will replace the old one, will probably orbit forever around the holy city (21:2).

V. CONCLUSION

This remarkable book ends with a fresh assurance to John that "these sayings are faithful and true." They are not idle dreams. They deal with realities—realities now coming rapidly into focus and awaiting only the rapture of the church before coming to a head.

Again the Lord assures us of His coming. "Surely I come quickly," He says. "Even so, come, Lord Jesus" is the response of His waiting people.

Appropriately enough, the last word in the book and the last word in the Bible is Amen—a name for the Lord Jesus (Revelation 3:14). Thus the Holy Spirit leaves us where the disciples found themselves on the mount of transfiguration when, the visions and visitation all over, "they saw no man, save Jesus only" (Matthew 17:8).

PREFACE

TO THE REVISED EDITION

H. A. Ironside's commentary on Revelation was first published in 1920. As might be expected in an exposition of prophetic Scripture, the author examined Bible prophecy in the light of then-current events and wove his observations into the commentary. Decades later some readers find certain of these references a bit puzzling.

During preparation of this revised edition we considered the possibility of eliminating or modifying observations that might be considered particularly dated. Ultimately we decided to retain these portions unchanged, believing that they provide valuable insight into the author's thinking and the way he examined current political events in the light of God's Word. The fact that none of Dr. Ironside's conclusions were subsequently invalidated indicates that there is much we can learn from his careful approach.

What the author wrote ten years after the first printing is still true: "The years that have elapsed have but given added proof that the system of interpretation followed is the Scriptural one. Everything in the church, in Jewry, and in the world moves on exactly as predicted in the Holy Scriptures."

The Publisher

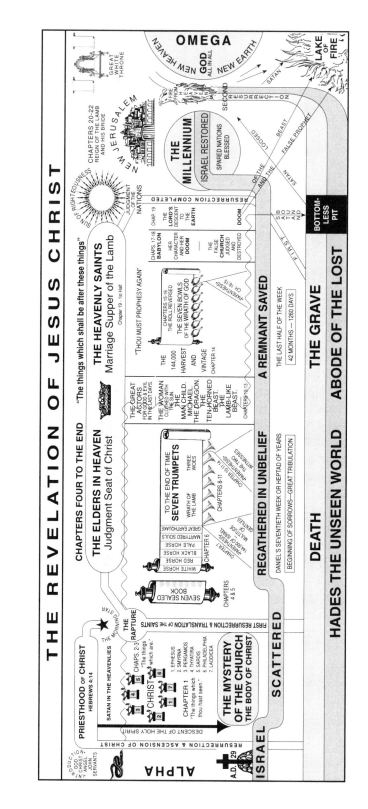

INTRODUCTION

It is regrettable that to so many Christians the book of Revelation seems to be a sealed book. That is not what God intended. The book of Daniel was to be sealed until the time of the end (Daniel 12:9), but of Revelation it is written: "Seal *not* the sayings of the prophecy of this book: for the time is at hand" (22:10, italics added). It is clearly evident that this portion of Holy Scripture was given for our instruction and edification, yet thousands of the Lord's people permit themselves to be robbed of blessing by ignoring it.

Significantly enough, the book of Revelation begins and ends with a blessing pronounced on those who read and keep what is written therein (1:3; 22:7). Surely God did not mean to mock us by promising a blessing on all who keep what they cannot hope to understand! Only unbelief would so reason. Faith delights to appropriate every part of the sacred record and finds that "they are all plain to him that understandeth" (Proverbs 8:9).

The true title is given in the opening verse. It is "The Revelation of Jesus Christ" not "The Revelation of St. John the Divine." There is no authority for this latter designation and it shows all too plainly how far some early editor had slipped away from basic principles. John was a saint as all believers are saints. He was not a divine! Such a title would have amazed him beyond measure. Nor is the book the revelation of John or of any other servant of God. It is the revelation of Jesus Christ Himself.

The word rendered "revelation" and sometimes "apocalypse" means literally "an unveiling." So this book is the unveiling of our Lord Jesus Christ. He is its one great theme. It presents Him as the Son of man in the midst of the churches during the present dispensation and as the Judge and the King in the dispensations to come.

If you want to learn to appreciate Christ more, read this book frequently and prayerfully. It reveals Him as the Lamb rejected, yet soon to reign in glory—the Lamb on the throne!

Observe the title is not in the plural. People often speak of the book of Revelations. There is no such book in the Bible. It is *the* Revelation—one blessed, continuous manifestation of God's unique Son, the anointed Prophet, Priest, and King. Revelation is the crowning book of the Bible. It is like the headstone of Zechariah 4:7 that completes and crowns the whole wondrous pyramid of truth.

The Pentateuch of Moses forms the broad, solid foundation of this vast pyramid. The covenant history is built on this foundation; then come the Psalms and poetical books followed by the prophetic series of the Old Testament. Higher up we have the Gospels and the Acts, then the Epistles with their deep spiritual instruction. To complete the glorious structure, this last solemn but exceedingly precious book, the Revelation, linking the rest of Scripture with the soon-to-be-manifested glory of God.

Or if you think of Holy Scripture as forming a great golden circle of truth, we start with Genesis, the book of beginnings, and go on through the Testaments until we come to Revelation, the book of the last things. We find it dovetails exactly into the book of Genesis and thus completes the inspired ring. The Word of God is one absolutely perfect, unbroken, and unbreakable circle. A comparison of Genesis and Revelation will readily show how we have the types in Genesis and the completion of the truth in Revelation—in the one book the beginning, in the other the consummation. Genesis gives us the creation of the heavens and the earth. Revelation presents a new heaven and a new earth.

Genesis shows us the earthly paradise, with the tree of life and the river of blessing lost through sin. Revelation gives us the paradise of God with the tree of life and the pure river of life proceeding out of the throne of God and the Lamb. We are shown paradise regained through Christ's atonement.

In Genesis we see the first man and his wife set over all God's creation. In Revelation we behold the second Man and His bride ruling over a redeemed world.

In Genesis we are told of the first typical sacrificial lamb. In Revelation the Lamb once slain is in the midst of the throne.

In Genesis we learn of the beginning of sin, when the serpent entered the garden of delight to beguile Adam and Eve with his sophistries. In Revelation that old serpent called the devil and Satan is cast into the lake of fire.

In Genesis we have the first murderer, the first polygamist, the first rebel, the first drunkard, etc. In Revelation all those who refuse to accept God's grace in Christ Jesus are banished from His presence forever.

In Genesis we view the rise of Babel, or Babylon. In Revelation we are called to contemplate its doom.

In Genesis we see man's city; in Revelation the city of God.

Genesis shows us how sorrow, death, pain, and tears—the inevitable accompaniments of sin and rebellion—came into the world. Revelation does not close until we have seen God wiping away all tears and welcoming His redeemed into a home where sin, death, pain, and sorrow never come.

And so we might go on contrasting and comparing these two books, but enough has been cited to stir each interested believer to study for himself. What we ourselves get out of our Bibles in the presence of God is worth far more than all that another passes on to us. We may learn from each other, but it is best to take nothing for granted. Like Ruth the Moabitess, we should "beat out that [which we have] gleaned" through meditation and prayer.

But before we examine this remarkable book, we should point out three very distinct views of Revelation held by commentators. They are generally known as the preterist, historical, and futurist. Each of the three systems of interpretation might be subdivided into various, conflicting schools, but the names give the main point of view in each case.

As a rule, the preterists see very little in the book beyond a weird religio-political document. It was supposedly written by some unknown person who took the name of John in order to give acceptance to his writings, or a John other than the apostle. Preterists hold that the author's real object was to comfort his Christian brethren

in a time of great persecution under one of the Roman emperors. So
he portrayed the final outcome of the stern conflict as a great victory for the saints, resulting in the overthrow of paganism and the
recognition of a glorious city of God in its place.

The historical school believe that the momentous events of the
last nineteen hundred years are the fulfillment of the seals, trumpets, and vials, and the other special visions of the book. According
to this view, Revelation cannot be understood apart from a thor-
ough knowledge of the history of the nations comprising
Christendom—the sphere where Christ's authority is nominally
owned. The schools of interpretation founded on this supposition
are many and varied.

The futurists consider that the largest part of the book applies to
a period still future. They believe that only the first three chapters
refer to the present church dispensation. Some extreme futurists even
relegate these chapters to the end times also; they do not see the
church in Revelation at all. Our position in expounding this book
will coincide with the futurists first mentioned. The basis for this
view will be addressed later.

Recall the occasion when the Lord Jesus restored Peter's soul
after his fall. He told him how when he was old another would lead
him where he would not want to go, thus indicating the kind of
death by which Peter would glorify God. Then Jesus said, "Follow
me." Peter turned and saw the disciple whom Jesus loved following, and said, "Lord, and what shall this man do?" The Lord answered, "If I will that he tarry till I come, what is that to thee? follow *thou* me" (John 21:18-22). Notice that the Lord Jesus very clearly
sets forth two things that are often confused by some Christian teachers—death and the second coming of Christ. He said, "If I will that
he tarry till I come, what is that to thee?" Jesus clearly put "tarry till
I come" in contrast with Peter's dying before His return. There is
no place in Scripture where death and our Lord's second coming
are confused. For death is not the second coming of the Lord; it is to
be swallowed up in victory at that second coming. But most of us
are extremists, so when the Lord said to Peter, "If I will that he tarry
till I come," the saying "that disciple should *not* die" was spread

among the disciples (23). Jesus did not say that he would not die, but "If I will that he tarry till I come." And, of course, time proved that the disciples' hasty conclusion was incorrect.

John died many years ago. Some years before the end of his earthly life, he was banished to the desolate island of Patmos for his faithfulness. There he had a wonderful vision unfolded before him of truth connected with our Lord Jesus' second coming. Through this vision *his ministry abides with us until Christ comes again.* John is absent from the body, but present with the Lord—has been for over 1900 years; but through the ministry given to us in this wonderful book of Revelation, John abides until Jesus comes. He continues to throw light on all the complex problems that God's people have to meet in this present dispensation. He also helps us understand, as no other ministry does, the great program that God Himself is soon going to carry out.

CHAPTER ONE
THE FIRST VISION

T urning to verse one of the text, we note that the Revelation of Jesus Christ was given by the Father to the Son, as David revealed to Solomon all his plans in connection with the building of the future temple. God is represented as being in counsel with our Lord Jesus Christ concerning "things which must shortly come to pass." It is the joy of His heart to communicate this knowledge to His servants. An angel became the messenger to make all known to the beloved apostle John. Note then the order through which the revelation came down to us. God gave it to Jesus Christ, who sent it by His angel to His servant John to show the coming things to His servants.

He is said to have "signified it"—that is, He made it known by signs or symbols. It is important to bear this in mind. Revelation is a book of symbols. But the careful student of the Word need not exercise his own ingenuity in order to think out the meanings of the symbols. It is important to recognize the principle that *every symbol used in Revelation is explained or alluded to somewhere else in the Bible.* Therefore, he who desires God's mind as to this portion of His Word must study earnestly with prayerful attention to every other part of holy Scripture. Undoubtedly this is why so great a blessing is in store for those who read and hear the words of this prophecy and keep the things written therein (1:3).

The Salutation (Revelation 1:4-8)

The book is particularly addressed, as a great general epistle, to "the seven churches which are in Asia." The term *Asia* does not refer to the continent that now bears that name, nor to Asia Minor.

Rather it was a Roman proconsular province distinctively called "Asia." In John's day there were many Christian churches already established in that province, and seven of these are selected to be addressed. Some might ask why these seven were selected in preference to others such as the churches in Colosse and Hierapolis, both of which were important churches. My answer is that the geographical position of these churches was in keeping with the vision presented in verses 12-18. They formed a rough circle with Christ in the middle as seen by John. Christ was standing in His priestly garb, taking note of all that was going on.

These churches were also chosen for their prevailing internal conditions. They were suited to portray the state of Christendom in seven distinct periods from the apostolic days to the close of the church's testimony on earth. Even the very names of the seven cities, when interpreted, help to make this plain. They become keys to the different periods to which they apply. The proof of this will be seen in our study of Revelation 2–3.

Observe how the three persons of the holy trinity are linked together in the salutation. "Him which is, and which was, and which is to come" is Jehovah (4). This is the literal meaning of the mystic name communicated to Moses. *Jehovah* is a compound formed from three words: the first meaning "He is," the second, "He was," the third, "He will be" or "He will come." Jehovah is the triune God, so the Father, the Son, and the Spirit are all called by this name. But in the present passage it is clearly God the Father who is in view. The Spirit comes before us in the next clause: "and from the seven Spirits which are before his throne." If it is hard to understand how the one, eternal Holy Spirit can be so pictured, turn to Isaiah 11:1-2. There we read of the seven Spirits who rest on the Branch of Jehovah, our Lord Jesus Christ. Note the order given:

1. The Spirit of the Lord
2. The Spirit of wisdom
3. The Spirit of understanding
4. The Spirit of counsel
5. The Spirit of might

6. The Spirit of knowledge
7. The Spirit of the fear of the Lord

There you have the one Spirit in the sevenfold plenitude of His power. Seven, mentioned so frequently in the book of Revelation, is the number of perfection and is so used here.

Finally with the Father and the Spirit we have Jesus Christ. He is "the faithful witness" when here on earth, "the first-begotten of the dead" in resurrection glory, and "the prince of the kings of the earth" when He comes again to reign (Revelation 1:5). No wonder an outburst of praise and worship follows at this full revelation of Christ's glories: "Unto him that loved us, and washed us from our sins in his own blood, and hath made us kings and priests unto God and his Father; to him be glory and dominion for ever and ever. Amen" (5-6). John's heart was full and overflowing. Adoration and praise were the spontaneous result of contemplation of Christ's person and offices as Prophet, Priest, and King.

Then he heralds the glad news of His coming again (7). He is going to return—not as a baby, born of woman, but the glorified One descending from Heaven. By a stupendous miracle, every eye will see Him, while "all kindreds of the earth shall wail because of him." I am persuaded this is the true meaning and refers to Zechariah 12:10-14; there all the tribes of restored Israel are seen by the prophet mourning over their past rejection of Christ and lamenting their folly while awaiting His return. John spoke for all the church when he cried with rapture, "Even so, Amen!" Does your heart take up the same glad welcoming shout? Or are you unready to meet Him and would dread His return?

In the 8th verse we read the words of the Son who declared Himself to be Jehovah also, One eternally with the Father. He is the Alpha and Omega—the first and last letters of the Greek alphabet—the beginning and the ending. He created all things; He will wind up all things and bring in the new heavens and the new earth. He is, and was, and is the coming One. He is *El Shaddai*—the Almighty—who of old appeared to Abraham. May our hearts be occupied with Him and His return be our "blessed Hope!"

The Vision of the Son of Man (Revelation 1:9-20)

In Revelation 1:9 the apostle John wrote that he was a prisoner for the sake of the Lord Jesus Christ. He was banished to the isle called Patmos—a little rocky island in the Mediterranean sea. There, shut away from all Christian fellowship, God had a greater mission for him than he had ever known in the past.

The devil really overreached himself when Domitian banished John to the isle of Patmos. If John had remained ministering the Word to the saints and preaching to the unsaved, he might not have been able to write the book of Revelation and we might not have the visions this book gives us. But on that lonely island, shut off from all his service, the veil was rolled back, and he was enabled to give us this wonderful record of the unveiling of Jesus Christ.

John wrote that he was "in the Spirit on the Lord's day." The Lord's day is a divinely given designation for the first day of the week. I know there are those who tell us the Lord's day in this verse is what the Old Testament calls the sabbath of the Lord. They tell us that the Jewish sabbath should still be observed, since it is not done away with in the New Testament. In answer to that, we may notice that nowhere in the New Testament, after the resurrection of the Lord Jesus Christ from the dead, do we ever have any special honor paid to the seventh day—Israel's sabbath. On that day, the Lord lay in the tomb. On the morning of the first day of the week, "in the end of the Sabbath" (Matthew 28:1), the Lord rose in triumph from the dead, and that new day became distinctly the Lord's day.

You find in the Word of God that following His resurrection on the first day of the week the Lord met with His own in the upper room (John 20:19). Also on the first day of the week the disciples gathered to break bread (Acts 20:7). In connection with their gathering thus together, 1 Corinthians 16:2 says, "Upon the first day of the week let every one of you lay by him in store, as God hath prospered him." Thus Christian giving and the weekly remembrance of the Lord are linked together. It is safe to say that if Christians everywhere carried this out, there would be no financial problem in the church of God today.

The first day of the week is preeminently the day for Christians.

Whenever the earliest Christian writers refer to the term *Lord's day*, they speak of it as the first day of the week—the day after the Jewish sabbath—the day we Christians call the Lord's day. I venture to say that people who lived from fifty to two hundred years after the apostle John were far more likely to know what was meant by the term *Lord's day* than people who live today. I know there are some prophetic students who confuse the *Lord's day* with the *great day of the Lord*, but there is a decided difference in the two terms. *Lord's day* is not in the possessive case in the original. The word translated "Lord's" is an adjective. If it were permissible to say "the Lordian day," we would have the exact meaning. Such an adjective has been formed from the word Christ. We say a *Christian* spirit, etc. So the Lordian or Lordly day is the day on which the Lord Jesus Christ broke the bonds of death and rose, never more to die. We Christians love to keep this day in memory of Him.

On that day, John says, "I was in the Spirit" (1:10). John was far away from any Christian assembly, but he found his pleasure in the things of God. Some Christians you know go to meeting every Lord's day when at home, but when on their vacations or away from town the Lord's day is just like any other day because nobody knows them. But John, shut away from any Christian association, was "in the Spirit on the Lord's day." It is good to see a Christian take his Bible with him when on a vacation and have daily intercourse with the Lord, or look up someone who does not know Jesus Christ and seek to make Him known to that needy one. See to it that you are in the Spirit on the Lord's day.

Being "in the Spirit" on the Lord's day, John had a glorious vision of the Lord Himself. First he heard a voice, then he saw a form. He heard a voice saying, "I am Alpha and Omega, the first and the last: and, what thou seest, write in a book...And being turned, I saw seven golden candlesticks" (11-12). If I understand it correctly, these were not like the candlesticks in the temple and in the tabernacle. Those were seven-branched—six side branches and the central shaft. But John saw seven separate lampstands. Christ is represented by the seven-branched candlestick in the holy place, and the Spirit of God is represented by the seven lamps on it. But during His absence—during the time of His priesthood in Heaven—His people are to be lights for Him in this world. So John saw in this first vision not one candlestick with seven branches, but seven distinct lampstands in the form of a circle. In the middle of them he saw One like the Son of man with a golden sash around His chest. It was a vision of the Lord judging in the middle of His assemblies.

Then we learn what these lampstands symbolize. They are the seven churches situated in the Roman proconsular province of Asia. These seven were selected from all the assemblies of God to picture the whole course of the church's history until the coming again of our Lord Jesus Christ. In His absence, the church of God is responsible to keep a light burning in the midst of the darkness. You remember He said while here on earth, "I am the light of the world" (John 8:12). Before He went away He said to His disciples, "Ye are the light of the world" (Matthew 5:7). He has gone up to the glory and all the members of His church are to shine for Him here. What kind of light are you giving out for Jesus? Do your neighbors appreciate your Christianity? Do the people that you do business with think much of it? I would rather get the testimony of the people you deal with on a daily basis than of those you meet in the public assemblies. When a man is really converted, it changes him through and through.

The church of God and individual assemblies of Christians are in this world to shine for Christ. We are here not merely to enjoy the things of Christ ourselves, but to hold up Christ to the world. Speaking of the Lord's supper the apostle Paul said, "For as often as ye eat this bread and drink this cup, ye do shew the Lord's death till he come" (1 Corinthians 11:26). The word translated "shew" in that passage is the same word that is used elsewhere for preaching: "you *preach* the Lord's death." The Lord's supper is a testimony to sinners as well as something for the church to enjoy. The church of God is here to shine for Christ, and we shine for Him as He is exalted in our gatherings and demonstrated in our lives.

"I saw seven golden candlesticks; and in the midst of the seven candlesticks one like unto the Son of man" (Revelation 1:12-13). In many respects He seemed different than how John remembered Him, except when on the mount of transfiguration. But he knew who He was—"One like unto the Son of man." John had known Him well on earth, and he knew Him the moment He appeared in that glorious vision.

Note how Christ is described, "clothed with a garment down to the foot, and girt about the [breasts] with a golden girdle" (13). He is seen in the long, white garments of the high priest with the golden sash around his chest. The sash or girdle speaks of service. We read of the servant girding himself and waiting on the table (Luke 17:8). In Revelation the girdle represents a high-priestly service. Our blessed Lord is now serving us at God's right hand. The girdle is a golden one, representing the fact that Christ's service is in full accord with God's holy and righteous ways. Looking back to the cross where Jesus hung in sacrifice for us, we rejoice to remember His dying words, "It is finished." Nothing can be added to and nothing taken away from that completed work. But there is another work He is now carrying on for His people. Although up in glory, He is serving us still. His people need His help all along the way. The moment you belong to the Lord Jesus, you are brought into living union with our great High Priest at God's right hand. "He is able also to save them to the uttermost that come unto God by him, seeing he ever liveth to make intercession for them" (Hebrews 7:25). He does not ask you to live in your own strength. Trust Him as Savior, and let Him fill your heart and control your life. He will live His life in you to His praise and glory. We are to come boldly to a throne of grace, that we may obtain mercy and find seasonable help.

Notice the 14th verse: "His head and his hairs were white like wool, as white as snow; and his eyes were as a flame of fire." I said previously that every figure, every symbol found in this book is explained somewhere else in the Bible. In Daniel 7:9-13 we read of the Ancient of days and of the Son of man. Now observe John said that the One in the midst of the seven lampstands was "like unto the Son of man." He was undoubtedly linking that up with the seventh chapter of Daniel. John described the Son of man as one whose hair is white as snow. He had all the appearance of great age, though the Lord Jesus was cut off at the age of thirty-three. Observe Daniel 7:9, "And the Ancient of days did sit,…and the hair of his head like the pure wool." Who is the Ancient of days? In the 7th chapter of Daniel, He is the Jehovah of Israel, and the Son of man comes to

Him. But we learn that the Son of man is Himself the Ancient of days. In other words, the Jehovah of the Old Testament is the Jesus of the New Testament. Christ is Himself "God manifest in the flesh."

Another Old Testament Prophet said, "But thou, Bethlehem Ephratah, though thou be little among the thousands of Judah, yet out of thee shall he come forth unto me that is to be ruler in Israel; whose goings forth have been from of old, from everlasting" (Micah 5:2). Who is the Savior born in Bethlehem? He is the One "whose goings forth have been from of old, from everlasting." The Lord Jesus Christ is the Ancient of days. This is one of the truths that Christians are called to contend for in these times of apostasy. Ministers are telling people that we are all sons of God. They deny Christ's virgin birth and deity and say that He is simply the greatest of all teachers sent from God. But that is not enough for the Christian. Christ is God, or we and those in Heaven are idolaters, for it is Christ who is worshiped there, and here. The Unitarian believes in God the Father, but not in the Son. He says, "Don't draw the lines too straight—Jesus is only a creature." If that Unitarian is right, I am an idolater, for I am worshiping Jesus Christ. I worship, not Buddha, not Brahma, but Jesus and own Him as God. Yet some would tell me that it does not make any difference! It makes a tremendous difference, for both time and eternity. It is going to mean all the difference between Heaven and Hell. For the Lord Jesus says, "Whither I go, ye cannot come,…for if ye believe not that I am, ye shall die in your sins" (John 8:21, 24). We confess Jesus Christ as God manifest in the flesh, the only-begotten Son of God, the anointed One who came in grace to save lost, guilty sinners. Are you trusting Him as your Savior?

So we see that this One in the midst of the candlesticks is the Son of man, yet God Himself. The Lord Jesus has that double character, and His place is always in the center. No company of believers deserves to be called a Christian company that does not give Him that place. But, "Where two or three are gathered together in my name," He said, "there am I in the midst" (Matthew 18:20). You remember when He hung on that cross between two thieves, He saved one of them who turned to Him in faith. When He rose from the dead and His disciples were gathered together in the upper room, "Then…

came Jesus and stood in the midst" (John 20:19). In the 5th chapter
of the Revelation, John looked and saw the Lamb "in the midst of
the throne and of the four beasts, in the midst of the elders." This is
the place that ever belongs to the Lord Jesus—the central place, the
preeminent place. God must have Jesus in the midst.

But let us turn back to Revelation 1. "His eyes were as a flame of
fire" (14). John did not know Him in that way on earth, except perhaps as He rebuked the Pharisees; but remember that all who do not
accept Him now are going to see His eyes like a flame of fire. There
will be nothing hidden from those eyes. They will discern everything that you would try to hide. All will be out in the light and
brought into judgment. Oh, have everything out with Him now. Do
you realize that the first time you meet God, you must meet Him
with all your sins on your soul? Have you had a meeting with Him
yet? If the first time you meet Him is at the day of judgment, it will
be too late. You can have your first meeting with Him in this world.
You can meet Him by faith. Do not try to improve or to make yourself better. Come just as you are, without one plea, except that He is
the sinner's Savior and invites you to come. You will find that those
eyes, that are as a flame of fire and look into the depths of your
soul, will become filled with tenderest love and will draw you to
Himself.

But John's description goes on to say: "His feet like unto fine
brass" (15). Brass in the Old Testament is the symbol of judgment.
The brazen altar that stood before the tabernacle was that on which
the fire of God's judgment was burning continually. It was overlaid
with brass because brass could stand the fire. (The peculiar metal
referred to was really a very hard copper alloy, but I use the word
brass as employed in the KJV.) You will find throughout Scripture it
is a symbol of judgment. And in Revelation the Son of man has feet
like brass, for His ways are unyielding in righteousness. The day is
coming when He will put His feet on everything contrary to truth
and righteousness. Everything unholy will be stamped out in divine
judgment.

"His voice [is] as the sound of many waters." When you stand on
the cliff by the seaside and hear the sound of many waters, you are
awed by their power. The ship, which looks so large and strong at

the docks, is helpless when at sea and the ocean rouses itself in furious anger. His voice is as the sound of the billows of the sea—a voice of power. That power put forth in grace means your salvation; put forth in judgment, it means your eternal damnation! You may pass from death into life by hearing His voice now. He can speak to your poor soul and in a moment create your heart anew. He has said: "The hour is coming, and now is, when the dead shall hear the voice of the Son of God: and they that hear shall live" (John 5:25, italics added). Hearing His voice, believing His Word, you live! Have you heard that voice of power? Soon His people will hear that same mighty voice calling them away from earth. "For the Lord himself shall descend from heaven with a shout,…and the dead in Christ will rise first," and the living saints will be changed (1 Thessalonians 4:16-17). Sometimes Christians become discouraged; but when that voice like the sound of many waters says from Heaven, "Arise, my love, my fair one, and come away," (Song of Solomon 2:13) we will be caught up in a moment to meet Him in the air.

"He had in his right hand seven stars" (Revelation 1:16). The stars speak of ministry committed to His saints, who are responsible to shine by His light and for Him in this world. "They that turn many to righteousness [shall shine] as the stars forever and ever" (Daniel 12:3). He holds the stars in His right hand. "Out of his mouth went a sharp two-edged sword." It is the Word of God (Hebrews 4:12). Men are trifling with that two-edged sword, but they will find out soon that it is powerful and irresistible.

"His countenance was as the sun shineth in his strength" (Revelation 1:16). In Malachi 4:2 we read, "But unto you that fear my name shall the Sun of righteousness arise with healing in his wings." When Saul of Tarsus was struck down, he saw a light greater than the brightness of the sun. It was the glory of God in the face of Christ Jesus. It was this that John saw, and he fell at His feet. But He laid His right hand on John and said, "Fear not; I am the First and the Last: I am he that liveth, and was dead; and, behold I am alive for evermore, Amen; and I have the keys of [death and of Hades]" (Revelation 1:18).

What is death? It is the body without the spirit: "The body without the spirit is dead" (James 2:26). There is no such thing in the

Bible as soul-sleeping. The spirit of the man is not in the grave. The body goes down to the grave, but the spirit is in the unseen world. Hades is the condition of the spirit without the body. Christ has the keys of both death and Hades.

In the 19th verse we get the threefold division of the Book of the Revelation: "Write the things which thou hast seen, and the things which are, and the things which shall be hereafter"—or "after these things."

"The things which thou hast seen" are the things of chapter one—the *first* division of the book of the Revelation.

"The things which are" follow in the next two chapters and make the *second* division, which deals with the present dispensation. The seven churches give us a picture of the whole professing church's history from the apostolic period to the coming of the Lord Jesus. These two chapters portray the condition of the church on earth in seven distinct periods. The church's history ends at the rapture, when Jesus comes as the bright and morning Star. That event closes the present dispensation.

"The things which shall be after these things," are the events described in chapters 4 to the end, and make the *third* and last division of the book. These are the things which will take place after the church's history ends—the great tribulation, the kingdom, and the eternal state.

CHAPTER TWO
THE SEVEN CHURCHES

(PART ONE)

We now turn to the letters addressed to the first four churches as found in Revelation 2. In the last chapter I tried to make it clear that the key to the structure of the book is found in Revelation 1:19. We have already studied the things that the apostle John had seen—that is, the first vision of the book where he beheld the glorified Lord in the midst of the lampstands. The third division is clearly indicated in the opening words of Revelation 4: "*After [these things]* I looked, and, behold, a door was opened in heaven" (italics added). Necessarily then, the second division must encompass the contents of chapters 2–3—"the things which are" (present, continuous tense)—the things which are now in progress. This is the only part of the Apocalypse that has to do specifically with the present church period; though it is all written for our instruction, our warning, and our encouragement.

In fact, I believe that the real value of the Revelation is that it gives us the full-grown trees which we now see as developing saplings. We need this book in order to judge correctly the various movements that are now going on. I am sure that if I did not know something of the teaching of Revelation, I would long since have been identified with many movements which I have come absolutely to distrust. I have learned by a careful study of the Apocalypse, what the end of these movements will be.

Let me illustrate: Someone asks concerning the so-called "church federation scheme." Wouldn't it be a wonderful thing if all the churches united and we simply had one great organization? All could agree to accept a common creed so worded that everyone could subscribe to it, and so the shame of Christendom's divisions would be ended. Now, why not support something like that? Would not this be the fulfillment of the prayer of our Lord, "that they all may be one" (John 17:21)? I might be caught by such a proposal. But in the book of Revelation I learn that just such a religious federation is going to arise after the church of God has been caught away to be with the Lord Jesus Christ. This big world-church is designated in the 17th chapter as "Babylon the great." The present movement is just a preparation for this. In the light of the book of Revelation, I see that if that is the way the movement for world-church unity is going to end, I should have no part in it now. Separation from evil—not fusion of diverse systems—is the divine order. So we see that the prophetic book throws the light of the future on events and movements that are in progress at present in order that we may take warning and be preserved from that which is contrary to the mind of God.

Before we begin our study of "the things which are," let me give you this parable. Sometime ago, rummaging through an old castle, some people came across a very strange looking old lock which secured a stout door. They shook the door and tried to open it, but to no avail. They tried one way and another to move the lock, but could not turn it. By and by somebody picked up a bunch of old keys from some rubbish on the floor and he said, "Maybe I can unlock it." He tried one key and it made no impression. He tried another and it gave a little; another and it gave a little more; and so on, but none would open the lock. At last he came to a peculiar old key. He slipped it into the lock, gave a turn, and the lock was open. They said, "Undoubtedly this key was meant for this lock."

You will understand my parable if I draw your attention to the fact that in Revelation 1:20, we are told that there was a mystery connected with the seven lampstands. The seven lampstands are said to symbolize the seven churches of Asia, but there was a mystery connected with them. While some have tried one key and some have tried another (there have been all kinds of efforts made to interpret this mystery), no solution was found. Then some devout students of Scripture weighing this portion said, "Since this section of the book presents 'the things which are,' perhaps God has given us a prophetic history of the church for the entire dispensation." But would the key fit the lock? They compared the first part of the church's history with the letter to Ephesus. Here it fit perfectly. They went on and compared the letter to Smyrna with the second part of the church's history, and the agreement was remarkable. They went on right down to the end. When they came to Laodicea they found that what is written to the church of Laodicea correlates exactly with the condition of the professing church in the days in which we live. They said: "There, the mystery is all clear. The lock has been opened; therefore we have the right key."

I have no doubt that this was the mind of the Lord in sending these letters to the seven churches. Seven churches were chosen because seven in Scripture is the number of perfection. You only have to read these seven letters, then take any good, reliable church history and see for yourself how perfectly the key fits the lock.

The Church of Ephesus (Revelation 2:1-7)

The names of the churches are significant in themselves. It would be impossible to reverse any of these names. If the order were changed they would not apply. The first one, *Ephesus* means "desirable." It is a term that a Greek applied to the young lady of his choice. Ephesus gives us a picture of the church as it was in the beginning. This is when the Lord held the stars (His servants) in His hand and controlled their ministry. He sent them here and there to proclaim the glad gospel of His grace and to minister to His saints. But human systems have largely changed all that. He walked in the midst of His churches. His eyes were on everything, and He was there to admonish, to correct, and to control. Observe that in the beginning His Name was the only center, and His saints gathered to Him.

Verses 2-3 tell us that the early church was walking in separation from the world. The Greek word *ecclesia*, translated "church" in our Bibles, means a called-out company. This is God's ideal, and every effort to amalgamate the church and the world is opposed to His mind. Such efforts will end in confusion for the church will never convert the world in the present dispensation. Someone once asked Dr. A. T. Pierson, "Don't you really think that the world is getting converted already?" "Well," he said, "I admit that the world has become a little churchy, but the church has become immensely worldly." If it were possible that the church could convert the world, that would be the end of the church. What do I mean? Simply this, that the church is a called-out company; if the world were converted, there would be nothing left out of which to call the church.

Believers in the days of Ephesus could not bear those who were evil. In our day, discipline in the church is almost at an end. In many quarters, anyone is welcome to full participation in all church privileges, particularly if they have a good bank account. In the beginning it was very different. That little Ephesian assembly said, "We don't want numbers if they are not holy numbers. We don't want growth at the expense of holiness." More than that, they were loyal to the truth. They tried those who claimed to be apostles, and if they found they were deceivers they refused them as liars. They did not say, "Oh well, you know Dr. So-and-so comes with such good recommendations. He is such a lovely man and so cultured. Though he doesn't happen to believe in the virgin birth, the deity of Christ, or His atonement, etc., he has so many good qualities that we mustn't be hard on him." The early church would have said, "Are you a servant of the Lord Jesus Christ?" and put a few serious questions to him. If he was not what he professed to be, they soon unmasked him and refused his unholy ministry. But in these days teachers can deny almost any truth of Scripture, and the professing church never knows the difference. Oh, for more of the zeal and piety of early days!

In verse three we learn that these saints were suffering for the sake of the name of the Lord Jesus. Their suffering was not for the name of any denomination or special theories. It was suffering for Christ's sake. For His Name's sake they bore trial and endured persecution.

Yet, even then, we have the evidence of early decline. Verse 4 says, "Nevertheless I have somewhat against thee, because thou hast left thy first love." The people of the Ephesian church had left their first love. Their hearts were drifting away from Christ. The decline that began in those first days of the church has continued and there has been no corporate recovery. That spirit of declension has gone on increasing until the present lukewarm Laodicean days.

The Church of Smyrna (Revelation 2:8-11)

In the next letter we see that the Lord, whose love never changes, permitted something to take place to arouse His people from their lethargy. *Smyrna* means "myrrh," a plant frequently mentioned in Scripture in connection with the embalming of the dead. Myrrh had to be crushed in order to give out its fragrance. This depicts the period when the church was crushed beneath the iron heel of pagan Rome. Yet it never gave out such sweet fragrance to God as in those two centuries of almost constant martyrdom.

"These things saith the first and the last, which was dead, and is alive" (2:8). What a blessed thing to know that the children of God are linked up with a resurrected Christ! The power of His resurrection works in them. He said, "I know thy works, and tribulation, and poverty, (but thou art rich)" (9). This describes the time when the church was hated, outlawed, and persecuted. Instead of worshiping in magnificent buildings, they gathered together in caves, catacombs, and other hidden places. Sentries were posted to warn them of the approach of their foes. Despised by the world and condemned as enemies of the Empire because of their faith in and loyalty to Christ, their lives were precious to God. They were rich in His eyes. They were poor in this world's goods, but rich in faith.

But even then all was not perfect. Christ said, "I know the blasphemy of them which say they are Jews, and are not, but are the synagogue of Satan"—referring to the Judaizing movement that came into the church in the early centuries. It was the leaven of Galatianism which had never been wholly judged and therefore made astonishing progress in the second and third centuries.

"Fear [not]...ye shall have tribulation ten days" (10). It is significant that in the two centuries of Roman persecution, from Nero to A.D. 312, there were ten distinct edicts demanding that governors seek out Christians everywhere and put them to death. The last edict was under Diocletian. He was the tenth persecutor. The early Christians believed he would be the last, and he was. "The blood of the martyrs is the seed of the church," said Augustine. The testimony of the dying often led their persecutors to receive the Lord Jesus Christ as their Savior because of the convincing power of the truth seen in the martyrs. Satan's effort to destroy Christianity by persecution was in vain. But those were days when it meant something to be a Christian. When God's people were being crushed like myrrh, a sweet fragrance of devotion and Christian love was wafted up to the very throne of God!

The Church of Pergamos (Revelation 2:12-17)

Pergamos has two meanings. It means "marriage," and "elevation." It represents the time when the church was elevated to a place of power and was married to the world. It depicts the time when church and state were united under Constantine and his successors.

The Lord Jesus judges everything by the Word. The word that He spoke will judge men in the last day. If you reject it now it will judge you then. "I know ... where thou dwellest," He says, even on "Satan's seat" (13). What was Satan's throne? If you had asked any of the Smyrna believers, they would have pointed you to the Emperor's throne in Rome. In Pergamos you find the church of God sitting on the imperial throne. How did that happen? Those of you who are familiar with Roman history and church tradition will recall that after the death of Diocletian and Galerius, Constantine and Maxentius contended for the throne. Constantine is said to have seen a vision of a cross of fire and to have heard a voice saying, "In this sign, conquer." He wondered what the vision could mean. He was told that the cross was the sign of the Christian religion and therefore his vision must mean that the God of the Christians was calling him to be the champion of the Christian religion. If he obeyed the voice he would be victor over the hosts of Maxentius and become emperor of the world. He called for Christian bishops and asked them to explain their religion to him. He accepted the new doctrine and declared himself to be its God-appointed patron and protector. Some writers make a great deal of this so-called conversion of Constantine, but it is questionable if he ever became a child of God by faith in Christ Jesus. He won a great victory over his opponent and thus became emperor of the world. One of his first acts was to liberate the Christians and to stop all persecution. He bestowed unwanted honors on the bishops; they sat on thrones with the nobles of the empire.

It was at this time that the truth of the second coming of Christ was given up. Before the days of Constantine the church was look-ing for Him. That was their expectation and hope. But after the great change in their circumstances, the church largely lost sight of this truth. Christian bishops said, "We have been looking for Christ's reign but we have been wrong. Constantine's empire is Christ's kingdom." They thought the church was already reigning and this thought continued until the days of the Reformation when the light began to dawn again.

But now note a most interesting thing. At the very time that the Lord said, "I ... know where thou dwellest, even where Satan's seat [or throne] is," He goes on to say, "Thou holdest fast my name, and hast not denied my faith" (13). Here is something very remarkable. At the same time that Christ sees them sitting on Satan's throne, He can commend them for holding fast His name.

It was at that time that the Arian controversy was fought out. Arius denied the eternity of the Word. John said, "In the beginning was the Word"—He always existed. When everything that had a beginning began, the Word was. Arius declared that the Word was the greatest of all beings that ever emanated from God. His oppo-nents insisted that the Word was one with the Father in one eternal Trinity—Father, Son, and Holy Spirit: one God in three persons. It was the most tremendous issue the church had ever been called to face. For over a century, it was the burning question that provoked heated controversy everywhere. For years the church was almost ripped apart over two words, h*omoiosian* ("of like substance")and *homoousian.* ("of the same substance"). The first was the battle cry of the Arians; the second of the orthodox, headed by Athanasius, Bishop of Alexandria. So irreconcilable were the contending par-ties that Constantine at last decided to intervene. He called a great church-council, which convened in the city of Nicea, to debate the question as to what the apostolic teaching really had been. Was Jesus truly God, or was He only the greatest being that God had

ever brought into existence? Over three hundred bishops met together, and Constantine, sitting on a golden throne, presided as the
acknowledged head of the Christian church. At the same time he
still bore the title Pontifex Maximus, or High Priest of the Heathen—the same title that the Pope bears at the present time.

The matter in question was examined from all sides. Again and
again Constantine was called in to quiet disturbances since feelings
ran so high. On one occasion it is related that a brilliant Arian seemed
to have almost silenced opposition. The great assemblage appeared
to be about to cast its vote in favor of the damnable Unitarian heresy. Then a hermit from the deserts of Africa, clad chiefly in tiger's
skin, sprang to his feet. He tore the skin from his back, disclosing
great scars (the result of having been thrown into the arena among
the wild beasts and his back dreadfully disfigured by their claws).
He cried dramatically, "These are the brand-marks of the Lord Jesus
Christ, and I cannot hear this blasphemy." Then he proceeded to
give a stirring address, setting forth clearly the truth as to Christ's
eternal deity. The majority of the council realized in a moment that
it was indeed the voice of the Spirit of God. Whether this story is
actually true or not I cannot say, but it illustrates the spirit that per-
vaded many who were in attendance, most of whom had passed
through the terrible persecution of Diocletian. The final result was
that the council of Nicea put itself on record as confessing the true
deity of our Lord Jesus Christ—"very God of very God," "Light of
lights," "perfection of perfection"—God and man in one blessed
person, nevermore to be separated. Thus was settled once and forever, in a public way, the acknowledged faith of the church of God,
which held fast His Word and did not deny His Name.

Did you ever stop to think what would have been the case if the
council had decided the other way? It would have meant this: Unitarianism would have henceforth borne the stamp of orthodoxy, and
the truth of the deity of Christ would have been branded as heresy.

We have no record as to who the Antipas was referred to in verse
13, but the name means "against all." Many years after the council
of Nicea, the Arian party was again largely dominant. Athanasius,
that doughty old champion of the truth, was summoned before the
Arian emperor Theodosius. He demanded that Athanasius cease his

opposition to the teaching of Arius—who was long since dead—
and admit the Arians to the table of the Lord. Athanasius refused.
Theodosius reproved him bitterly for what he considered his
insubject spirit and asked sternly, "Do you not realize that all the
world is against you?" The champion of the truth drew himself up
and answered the emperor, "Then I am against all the world." He
was a true Antipas, a faithful witness to the end of his days, despite
banishment and opposition of various kinds. Oh, my brethren, God
wants such men today who are willing to stand against all the world
for the truth's sake!

We now turn to consider another phase of things in the Pergamos
period—the introduction of the doctrine of Balaam and the teaching of the Nicolaitanes in the church. Balaam taught Balak to cast a
stumbling block before the sons of Israel by leading them to make
unholy alliances with the Midianite women, as recorded in Numbers 25:1-9. In figure this is the union of the church and the world.
During the Smyrna period, Satan sought to destroy the church by
persecution. In the next three centuries he tried different tactics: he
endeavored to ruin the testimony by worldly patronage from without and the introduction of false principles from within.

It is far more dangerous for the church to be patronized by the
world than for the world to stand openly against it. For example,
when were any of the denominations in Christendom shining most
brightly for the Lord? It was in the days of their first love, when
they were suffering from the world and were the objects of its bitter
persecution. But when the period of persecution ended and the world
began to look at them with complacency, to greet them with the
outstretched hand and the smiling face, instead of with the sword
and the frown, in every instance decline set in. So it was in the
Pergamos period. Constantine's patronage did what Diocletian's
persecution could not do. It corrupted the church, and she forgot
her calling as a chaste virgin espoused to an absent Lord. She gave
her hand in marriage to the world that had crucified Him, thus en-
tering into an unholy alliance of which she has never really repented.

In close connection with this we have the introduction of wrong
principles from within the church—the teaching of the Nicolaitanes
(15). Others have often pointed out that this is an untranslated Greek

word meaning, "rulers over the people." Nicolaitanism is really clerisy—the subjugation of those who were contemptuously styled "the laity" by a hierarchical order who lorded their position over them as their own possessions. They forgot that it is written, "One is your Master, even Christ; and all ye are brethren" (Matthew 23:8). In the letter to the church in Ephesus the Lord commended them for hating the deeds of the Nicolaitanes, those who, like Diotrephes, loved to have the preeminence among them (3 John 9). But, in the Pergamos letter, we have Nicolaitanism designated as a distinct system of teaching. It was during that period that the clergy was accepted as of divine origin, and therefore something that must be bowed to.

All this prepared the way for the Thyatira period, according to the next letter.

The Church of Thyatira (Revelation 2:18-29)

Thyatira is perhaps the most difficult of all the names to define. Scholars tell us that it comes from two words, one meaning a sacrifice, or an incense-offering; the other, that which goes on continually. A suggested interpretation, therefore, is "continual sacrifice." And this is very significant, because Thyatira undoubtedly illustrates the period that was the result of the union of church and state already noticed. It was in the seventh century that the Bishop of Rome was first regularly recognized as Christ's vicegerent and visible head of the church. This was, properly speaking, the beginning of the papacy. There was no Roman Catholic church, in the full sense, until the pope was the acknowledged head of Christendom. It is important for Protestants to keep this in mind. You will often hear papists say, "You know the first church was the Roman Catholic church, and all the different branches of the Protestant church have simply broken off from Rome. There was no Protestant church until the days of Luther." That is an absolute sophistry. There was no such thing as the papacy until the seventh century of the Christian era. For six centuries before that, the church was becoming more and more corrupt and drifting further away from the Word of God. Then in the seventh century, men professing themselves to be servants of God were ready to acknowledge the pope as head of all Christendom. A Roman Catholic once asked a bright Protestant school-girl, "Where was your church before the days of Henry the VIII?" "Why, sir, where yours never was, *in the Bible*," was her sensible and correct reply. It was a far cry from the simplicity of early Christianity when in the seventh century Christians were ready to own the pretensions of the bishop of Rome.

I said that Thyatira seemed to imply a continual sacrifice. You will see the significance of this in the great fundamental error of the church of Rome—the sacrifice of the mass. The Roman Catholic priests declare that in the mass they offer a continual sacrifice for the sins of the living and the dead. Other errors of the church of Rome spring from that teaching. There are many things that Protestants might be able to condone. This doctrine is the central blasphemy—the denial of the finished work of the Lord Jesus on Calvary's cross which was the one, only, and all-sufficient offering for the sins of a guilty world. Every time the priest stands at Rome's altar to offer the sacrifice of the mass, he denies the unchanging efficacy of the work wrought by the Lord Jesus on Calvary's cross.

I have often pressed this question home to Catholic priests: "What is your function as a sacrificing priest?" They say, "It is my privilege to offer up the Lord Jesus from time to time a continual sacrifice for the sins of the living and the dead." I generally put it like this: "Well, Christ has to be slain that He may be offered up, doesn't He?"—"Yes." "You claim then that every time you offer the sacrifice of the mass, every time you pronounce the blessing, you are sacrificing Christ for the sins of the living and the dead?"—"Yes." "Well then, you kill Christ afresh every time you offer that sacrifice!" Then they begin to hedge. But there is no escape from this horrible conclusion. The Roman priest says that when he offers the sacrifice of the mass he is presenting Christ again for the sins of the living and the dead. The only way that Christ can be a sacrifice is to be put to death; therefore, the priest kills Him afresh every time he offers. They cannot get away from it. The apostle Peter said at Pentecost, "Him, being delivered by the determinate counsel and foreknowledge of God, ye have taken, and by wicked hands have crucified and slain: whom God hath raised up, etc." If Christ has to be offered continually then every priest is guilty of murdering the Lord Jesus Christ in the sight of God.

God is going to judge Rome in a little while, so Christ's letter to Thyatira properly speaks of this central blasphemy of the church of Rome. Continual sacrifice? Never! No other sacrifice is needed. The dignity of the Lord is so great, the value of His blood is so absolutely infinite, that it is vain for you or any other man to speak about a new sacrifice.

You may say, "I agree with you." Well let me ask, do you have a personal interest in that one offering made once on the cross? Can you say, "Thank God, He gave Himself a propitiation for my sins, and He is my Savior. I need no other sacrifice. My soul is resting on the finished work of Christ. I require nothing more on which to enter the presence of God"?

It is very significant that the Lord presented Himself in each one of these letters in such a way so as to meet the special condition in which each church is found. When He addressed Himself to the church of Thyatira, He spoke solemnly as "the Son of God" (18). Why did the Lord Jesus Christ in writing to this church emphasize the fact of His deity? Because Rome everywhere has accustomed people to think of Him as the Son of Mary. I once talked with a woman who told me she would rather go to Mary than to Christ or the Father. She said, "There is nobody that has so much influence with a son as his mother. If Jesus Christ is inclined to be a bit hard-hearted, I just go to His good, kind mother, and I ask her to please say a good word to Him for me." What a caricature of our Lord Jesus Christ! Think of having to go to anybody else to win His favor. Who else could be compared with Him? Thus Christ is degraded into the position of the Son of Mary, rather than the Son of God who came in infinite grace to save poor sinners.

Observe that He has "eyes like unto a flame of fire, and his feet are like fine brass." This speaks of His holiness and righteousness. He must judge all that is evil. Yet He never overlooks what can be commended. He goes on to say, "I know thy works, and charity, and service, and faith, and thy patience, and thy works: and the last to be more than the first" (19). The Lord gave Rome credit for a great deal that is good. Remember from the seventh century to the

present there has been a great deal in the way of good works in the
Roman Catholic church that cannot be overlooked. There have been
Roman Catholic nuns and monks who have been ready to lay down
their lives for the needy and the sick. Centuries before Luther every
hospital in western Europe was simply a Roman Catholic monas-
tery or convent. The Lord does not forget all that. Where there is a
bit of faith, His love takes note of it all. If there are hearts in the
church of Rome that, amid the superstition, reach out to the blessed
Lord Himself, He meets them in grace and demonstrates His love to
them. But having done this, He continued by putting His finger on
the sore spot: "Notwithstanding, I have a few things against thee,
because thou sufferest that woman Jezebel, which calleth herself a
prophetess, to teach and to seduce my servants to commit fornication, and to eat things sacrificed unto idols" (20).

To understand verse 20, we need to go back to Israel's history in
the days of King Ahab. Jezebel was adept in the art of mixing. She
undertook to unite the religion of Israel and the religion of Phoenicia.
That is just what Romanism is—a mixture of heathenism and Christianity and Judaism. It is not Christianity—yet there is in it a little
that is Christian. Where did its superstition and image worship come
from? It was all taken bodily over from heathenism under the plea
that it would help to convert the pagans. The church became very
accommodating. In the fourth, fifth, and sixth centuries the church
compromised with heathen rites and heathen ceremonies to such a
degree that by the seventh century one could hardly tell heathen
from Christian temples. The amalgamation is such that it is almost
impossible to separate the one from the other. Go to a Roman Catholic church. After sitting through the whole ceremony, take your Bible
and search it from one end to the other and ask yourself, "Is there
anything like that in the Book?" You will say, "No." Where does it
come from then? Go from there to a heathen temple. Observe its
ritual, and you will say, "Yes, they are the same."

Romanism is Christianity, Judaism, and heathenism joined together and the Lord abhors the vile combination. Note two things
that He holds against Rome—spiritual fornication and idolatry. The
first is the union of the church and the world and "the friendship of
the world is enmity with God" (James 4:4). Idolatry is the worship

of images, strictly forbidden in the second commandment (Exodus 20:4-5). God gave the church time to repent and she repented not. Go back to the days of Savonarola in Italy, Wycliffe and Cranmer of England, John Knox in Scotland, Martin Luther in Germany, Zwingli in Switzerland, Calvin in France—all those mighty reformers whom God raised up throughout the world to call Rome to repent of her iniquity, but "she repented not."

Mark this, you could not transpose these churches. You could not put Thyatira in the place of Smyrna. It could not be said to the church in that early day, "I gave her space to repent, and she repented not;" but it is fully applicable to the church of Rome. God gave Rome space to repent. If she had had any desire to get right with Him, she would have repented in the sixteenth century.

Since the sixteenth century Rome has added to her blasphemies and errors the declaration of the absolute sinlessness of the virgin Mary. The church of Rome has lifted her to the position of a female God and declared that she was caught up to Heaven without dying and crowned queen of Heaven.

At the Council of the Vatican, the church of Rome produced another of her wretched dogmas—the infallibility of her popes. This dogma was so utterly without reason that many bishops said, "This is going too far. We know that popes have reversed each other over and over again." But Rome never repented; she has added sin upon sin to the heavy list God had against her in the middle ages and will remain the same to the end. It behooves Protestants to keep clear of it all. God says He is going to cast her into the great tribulation.

The age of Ephesus ended; the age of Smyrna ended about A.D. 312; also Pergamos ended. But Thyatira began in the seventh century and goes right on into the great tribulation and shows herself at last as Babylon the great. Her children are to be judged. But wherever there is a remnant found who "have not known the depths of Satan," the Lord owns them as His and exhorts them to hold fast what they have until He comes (24-25). To the overcomer He promises what Rome has always pursued—power over the nations. They will rule with Him when He comes again (26-27). Thus the hope of the second coming of Christ is put before them and this event has a large place in each of the rest of the church letters.

CHAPTER THREE
THE SEVEN CHURCHES

(PART TWO)

We now go on to look at the next part in the marvelous series of this great annotated timetable of the church's history.

Church of Sardis (Revelation 3:1-6)

Chapter 3 begins with the letter to the church of Sardis. *Sardis* means "a remnant," or, "those who have escaped." This name is very significant and tells its own story too plainly to be misunderstood. It brings before us, prophetically, the great state churches of the Reformation. These churches escaped from Rome, only to fall eventually into cold, lifeless formalism.

The first verse indicates that there was a measure of return to early principles in Sardis. The Lord's introduction of Himself to this church is very similar to that in the letter to Ephesus, and yet the difference is most marked. Here He is said to *have* the seven stars; in the letter to Ephesus He was said to *hold* the seven stars in His right hand. It is, at least, the recognition that ministry belongs to Christ. Ministers are Christ's ministers—not the church's. Yet even in the glorious days of the Reformation, the truth was not fully apprehended that ministers are to be controlled by, and subject to Christ without any human intermediary. While the Protestant ministry is very different from the Roman hierarchy, unfortunately human ordination has done much to obscure a proper conception of the servant's responsibility to the Master.

The Lord declared solemnly, "I know thy works, that thou hast a name that thou livest, and art dead" (3:1). How sad and solemn the indictment! One might well ask in amazement, how such things could be after the blessing and revival of Reformation days. We need to remember that historically the state churches included all the population of a given country who were supposed to be made members of the church and kingdom of Christ by baptism in infancy. We can then readily understand why such churches, though possibly strictly orthodox, may yet be largely composed of persons still dead in trespasses and in sins. Nothing can be much sadder than vast congregations of people, baptized, banded together as Christians, taking the sacrament of the Lord's supper, zealous for church and Christianity, and yet often devoid of personal, saving faith in Christ. They trust in forms and ceremonies, and what some have called "birthright membership," rather than in new birth through the Word and Spirit of God.

What is needed everywhere is a great revival of decided gospel preaching, pressing home on the consciences of men and women their lost condition, despite church membership, if they have not personally received the Lord Jesus Christ. The Word says, "Break up your fallow ground, and sow not among thorns" (Jeremiah 4:3). People often say they would like to see more old-time conversions. Well, there must first be the old-time preaching of the exceeding sinfulness of sin and the lost condition of all men by nature as well as practice. Then the old-time conviction will seize on the souls of Christless people and the old-time gospel will be hailed as the only relief.

No wonder the Lord says to Protestantism, "Be watchful, and strengthen the things which remain, that are ready to die: for I have not found thy works perfect before God" (3:2). He calls on them to remember how they had received and heard and to hold fast and repent. With careful examination it is clear that this message would not have been as applicable to the Thyatira as to the Sardis period. Such words would not have the same force when addressed to Rome as when addressed to the churches of the Reformation.

What did these churches of the Reformation receive and hear? Clearly the great truths were proclaimed fearlessly in the days of the Reformation. These truths were embodied in the creeds of the sixteenth and seventeenth centuries for the instruction of future generations. I am not one of those who waste time denouncing creeds. *Credo* means "I believe." Any man who believes anything has a creed. All the great creeds of Protestantism are the carefully drawn-up declarations of the faith of those who had escaped from Roman superstition. They wrote these creeds to make clear to their children what they recognized as the truth which they had received from God. We need not be surprised if we find in these creeds some statements that fuller light and knowledge would lead us to refuse or revise. But these statements of faith hold within them *fundamental* truths of the Word of God. Take the Augsburg Confession of the Lutherans; the Westminster Confession of the Presbyterians; the 39 Articles of the Church of England; and others too numerous to mention. Every one of these creeds insists on the true deity of Christ and the efficacy of His atoning work on Calvary's cross. All declare that salvation is only through faith, apart from works.

Those creeds stand for the fundamental truths of Christianity. It is not to any minister's credit today to stand up in the pulpits of denominations advocating such creeds and say, "I have thrown the creed of the church overboard." When a man reaches that point he either ought to be thrown out of the church whose principles he no longer believes, or he should be honest enough to take himself out. One of the worst features of the present apostasy is that there are thousands of men occupying supposedly orthodox pulpits who, if they could, would destroy everything for which their respective denominations stand.

So we may thank God for the truths contained in these creeds, yet recognize that where the Word of God is bowed to, no creed drawn up by humans is needed. Nevertheless, I believe it is in view of these very confessions that the Lord says, "Remember therefore how thou hast received and heard" (3:3). He calls on Protestants to remember the great truths committed to them at the Reformation and hold them fast. They should repent for the slack way in which they have treated these truths in the past.

Once again the Lord spoke of His approaching advent: "If therefore thou shalt not watch, I will come on thee as a thief, and thou shalt not know what hour I will come upon thee" (3). How different this verse is from 1 Thessalonians 5:4 where Paul wrote of that same wondrous advent: "But ye, brethren, are not in darkness, that that day should overtake you as a thief." It is very evident, therefore, that the coming of the Lord should be the daily expectation of His own beloved people. It is only to the great mass of mere professors that His return will be as the coming of a thief—that is, as the unexpected and unlooked-for One whose coming will spread dismay instead of gladness.

It is blessed to know the declaration and promise of the Lord in verse 4. Even in Sardis He saw a few names that had not defiled their garments. He declared that they will walk with Him in white for they are worthy. His blood alone has made them so. There are thousands in Christendom who are linked up with much that is unscriptural and are often almost undistinguishable from the mass. Yet they are plainly discernible to His eye, for it is written, "The Lord knoweth them that are his." To these overcomers the promise is made that they will be clothed in white raiment. Their names will not be blotted out of the Book of Life. Whereas thousands of names, representing a Christless profession, will be expunged from the records in that day of manifestation.

It is not a question of people who have been truly born of God losing that eternal life given them in Christ. As many other Scriptures show, that is an impossibility. In fact, were it otherwise it would not be *eternal* life at all. But the Lord is referring to those who have a *name* to live, but are *dead*. Their names are registered among those who profess to have life in Christ. In reality they are, as Jude wrote, "twice dead"—dead in trespasses and sins and dead to their profession of life.

So in the day of manifestation their names will be eliminated. Only those who have proven by persevering in well-doing that they truly have life in Christ, will be left. They will be confessed before the Father and the angels at the Lord's second coming.

The Church of Philadelphia (Revelation 3:7-13)

The next in order is the letter to the church in *Philadelphia*, which means "brotherly love." This letter, I believe, brings us to what we may call the revival period. Following the Reformation there came a time when a cold, lifeless formalism seemed to settle down over all Protestant Christendom. It was an era in which men were content simply to confess a creed. As we have already mentioned, they were presumed to be united to the church by baptism. But in the eighteenth and nineteenth centuries there came a great wave of blessing over all those lands where the Reformation had gone. God began to work afresh in mighty power. There were marvelous awakenings all over northern Europe and the British Isles. A half century later the same mighty power began to evidence itself in America. Spirit-filled servants of Christ went through these various countries like firebrands of the Lord, calling on sinners to repent and saints to awaken to their privileges. A little later, in the early part of the last century, God began to arouse many of His people to a deeper sense of the value of His Word and its all-sufficiency for the guidance of His people. This led to the recognition of the fact that Christ Himself is the gathering center for His people. For His name's sake thousands left all human systems and began to meet in simplicity, seeking to be guided alone by the Word of God.

Now I do not mean to imply that we are to understand any special movement or association of believers to be in itself Philadelphia. But, just as the church of Sardis depicts state churches of the Reformation, so I believe the church of Philadelphia illustrates those in Protestantism who emphasize the authority of the Word of God and the preciousness of the name of Christ. For any particular company to claim to be Philadelphia is but detestable ecclesiastical pretension; God has very evidently frowned on all such conceit.

Notice what would mark in a special way those who seek to walk as Philadelphians. In the first place the very name of this church—"brotherly love"—implies that its members love as brethren. They are born of God, and His love is shed abroad in their hearts by the Holy Spirit given unto them. They are characterized by love to all who are Christ's. How little this characteristic is seen among many who make very loud assertions to being the testimony of the Lord at the present time. There may be much truth and a great pretension to divine ground and maintaining of scriptural principles, but if this first mark of brotherly love is missing you have not yet found Philadelphia.

In the second place, observe the character in which the Lord presented Himself to this church. "These things saith he that is holy, he that is true" (3:7). These words embody a challenge to separation from evil in life and error in doctrine. If we would walk in fellowship with the holy One we must remember the admonition, "Be ye holy, for I am holy" (1 Peter 1:16). And if we would enjoy communion with Him who is the Truth, we must refuse Satan's lies, and love and live the truth ourselves. Hence it follows, as others have stated, that "separation from evil is God's principle of unity." Not separation in a cold, pharisaic sense, but separation *to Christ* from that which is evil.

Next, the Lord spoke of Himself as "he that hath the key of David, he that openeth, and no man shutteth; and shutteth; and no man openeth" (3:7). This verse is clearly a reference to Isaiah 22:22. In that Isaiah passage he who had the key of David was the treasurer of David's house. There it is said of Eliakim, "The key of the house of David will I lay upon his shoulder; so he shall open, and none shall shut; and he shall shut, and none shall open." The remainder of the passage shows that Eliakim was a type of the Lord Jesus Christ, the one on whom should be hung all the glory of His Father's house. He, by His Spirit, opens the great treasure-house of divine truth, and none can shut it. On the other hand where there is perversity of spirit and an unwillingness to walk in the truth, He shuts and none can open. So He has said elsewhere, "If therefore the light that is in thee be darkness, how great is that darkness" (Matthew 6:23).

It is blessed to realize that, while Christ is said to have the key of David, there is another sense in which we see that He is the key. By the presentation of Himself to the souls of His people He opens up the treasures of His Word. Thus Christ is the key to the Holy Scriptures, and no other is needed. To understand the Bible you need only to know Christ.

Perhaps there is another sense in which we might apply the words in regard to opening and shutting; they may have an application to service. The Lord Himself opens the doors for those whom He sends forth, and He it is who closes them when He so wills. This is one thing that Philadelphian believers, generally, have found to be true. Christ is Son over His own house, and He has commanded His servants to go into all the world and preach the gospel to every creature. Acting on this truth, thousands have gone forth in dependence on Him alone in the homeland and to lands beyond the seas without any organization behind them. They have found the Lord Himself all-sufficient to meet every need and to open and close just as He will. "Faith can firmly trust Him, come what may." I think the 8th verse emphasizes this second application. There He says, "I have set before thee an open door, and no man can shut it: for thou hast a little strength, and hast kept my word, and hast not denied my name."

Observe these important characteristics of Philadelphia. His Word is kept and His Name is confessed. The keeping of His Word involves a great deal more than just believing the Bible or reading and studying it. It implies *obedience* to the revealed will of the Lord. It is a blessed thing to realize that "all scripture is given by inspiration of God, and is profitable for doctrine, for reproof, for correction, for instruction in righteousness: that the man of God may be perfect, throughly furnished unto all good works" (2 Timothy 3:16). What immense scope is there here for faith to act on! This blessed book of God marks out all my path. As long as I seek to walk in obedience, I will never be found in circumstances where this Book cannot guide me. I believe this is what is involved in keeping His Word.

The denial of His Name is demonstrated by the increasing apostasy around us on every hand. Those who have not denied His Name refuse all fellowship with those who dishonor God. Christ is more precious to them than all else. Even for the sake of service, they refuse to link themselves with that which dishonors or blasphemes that worthy name whereby they are called.

It is significant that wherever Philadelphian truth has been proclaimed, the devil has raised up a counterfeit to draw people's hearts away from the truth. So in verse 9 the Lord spoke of those who will be revealed as the synagogue of Satan, "which say they are Jews, and are not, but do lie." The day will come when they will have to worship before the feet of those who are faithful to the Lord and will know that He has loved them. This verse is undoubtedly refer-ring to the false Judaizing system. Its advocates everywhere oppose the truth of grace and seek in every way to hinder the carrying out of those principles that please the Lord. In their ignorance, these teachers give up the true Christian position, claiming to be the spiri-tual Israel. They appropriate to themselves Jewish promises and Jewish hopes and would put the consciences of Christians under the bondage of Jewish legalism. Thus they are really doing Satan's work.

The promise of verse 10, like all the promises to these different churches, is for every true child of God: "Because thou hast kept the word of my patience, I also will keep thee from the hour of temptation, which shall come upon all the world, to try them that dwell upon the earth." This is the Lord's own pledge to those who love His Name and seek to keep His Word—they will not be left down here to pass through the appalling tribulation that is just ahead of those who "dwell upon the earth." This expression is found fre-quently in the book of Revelation. It does not simply mean those who live in the world. A careful reading of the various passages in which this peculiar term is found will make it clear that "the earth-dwellers" are in contrast to those whose citizenship is in Heaven. They are persons who, while professing to be Christians, refuse the heavenly calling. They prove by their earthly-mindedness and worldly ways that they really belong to this world. All their hopes and their treasures are here. The Lord has said, "Where your trea-sure is, there will your heart be also." The coming great tribulation will be a time of fearful trial for them.

The bulk of the book of Revelation considers this hour of tur-moil, as we will demonstrate in future chapters. But when that hour comes the church of the present dispensation will have been caught up to meet the Lord (1 Thessalonians 4:13-18). Revelation 3:11 speaks of this, "Behold, I come quickly: hold that fast which thou hast, that no man take thy crown." The Lord's return is the hope of every Christian heart. They long to see Him who loved them and gave Himself for them. At His return, they will be revealed before His judgment seat and be rewarded according to service here. Then

He will give out the crowns for service in this day of His rejection. Observe that the warning is let "no man take thy crown." It is not, "Let no man take thy life," or "thy salvation." That is eternally secure in Christ. Being born of God, I cannot lose my salvation; but, if I am not a faithful servant, I may lose my *crown*.

The overcomer will be made a pillar in the temple of the God of our Lord Jesus Christ and will dwell in the Father's house forever. The name of God, the name of the holy city, and Christ's new name will be written on him. All that is involved in this is beyond our poor, finite comprehension. It speaks of stability, of security, of fellowship, of intimacy with the Lord Himself, which will make Heaven to the believer—his blessed and eternal home.

The Church of Laodicea (Revelation 3:14-22)

Laodicea completes this septenary series. It brings us down, practically, to the last stage of the professing church's history on earth— the close of the present dispensation. *Laodicea* is a compound word and means "the rights of the people." Could any other term more aptly describe the condition of present-day church affairs? It is the era of democratization, both in the world and in the church. The masses of the people are realizing their power as never before. The terrific slogan, *vox populi, vox Dei* (The voice of the people is the voice of God), is ringing through the world with clarion-like distinctness. Imperialism and every form of aristocratic government is disappearing—at least for the time being. The age of anarchy is almost upon us. Statesmen and capitalists never were more anxious and nervous than at the present time. In World War I we were told our soldiers were fighting to make the world safe for democracy. Soon statesmen will be attempting to raise armies to make the world safe from democracy. The spirit of this ultra-democratic age has invaded a large portion of the professed church. The authority of God and His Word is rapidly being denied. The spirit of the age is exhibited by a large part of the church; hence the striking correspondence between this letter to the Laodiceans and the latitudinarianism so prevalent about us.

In a day when faithful witnesses to God's truth are becoming fewer and fewer, the Lord addresses Himself to the church as "the Amen" (that is, the establisher of all God's promises). He is the faithful and true Witness, who will maintain to the end what is of God, though the great majority of those who profess to follow Him be swept away by the apostasy. He reproves the church for its lukewarmness and indifference to Himself and the truth. He says, "Because thou art lukewarm, and neither cold nor hot, I will spue thee out of my mouth" (3:16). There is neither burning zeal for His Word, nor yet absolute repudiation of Christ and the Bible. Instead there is a nauseating, lukewarm condition that is abhorrent to the Spirit of God. Lukewarm water is, in itself, an emetic, and this is the figure the Lord here uses. He cannot tolerate such conditions much longer, but will spew out the whole disgusting mass in judgment.

Meanwhile the church goes on in its pride and self-satisfaction, saying, "I am rich and increased with goods, and have need of nothing." The church does not know that in God's eyes, it is "miserable, and poor, and blind, and naked" (17). Never were church dignitaries and carnally-minded religious leaders more satisfied with themselves and their great work than at the present time. Anything and everything is advocated that will make the church popular. The rights of the people alone must be considered; the rights of the Lord Jesus Christ are not even thought of. We have come to a time when, in many places, it is easier to get on without Christ than with Him; it is easier to carry on religious programs without the Holy Spirit than if He were working among us in mighty power. No wonder He says, "I counsel thee to buy of me gold tried in the fire [that is, divine righteousness], that thou mayest be rich; and white raiment [that is, practical righteousness], that thou mayest be clothed…and anoint thine eyes with eyesalve [that is, the anointing of the Holy Spirit], that thou mayest see" (18). Yes, there is lots of fleshly energy and human effort being exerted to reclaim the world and make it a comfortable place for men to live in apart from Christ. But the great things of God's truth are largely neglected. Myriads of so-called church-workers are utter strangers to the new birth, without which no one can see the Kingdom of God.

So we see the Lord standing at last outside the door of the professing church and saying so tenderly, "Behold, I stand at the door, and knock: if any man hear my voice, and open the door, I will come in to him, and will sup with him, and he with me" (20). Beloved friends, it is getting late in the dispensation. The Lord who, in the beginning, was in the midst of His church, stands *outside* that lukewarm system which calls itself by His name, and He knocks in vain for entrance! Yet, individuals here and there open to Him and find His presence offers more than all the earth or the professing church can afford.

We have come down to the closing days of the present dispensation of grace. The Ephesus period passed away long ago, and the same is true of the Smyrna and Pergamos periods. Thyatira, which as we have seen speaks of Romanism, began properly when the pope was recognized as universal bishop, is with us still, and will go on to the end. Sardis, which began centuries later, remains to the present time and will remain until the Lord comes. Philadelphia, thank God, is also here; although it only has a little strength, it will also abide to the end. But Laodicea is more and more in evidence and seems to be almost swamping everything that is of God.

The next great event is the coming of the Lord Jesus Christ and our gathering together unto Him. For this we wait, and our longing hearts cry, "Even so, come, Lord Jesus" (Revelation 22:20).

CHAPTER FOUR
THE FIRST VISION OF HEAVEN

As we turn from chapter 3 to chapter 4, the scenes are very different! We are no longer occupied with the professing church in the place of testimony, nor with events on the earth at all. A door is opened in Heaven, and escorted by John we are carried far above the shifting scenes of this poor world. We are permitted to gaze with awe-struck eyes on a scene of indescribable glory and to hear things kept secret from the foundation of the world.

The opening verse begins the third great division of this book—the "things which must be hereafter." It describes the stirring panorama of wonders, both heavenly and earthly, which must take place after the church's history is ended. From the close of chapter 3, we never see the church on earth again through the rest of this solemn book. We read of "saints," but they are distinct altogether from the church of the present dispensation. Israel comes into view and a great multitude of Gentiles saved out of the great tribulation; but there is no church, no body of Christ, no bride of the Lamb any more on the earth!

The Throne (Revelation 4:1-3)

I believe that we must understand the rapture of 1 Thessalonians 4:16-17 as transpiring between Revelation 3 and 4. The apostle is the symbol of this rapture. He sees the door opened in Heaven. His attention is turned from earth to glory. He is caught up in spirit, and far above all the mists of this world he sees a throne set in Heaven and someone sitting on it. He cannot even attempt to portray the likeness of this august being. He only tells us he beheld a presence whose glory was like a jasper and a sardius.

The jasper of the Revelation is not the opaque stone we know by that name. It is later described as clear as crystal (21:11). It is probably the diamond, the most brilliant of all the precious jewels. The other stone is blood-red and may really be the ruby. Thus the two together give the idea of glory and of sacrifice. Remembering that many of the first readers of the Revelation were converted Jews, we might ask what these stones would suggest to them. Surely every instructed Hebrew would instantly recall that they were the first and last stones in the breastplate of the high priest (Exodus 28:17-21). These stones were engraved with the names of the tribes of Israel, arranged according to the births of the twelve patriarchs; so the ruby would suggest at once the name Reuben, "Behold a Son," and the Jasper Benjamin, "Son of my right hand." It is Christ enthroned, the Son about to reign in power who is before the seer's vision. Around the throne a rainbow, like an emerald, the stone of Judah ("Praise") is seen. This suggests the perpetuity of the Noahic covenant and God's unchanging goodness, despite all man's failure, folly, and wickedness.

The Elders (Revelation 4:4-5)

The fourth verse brings before us a sight never beheld in Heaven on any previous occasion: twenty-four thrones (not merely "seats") surrounding the central throne and on them twenty-four elders seated with victors' crowns (not diadems) on their heads, and clothed in priestly robes of purest white. Who are these favored ones gathered around the glorious central Being? I think their identity is clear if we compare Scripture with Scripture and distrust our own imagination, which can only lead us astray.

In 1 Chronicles 24, we read of something very similar; again I would remind you that many of John's first readers were Hebrews, thoroughly familiar with the Old Testament. Every Jewish believer would remember the twenty-four elders appointed by King David to represent the entire Levitical priesthood. He divided the priests into twenty-four courses, each course to serve for two weeks at a time in the temple which Solomon was to build. The same arrangement was in force when our Lord's forerunner was announced. Zacharias was "of the course of Abiah," the eighth in order (Luke 1:5).

The thousands of priests could not all come together at one time; but when the twenty-four elders met in the temple precincts in Jerusalem, the whole priestly house was represented. I submit this is the explanation of the twenty-four elders in Heaven. They represent the whole heavenly priesthood—that is, all the redeemed who have died in the past or who will be living at the Lord's return. In vision they were not seen as millions of saved worshipers, but just twenty-four elders symbolizing the entire company. The church of the present age and Old Testament saints are both included. All are priests. All worship. There were twelve patriarchs in Israel and twelve apostles introducing the new dispensation. The two together would give the complete twenty-four.

Then, observe that these persons are not angels. They are redeemed men who have overcome in the conflict with Satan and the world. They wear victors' wreaths on their heads. Angels are never said to be crowned, nor have they known redemption.

There are two kinds of crowns mentioned in this book: the victor's crown and the ruler's diadem. The former is the word used here. It refers to the laurel or pine wreath placed on the victor's head in the Greek games. It is the same word so often used in the New Testament regarding reward for service. Note carefully that no saints will ever be crowned until the apostle Paul receives that crown of righteousness which the Lord revealed to him as his reward. In 2 Timothy 4:8 he says: "Henceforth there is laid up for me a crown of righteousness, which the Lord, the righteous judge, shall give me at that day: and not to me only, but unto all them also that love (or have loved) His appearing." The expression "at that day" refers to the day of Christ when He will come for His own, and they will all be confirmed before His judgment seat. He says: "Behold, I come quickly; and my reward is with me, to give every man according as his work shall be" (Revelation 22:12). Surely it follows then that no rewards are given out until He returns for His saints. Therefore there can be no crowned elders in Heaven until after the rapture.

I believe this is a point of great importance today. Many are being troubled by the thought that perhaps the great tribulation, which is the subject of a large a part of the book of Revelation, has already begun. But all such fears are set at rest when the facts I have been emphasizing are kept in mind. I want to dwell a little on this in the next chapter, so I refrain from further comment now. Only I trust it is clear to all that the elders are the *heavenly* saints surrounding the Lord in glory, God the Son sitting on the central throne.

Lightnings, thunderings, and voices emanating from the throne make it clear that a dreadful storm is about to burst on that world below. As we go on in the study of the book, we will see more alarming conditions added from time to time as the scene becomes increasingly solemn.

Following out the symbolism of the tabernacle, seven lamps of fire are seen burning before the throne, as the seven-branched lampstand burned just outside the veil, before God's throne on earth—the ark of old. These lamps are said to be "the seven Spirits of God." As we have already seen (1:4) this figure illustrates not seven distinct Spirits, but the one Holy Spirit in the sevenfold plenitude of His power.

The Adoration (Revelation 4:6-11)

The sea of glass of verse 6 calls to mind the sea of brass in Solomon's temple, which like the laver, symbolized the Word of God. It contained the water used for priestly cleansing, and we are sanctified and cleansed by "the washing of water by the word." But the sea in Revelation is not for cleansing, so it is like crystal and later we find the martyred tribulation-saints standing on it. It is the Word of God still, but no longer needed for cleansing because desert experiences are viewed here as forever passed. But the Word abides, stable and sure forevermore—a glassy sea filled with crystal. It is firm and glorious and on it the people of God can stand eternally.

It is well known that instead of four "beasts" surrounding the throne, a better translation would be "four living ones." They are not beasts. The word is very different than that used in Revelation 13. They are not created beings, for they are in the midst of the throne, where only Deity can dwell. They are linked with it round about. They represent the attributes of the living God. The lion is the well-known symbol of divine majesty. The young ox symbolizes the divine strength graciously serving man. The face of a man indicates intelligence and purpose; it tells us that Deity is no mere blind force, nor is He simply the "great first cause" or impersonal law. The eagle suggests swiftness in detecting evil and executing judgment. The living creatures are six-winged and full of eyes suggesting incessant activity and omniscience. "The eyes of the Lord are in every place, beholding the evil and the good" (Proverbs 15:3). The creatures cry, "Holy, holy, holy, Lord God Almighty, which was, and is, and is to come," (Revelation 4:8) for all God's attributes glorify the eternal Son.

The elders bow in worship at this announcement and cast their crowns at the feet of Him that sits on the throne. They adore Him as Creator, saying, "Thou art worthy, O Lord, to receive glory and honour, and power: for thou hast created all things, and for thy pleasure they are and were created." A higher note is struck in chapter five, but the blessed truth is here proclaimed that He who died on the cross is worshiped by all the redeemed in Heaven. There can be no mistake as to the identity of the person on the throne. If John 1, Colossians 1, and Hebrews 1 are all carefully compared with this closing verse, it becomes perfectly clear that it is Christ Jesus, the Son who created all things. Without Him was nothing made. All things are by Him and for Him. So He it is who fills the throne and is the center of the worship here described.

In our day Christ's glory as the eternal Son is so often denied. His true deity, His virgin birth, His sinless humanity are all alike flouted by apostate teachers as so much traditional lore to be rejected at will. How refreshing to the soul to turn from earth to Heaven and contemplate His glory as displayed there and the unhindered adoration of His own as they prostrate themselves before His throne. If He is not God, then Heaven will be filled with idolaters, for it is written: "Thou shalt worship the Lord thy God, and him only shalt thou serve" (Matthew 4:10).

But we need not for a moment enter such an "if." He is "God over all, blessed forever," and He is also man. God the Son in grace was born of the virgin, and it is He who fills the throne above. Nor will He ever abdicate that throne, even though He will soon descend to gather His own to Himself and to reign over all the earth as Son of man, sitting on the throne of His father David. Both thrones are His, for all glory belongs to Him by the Father's firm decree. Thus all men will eventually honor the Son even as they honor the Father.

I add a further word as to the living creatures. In chapter 4 we see them linked especially with the throne. In chapter 5 they are most particularly linked with the elders. We have suggested that they represent the divine attributes. During the present age and before the Lamb takes the book of judgment these are largely seen in angelic ministry. But "unto the angels hath he not put in subjection the [age] to come" (Hebrews 2:5). In that day God will work through His redeemed ones; hence the living ones join in the new song, voicing the joy of the saints in whom the divine glory will be displayed. The living creatures of Ezekiel's vision and the cherubim on the mercyseat tell the same story.

CHAPTER FIVE

THE SEVEN-SEALED BOOK

In Revelation 5 we are still occupied with the same vision as in chapter 4. There we saw the Lord Jesus Christ worshiped as Creator. Here a higher glory is His—He is worshiped as Redeemer. " 'Twas great to speak a world from nought; 'twas greater to redeem."

The Book (Revelation 5:1)

The first thing that attracts our attention is what is said of the seven-sealed book in the right hand of Him who sits on the throne. We have already seen in chapter 4 that the Son is on that throne; but we must not forget that it is likewise the throne of God the Father. And so here we have in the Father's right hand a book written within and on the backside and sealed with seven seals. When we read of a *book* we must not think of a volume such as we are familiar with but rather of a roll of parchment. The ancient books of Israel were generally sheepskin rolls. When we are told that this book was sealed with seven seals, we are to understand that the book was rolled up to a certain point, and there a seal was put on the edge so that it could not be opened until that seal was broken. It was rolled up a little farther and another seal put on, and so on until there were six seals on the edge of the book and one seal closing the entire scroll. When the first seal was opened a certain portion of the book was exposed to view and so with each one following. When the seventh was broken then the entire book would be unrolled.

What is this sealed book? I will again remind you of a principle which I want to keep before you throughout our study. In studying the book of the Revelation it is never necessary to fall back on our own imagination as to what a particular symbol means. Every symbol is explained, or alluded to, somewhere else in the Bible. We will turn to the book of Jeremiah for an understanding of this seven-sealed book. The prophet Jeremiah lived in a day just previous to the fall of Jerusalem under Nebuchadnezzar. He had been telling the people of Israel that they were going to be carried captives to Babylon. For seventy years they would be in captivity. At the end of that time, they would be restored and would build again the waste places (Jeremiah 29:10). Hanameel, Jeremiah's cousin, had a piece of ground and knew well that it was soon to be absolutely worthless. He was anxious to get it off his hands and realize what he could from it. He concluded to try to sell it to his prophet-cousin who was in prison at the time for the truth's sake. The Lord told Jeremiah to buy the field. He was commanded to accept it as though it were really worth having, because the time was coming when it would be worth having; for just as surely as God's people were going down into Babylon, so surely were they coming back again. That land would be worth far more in that day, and he would have it in his family.

So we are told in Jeremiah 32:8 that Hanameel came and begged Jeremiah to buy the field. Jeremiah acquiesced. The title deed was made out and sealed and hidden away. The land was purchased by Jeremiah, but he was not going to enter into possession of it for he too was to be driven out—to be rejected and set to one side. Someday when the restoration took place that sealed roll would be of great value. He gave it to his secretary to hide away with a view of making known to his heirs where the deed was which would give them the title to the land. The sealed book was the title deed to Jeremiah's inheritance. When the people of Israel came back from Babylon there would be a man who could go into court and say, "This deed belongs to me. I am Jeremiah's heir. I have the right to break the seals and take the property." With this illustration from the Old Testament before us, we have no difficulty in seeing what the seven-sealed book in Revelation means. The book that John saw in the hand of Him that sat on the throne is the title deed to this world. When God said, "Who is worthy to open the book, and to loose the seals thereof?" (5:2) it was just another way of saying, Who is the rightful heir? Who can say, "I have title to break those seals, title to claim that world, it belongs to me?" Who is worthy to take possession of that world and subject it to himself?

The Rightful Heir (Revelation 5:2-7)

Adam, what about you? Wasn't that world given to you? When God created you and placed you in the garden of Eden, did He not say that all of this was yours? Why do you not come forward and take this title deed and claim your property? Adam says, "I forfeited my inheritance because of sin. It was mine, but I sinned it away. The devil cheated me out of it, and I no longer have any title to it." Is there any angel who can step up and take the book? No, not an angel among all the serried ranks of Heaven's hosts can say, "I have title to that world." Not a man in all God's universe can say, "It is mine."

John said, " I wept much, because no man was found worthy." But as he was weeping, one of the elders said, "Weep not: behold, the Lion of the tribe of Juda…hath prevailed to open the book, and to loose the seven seals thereof" (5:5). And John looked for the Lion of the tribe of Judah, the majestic roaring king of beasts, ready to spring on the prey; but he saw a Lamb. Why, the Lamb is the Lion! The Lamb of God is the Lion of Judah's tribe. The lamb that depicts innocence, meekness, gentleness, and sacrifice is the One who is to go forth as the mighty conqueror. He will claim this world as His own and drive all His enemies from before His face. I like the translation of Weymouth here. He says, "I saw in the midst of the throne a lamb that looked as though it had been offered in sacrifice,"—the Lamb in the very glory of God that will have through all eternity the marks of death on His glorified body! It is right to sing as we sometimes do,

> I shall know Him, I shall know Him,
> As redeemed by His side I shall stand;
> I shall know Him, I shall know Him,
> By the print of the nails in His hand.

When He came out of the tomb the print of the nails was there. When John saw Him many years after in vision in glory, he saw a Lamb that looked as though it had once been offered in sacrifice. When we get home to Heaven we will never make any mistake in identifying Him. We will never be found worshiping Gabriel instead of Christ. We will not even mistake so loving an apostle as John for his Lord. We will have eyes only for the Lamb on whose body will be for all eternity the marks that tell of our redemption. Ah, what a sight that will be for God's beloved people—when we look on His face, feel His gentle touch, behold the print of the nails in His hands and feet, and see the mark left by the Roman spear in His side!

The prophet Habakkuk described Him as having "bright beams coming out of His side, and there was the hiding of His power" (Habakkuk 3:4, literal trans.). There, where the cruel spear pierced Him, is the hiding of His power.

> Oh, the Lamb, the bleeding Lamb,
> The Lamb of Calvary;
> The Lamb that was slain, that liveth again,
> To intercede for me.

Do you know this blessed Lamb of God? Are you acquainted with Him? Is He your own Savior? Have you thrown yourself on His mercies?

It says that the Lamb in the midst of the throne had seven horns. Horns represent power. In the Old Testament we read of the "strong bulls of Bashan," of great heads, thick necks, and powerful horns. Israel would thus be accustomed to connect the thought of power with the horns. Yet it is not a mighty bull that is seen, but a lamb and the diminutive form of the word, "a little lamb," with seven horns! Just as horns speak of power, seven speaks of perfection. Perfect power belongs to the Lamb of God. And we are told He had seven eyes, which is interpreted as meaning "the seven Spirits of God sent forth into all the earth" (5:6). We have connected this phrase with Isaiah 11:1-2. The Holy Spirit is the Spirit of Christ. "In him dwelleth all the fulness of the Godhead bodily" (Colossians 2:9).

All spiritual graces are His. He is anointed with the oil of gladness and He it is who gives the Holy Spirit to us.

He came and took the book out of the right hand of Him that sat on the throne. What right had He thus to act? Because He went to the cross in infinite grace to pay the great debt of sin, thus to redeem this forfeited inheritance and free it from Satan's domination. The Lamb has title to the book! The Lamb can claim the title deed to this world because when He died on Calvary's cross He purchased the entire world to be His own. The glory of God is to be displayed in this world through a thousand wondrous years. It was His because He created it. He gave it to man, but man forfeited it through sin. The Lord Jesus Christ bought it all back when He hung on Golgotha's tree; but for almost two thousand years He has been waiting patiently up there in the glory until the appointed time for claiming His inheritance. So the book of the title deeds has been sealed. In this interval, men have been having pretty much their own way down here. The devil has been running things to suit himself, but in a little while Christ is coming again. He is going to put everything right, but He will have to act in judgment to do so. For the very world in which the Lord Jesus died is going to be the sphere in which the glory of God will be displayed. This will be true not only in the millennium, but afterward in the new earth as well as in the new heaven.

The Lamb is Praised (Revelation 5:8-14)

The moment that the Lamb takes the book, the four living ones and the four and twenty elders fall down before Him. Every one of them has harps and golden bowls full of odors, which are the prayers of saints. I am very sentimental about the harp. I love it. When I hear the harp being played I always think that it is the instrument I am going to play in Heaven. It is a symbol, of course, but a very lovely one. "And they sung a new song, saying, Thou art worthy to take the book, and to open the seals thereof: for thou wast slain, and hast redeemed us to God by thy blood out of every kindred, and tongue, and people, and nation; and hast made us unto our God kings and priests: and we shall reign on the earth" (9-10). They sing, not merely of themselves but of all the redeemed; so the living ones, the divine attributes, join in it too. And note the great throng suggested by the words of the song. Far more people will be in Heaven than will ever be lost in Hell! All the babies that died in infancy will be there. What a throng will fill that home and how wonderful the fellowship will be! We will have the society of all the pure and holy, made pure by the blood of Jesus. But notice carefully what they sing up there. They ascribe their redemption entirely to the Lamb and His work. Those are the saints of God. There are angels too but the inner circle is composed of sinners that were redeemed. That will be the glory of Heaven.

You often hear of the angels singing. But it is remarkable that when you go to the Bible (King James version) there is only one place where you read of angels singing; it is in Job 38. The morning stars there are angels, and they sang together when this world in its pristine beauty sprang from God's hand. But that ancient song was stilled. Sin came in and marred that beautiful creation, and from the time that sin came in we never read again that angels sang. At the birth of our Lord Jesus a multitude of the heavenly hosts praised God, *saying*, "Glory to God in the highest" (Luke 2:14); but we do not read that they *sang*. It is *the redeemed* that sing, and they sing a new song—the song of redemption. Will you be able to sing that song?

We next read of the host of angels that surround the throne. You would think that God had enough without us. John Bunyan said, "Oh, this Lamb of God! He had a whole heaven to Himself, myriads of angels to do His pleasure, but this could not satisfy Him. He must have sinners to share it with Him!" If you are ever going to sing up there you will have to start in down here. Can you say, "Thou wast slain, and hast redeemed *me*...by thy blood"?

The angels stand in an outer circle. In other words, the angels stand off and look on and say, "The Lamb deserves all the honor He is receiving." Then there is a third company, a third circle, embracing all creation. John looks throughout the universe, and he sees every creature extoling the Lamb. The day is coming when all created intelligences will join in saying, "Glory to the Lamb."

In Revelation 6 we read that the Lamb, having taken the book, proceeded to open the seals. Here I want to pause for a moment in the course of the exposition. Many have asked if perhaps the great tribulation has already commenced. My answer is this: There can be no period of tribulation such as is depicted in the book of Revelation until the Lamb breaks the seals of the seven-sealed book. But the Lamb does not break the first seal of this book until the redeemed are seen crowned in Heaven; and no redeemed one will ever get his crown until he is taken up at the coming of the Lord Jesus Christ to the air and the setting up of the judgment seat. All the crowns are going to be given out at the judgment seat of Christ before the Lamb takes the book and before the seals are broken.

During World War I a lady said to me, "But, dear brother, what tribulation could be worse?" Well, conditions were certainly terrible, but never before had there been a war in which the organizations that profess to stand for righteousness did as much for the soldiers, and the relatives, and the afflicted, as in that awful conflict. Consider the Red Cross, for instance. It was the spirit of sacrifice that caused people to start the society, and many of the founders of it were devoted to Christ; wherever the red cross was seen it was the reminder of the cross of Christ. There will be no Red Cross in the great tribulation. The cross of Christ will be so hated then that it will never be seen anywhere. Then look at the Y.M.C.A. I know all about the criticisms, and I have had to speak plainly myself, but the Y.M.C.A. movement was started by a man of God, and its original objective was to bring men to Christ. Much of their recent work is indeed open to just criticism; it is a shame that it has added to and detracted from its original purpose, yet we can thank God for its distribution of the New Testament and the comfort it has brought to millions of men. Take the work of the Salvation Army: I have heard scores testify about the Salvation Army preaching the gospel of God in the trenches. Now think of a greater war than this (and it is in the future), a war in which there will be no Salvation Army, no Y.M.C.A., no Red Cross, no Bible Societies, no Christian workers —absolutely no spiritual ministry of any kind to alleviate the awful conditions that will then prevail. The thought is unspeakably terrible, but such a war is predicted in this book of Revelation.

CHAPTER SIX
SIX SEALS OPENED

As we begin our study of Revelation 6, I wish to repeat that the great tribulation cannot begin until the redeemed are gathered around the Lord in glory and crowned there. It cannot be emphasized too much that no saints in Heaven now have crowns. The apostle says, "Henceforth there is laid up for me a crown of righteousness, which the Lord…shall give me at that day: and not to me only, but unto all them also that love his appearing" (2 Timothy 4:8). "That day" when the saints are gathered around the judgment seat of Christ is the day when they will get their crowns.

Well then, after the church has gone, what is going to take place in the world? Look at this chapter from the standpoint that we are in Heaven already, the rapture having taken place. Let us suppose that last night, while things were going on in the ordinary way, suddenly there was a heartening shout heard from the glory. Every redeemed one responded to the trumpet of God. In a moment the graves were opened, and in every place where the believing dead were resting, the bodies were raised and the living saints were changed. We found ourselves caught away. We entered with Him into the Father's house and gathered around the throne and fell down to worship. We will say that we have had twenty-four hours in Heaven. At first our hearts would just be too full of Christ to think of anything else. (O sinner, you wouldn't be there. It is *saved* people I am talking about.) But He, Himself, stirs us at last to think of what He is about to do. We say to ourselves, What is going to happen next in that world we have left behind? We look down to that poor scene where we lived yesterday. Men are going on much as before, only in great excitement. Look at the streets of the great cities. We can see the headlines, "A great number of people have disappeared!"

There is a rush to get the newspapers to find out all about this strange event. Throngs are crowding the popular churches to hear the preachers give their explanation of the great disappearance of so many people.

I believe there will be lots of church-going for a little while after the rapture of God's people; those left behind will be crowding into the churches as never before. I think I see the Rev. Mr. Smooth-things standing in his pulpit, with pale, wan face. He looks at scores of parishioners he hasn't seen for many years and thinks to himself, "Now, I have to explain to these people. I have been telling them for twenty years that this talk of the second coming is false." People who believed in the second coming were looked on as idiotic ranters who didn't know what they were talking about. I think I hear mutterings down in the congregation: "We trusted our souls to you. You had been to the colleges, seminaries, and universities, and read a whole library of books. We believed you when you told us the old idea of salvation by the blood of Christ was all worn out and that we could save ourselves by culture. We believed you when you said Christ's second coming was only a fantastic notion. Now explain this to us." Another cries, "What about my grandmother? She believed in her Bible to the end. She was reading just the other day, 'In an hour when ye think not, the Son of man cometh.' Now Grandmother is gone, and I am here. Now, Doctor, explain all this." Oh, there are going to be some wonderful meetings after the Lord has come! There is that world seething with corruption, men's hearts failing them for fear. Christian statesmen will have gone; Christian business men and people of all ranks who knew Christ will have disappeared. Cities and communities will be in turmoil. What are they going to do? Let's look at the Book and see.

The First Seal (Revelation 6:1-2)

We behold the Lamb as He breaks the first seal, and John hears a noise as of thunder. Thunder speaks of a coming storm, though the scene seems peaceful enough. A warrior comes forth on a white horse with a bow in his hand. A bow signifies distant warfare. Horses, as in Zechariah 1, symbolize providential movements. This rider on the white horse evidently pictures man's last effort to bring in a reign of order and peace while Christ is still rejected. It will be the world's greatest attempt to pull things together after the church is gone. It will be the devil's cunning scheme for bringing in a mock millennium without Christ. How long will it last?

The Second Seal (Revelation 6:3-4)

As the Lamb opened the second seal a red horse appeared. It's rider brought anarchy and bloody warfare! "When they shall say, Peace and safety; then sudden destruction cometh upon them" (1 Thessalonians 5:3). The first effort in the world we have left behind will be to bring in universal peace apart from Christ. But it will end in universal, bloody warfare, greater far than has ever been known. The rider on the blood-red horse has a sword representing a different type of warfare than that of the bow: man wrestling with man, nation with nation. Internal strife, class wars, civil wars, the breaking up of all established order is illustrated here.

The Third Seal (Revelation 6:5-6)

When the Lamb had opened the third seal, a black horse appeared, with his rider holding a pair of balances. We have that which inevitably follows worldwide war—worldwide famine. We understand a little more now what this vision means than when these things were first opened up by men of God. We have had our food sold to us by measure, and we have known much of the high cost of living. But in this coming day, conditions will be so dreadful that it will be a measure of wheat for a penny or three measures of barley for the same amount. The word translated "measure" means just enough wheat to make a man one meal, and the penny or denarius was a full day's wages. It will cost a whole day's wages for enough food for one meal—that is, if one is going to eat wheat. Now if they will take barley they will get three meals for a day's work. What hard conditions! Prices are going to be unprecedented in those days of the tribulation.

"And see thou hurt not the oil and the wine" (Revelation 6:6).

The oil and the wine are put in contrast with the wheat and the barley. The wheat and barley are the food of the poor—almost out of reach; but the food of the rich, or the luxuries, are not touched.

The Fourth Seal (Revelation 6:7-8)

Next the Lamb opened the fourth seal, and a pale horse ridden by Death appeared. The word rendered *pale* means "chrome green." A better translation would be a *livid* horse, in the sense of being the color of a corpse. It pictures pestilence, which always follows war and famine.

The Seventy Weeks of Daniel 9

Before examining what is written concerning the breaking of the fifth and sixth seals, it is necessary to say something as to God's dispensational dealings with His earthly people Israel. We will endeavor to show how the book we are studying links up with the older prophecy of Daniel.

For fifteen hundred years before the cross, God was dealing in covenant-relationship with the people of Israel. He had chosen them to be peculiarly His own, in accordance with His promise to Abraham, Isaac, and Jacob. He separated them to Himself and gave them the land of Canaan as their inheritance, so long as they remained faithful to Him as their unseen King. He gave them His holy law and declared that if they obeyed His voice they would be the head of all nations and His witnesses to the ends of the earth. On the other hand, He warned them that if they were disobedient to Him, if they did not keep His testimonies, if they broke His commandments, if they turned to the false gods of the surrounding nations, He would no longer protect them from their enemies. He would give them up to desolation and scattering until they judged themselves and turned from their sins. Then He would remember His covenant with their fathers and would restore them to their own land and fulfill all His promises.

They completely broke down under every test and in accordance with God's word ten tribes were carried away by the king of Assyria.

A little later the remaining two tribes were deported to Babylon, where they remained in bondage for seventy years. At the end of this prophetic period they were permitted to return to their own land, that they might be there to welcome their promised Messiah when He would be revealed. Only a remnant of the Jews availed themselves of this privilege and their descendants were living in Palestine when the Lord Jesus Christ appeared in the fullness of time. Yet He was rejected by the very nation that had waited for Him so long.

The time of His coming had been very definitely foretold in the book of Daniel. In the ninth chapter we are told that a heavenly messenger brought word to the prophet that God had appointed seventy weeks to His people and their holy city. These are not to be understood as weeks of days, but sevens of years. The term "weeks" might better be simply rendered sevens. Seventy times seven years would be 490 years. It is an appointed period in the course of time and has to do especially with the Jews and Jerusalem.

This period was divided into three parts: 7 weeks, or 49 years, in which the streets and the wall of the city were to be rebuilt; then 62 weeks, or 434 years, immediately following the completion of this work until the appearing and cutting off of Messiah the Prince; and one final week, or 7 years, to complete the cycle. At the end of this week the King would be reigning in the holy city and all prophecy fulfilled by the establishment of the kingdom so long foretold. The starting point is clearly defined as, "The going forth of the commandment to restore and to build Jerusalem" (Daniel 9:25). This is the decree of Artaxerxes as recorded in Nehemiah 2. During the next 49 years the city was rebuilt. Then, 434 years later, our Lord rode into Jerusalem and was acclaimed by the multitudes as King, the Son of David. But a few days later He was rejected and crucified. Thus Messiah was cut off and had nothing.

What about the last week? Has it been fulfilled? It has not. When His Son was cast out, God cast off the nation of Israel. That week will not be fulfilled until a future day when He takes up Israel again.

The angel-revealer said to Daniel, "Unto the end of the war desolations are determined" (Daniel 9:26). This gives the whole history of Palestine for the past 1900 years. It has been a great battleground and a scene of almost unparalleled desolation because Israel knew not the time of their visitation. Their times are not in progress now. God is doing another work. While the Jews are blinded in part, He is gathering out the church. This body of Christ, a heavenly company, will reign with Christ when He establishes His kingdom of righteousness on the earth. The last week of 7 years cannot begin to run until the Jews are again in the land, and Jerusalem becomes the Jewish capital, after the church has been caught up to meet the Lord in the air. The greater part of the book of the Revelation treats this last week. It is only when this is seen that all becomes plain and the prophecy becomes intelligible.

The church began on the day of Pentecost when the Holy Spirit, sent by Christ glorified, came on the disciples. Yet the full truth of this wonderful mystery was not made known until Saul of Tarsus became Paul the apostle. The truth of the present dispensation was made known to him and through him to us. The church of Christ is one, though men who take His name and claim to be His followers have become sadly divided. They have formed many systems, often embracing saved and unsaved alike. But God's church consists only of those who are born of the Spirit and baptized by the same Spirit into the body of Christ. This special work will cease at the return of the Lord to the air, which is the first stage of His second coming. The second stage will be when He comes to earth to reign in glory. The 70th, or last week of Daniel, comes in between these two momentous events. The Lord spoke of this period as the "end of the age" in Matthew 24. He divided it into two parts, "the beginning of sorrows" and "the great tribulation."

A careful comparison of our Lord's great prophecy with Revelation 6 will make it plain that the first six seals correspond to the first half of the week—"the beginning of sorrows". From the opening of the seventh seal (Revelation 8) we are introduced to the great tribulation itself with all its attendant horrors. Jesus' warning as to false Christs, implying false hopes of a lasting peace (Matthew 24:5) corresponds to the first seal. His declaration that wars and rumors of wars will follow (24:6) fits perfectly with the second seal. In like manner His solemn warnings of famine and pestilence (24:7) find their counterparts in the third and fourth seals. The Lord then goes on to foretell a time when His followers will be ruthlessly slain (24:9) bringing us to the breaking of the fifth seal. It will be all one's life is worth to confess His name.

The Fifth Seal (Revelation 6:9-11)

John saw under the altar the souls of those who had been beheaded for the Word of God and the testimony of the Lord. Who are these martyred saints, and to what dispensation do they belong? They cannot belong to the church. We have already seen, that the church is represented by the throned and crowned elders in Heaven before the first seal is broken. But Romans 11 makes it clear that after the fullness of the Gentiles has come in—after the present dispensation has come to an end and the church has been removed to Heaven—the blindness will pass away from Israel. They will realize their true condition and their sin in rejecting their Messiah. Then they will call on Him for deliverance. Thus a new company of saints will be formed on the earth, altogether different from the present heavenly company. Many of these Jewish believers will be martyred by the Satanic hosts of the last days. It is these who are seen as having been sacrificed and their souls poured out at the bottom of the altar.

They cry for vengeance on their adversaries, for this is fully in keeping with the dispensation of judgment to which they belong, whereas it would be thoroughly contrary to the grace of the present gospel dispensation. God's people are taught of His Spirit to pray according to the ruling principle of the specific time in which their lot is cast. This accounts for what often disturbs and even shocks sensitive souls—the so-called imprecatory psalms. They cannot understand the cries for vengeance that seem so opposed to the grace of God as now made known. It is no wonder they are troubled and hesitate to speak such words, for those psalms do not belong to us at all. But they will be exactly suited to the remnant of Israel, suffering for Jehovah's sake, but with no clear knowledge of an accomplished redemption. They will be waiting for their Messiah to appear and overthrow the last great Gentile confederation, which, as we will see when we come to chapter 13, will be bent upon their absolute extermination.

White robes are given to these souls under the altar who are invoking the judgment of God on their merciless adversaries. They are told that they must wait a little season till the time of Jacob's trouble is ended and they are joined by their brethren who are yet to be slain. The hatred to God and His Christ rises ever higher until the Lord Jesus will be revealed from Heaven in flaming fire, taking vengeance on those who do not know God (2 Thessalonians 1:8).

The Sixth Seal (Revelation 6:12-17)

The opening of the sixth seal gives a marvelous symbolic picture of grave import. It should be evident from the balance of the book that we are not to take this as a literal earthquake, though our Lord's words in Matthew 24 show us that there will be such phenomena in various places, terrific in character as the end draws near. Already we have had some noteworthy reminders and warnings of this nature that shocked the civilized world, but are apparently so easily forgotten within a very short time. But the earthquake of the sixth seal is of a different type altogether. It cannot be merely literal, as the actual islands, mountains, and seas, together with the cities of the nations are still seen to be in existence long after this vision has had its fulfillment. Rather it illustrates the complete breaking up of society as now constituted, the destruction of the boasted civilization of our present day. Looked at from this standpoint, we have abundant Old Testament Scripture to throw light on it and to make plain its awful portents.

We will be helped, too, if we remember that in the very beginning of the book of Revelation we are told that the Lord sent and "signified it by his angel unto his servant John" (1:1). That is, He revealed those "things which must shortly come to pass" through signs or symbols. If this is kept in mind we will be preserved from taking literally what God meant us to take symbolically. We will be more likely to get the mind of the Spirit in regard to the future of both Christendom and Judaism, the two spheres with which this book deals.

Therefore the sixth seal does not introduce a worldwide, literal earthquake. Rather it is the destruction of the present order—

political, social, and ecclesiastical—reduced to chaos; the breaking down of all authority; and the breaking up of all established and apparently permanent institutions.

We may see, I believe, a foreshadowing of this in what has taken place in Russia (1917-1920): the overturning of the throne; the blotting out of the Romanoff Dynasty; the wrecking of all industrial and social order; the fearful orgies of fanatical Bolshevism; blood-red anarchy everywhere holding sway, making wild promises of liberty while destroying every safeguard against the unrestrained brutality of beast-like men. Take as but one horrible instance the attempted abolition of marriage (that which God Himself instituted, at the very beginning of human history, for the sanctity and blessing of His creatures), and the substitution of the degrading custom of forcing all women to be common property, taken by whoever may desire them, and all children born in these abominable conditions to be separated from their parents and reared as children of the state. Natural affection at once receives its death-blow, and all restraint on man's animal propensities is at an end. Another event that has shocked the world has been the overturning of Russia's state church. It is true that it had become unspeakably corrupt, but in their wild desire to destroy it the Soviet government has declared war on all that bears a religious name, whether human or divine. "No God and no church" is the cry ringing through the unhappy land, and who can foretell what the dreaded future has in store?

Many thought in the past century that they saw the French Revolution portrayed in this sixth seal, and it was indeed but an earlier sample of the same conditions we have been considering; so was the break-up of the Roman Empire in the fifth, sixth, and seventh centuries. But none of these cataclysms, stupendous as they were, fully met the requirements of the prophecy. The church of the First-born is still here, and the gospel of the grace of God is still being proclaimed to a guilty world. But we have already seen that when the seals are broken the church will be with Christ, waiting for the moment when He will descend to take His world kingdom and establish His authority in righteousness.

But we must now proceed to look at the passage in detail that we may better grasp its true import. The sun, we are told, became black as sackcloth of hair. The sun, the source of light and life for this planet, symbolizes supreme authority. It is the well-known type of the Lord Himself. "Unto you that fear my name shall the Sun of righteousness arise with healing in his wings" (Malachi 4:2). Such is Malachi's declaration concerning the coming of Christ the second time. At present Christendom, at least nominally, acknowledges His lordship. We speak of Him as our Lord and profess to receive our governments from His hand. But soon He will be entirely rejected and His Word utterly despised. Thus will the sun be blotted out from the heavens, and God will seem to have been dethroned.

Naturally enough this will mean the complete destruction of all derived authority, so we read next, "the moon became as blood" (6:12). The moon gets all its light from the sun, just as "the powers that be are ordained of God" (Romans 13:1) and are appointed by Him for man's blessing. But all government being overthrown, the lurid glare of anarchy will take its place, for a time at least.

The stars falling from heaven indicate the downfall and apostasy of great religious leaders, the bright lights in the ecclesiastical heavens. In Daniel, those who turn many to righteousness shine as the stars. In the first part of our book the stars are said to be the messengers of the churches. So it would seem clear that we are to understand the symbol in the same sense here. After the true church has been caught up to meet the Lord in the air, there will be a vast host of unconverted ecclesiastics left behind. Thousands of Protestant and Catholic church dignitaries looked on as spiritual guides will be revealed as utterly bereft of divine life. These professional clergymen, despite their pretensions and exalted calling, are simply natural men intruding into spiritual things. They are like the Philistines of old who lived in the land of Canaan. They gave their name, Palestine, to the whole region as though it rightfully belonged to them, while all the time they were unwarranted intruders of Egyptian descent. These are the stars who will be hurled from their places of power and eminence in that awful day of the wrath of the Lamb. Apostatizing from the last vestiges of Christianity, they will soon become leaders in the worship of antichrist.

Thus the heavens, symbolizing the ecclesiastical powers of every description, will depart as a scroll when it is rolled up. The whole fabric of Christendom will be wound up as something obsolete and out of date. Religious leaders have often questioned the finality of the Christian religion. They attempt to formulate a new religious system, which results in the worship of humanity. They teach that God lives in all men and can only be found within the heart of man. But as long as the Holy Spirit is here on earth, dwelling in the church of God, the full development of this mystery of iniquity is checked. As soon as He goes up with the church, the whole profession that is left will be destroyed. Out of its ruins will arise the final Satanic masterpiece of the last days.

The destruction of all organized religion will intensify the frightful conditions of that dreadful time. Men drunk with their false liberty, and rejoicing in the triumph of a blatant God-defying demagoguery, will for a brief period turn this earth into a great madhouse. The vile orgies of those days will be indescribable until it dawns on multitudes that the Lamb of God whom they had rejected and whose gentle rule they had spurned has in some way brought the punishment for their sins on their own heads. Then we have depicted what someone has called "the greatest prayer meeting of all history." "The kings of the earth, and the great men, and the rich men, and the chief captains, and the mighty men, and every bondman and every freeman, hid themselves in the dens and in the rocks of the mountains." They will cry out in their distress for the mountains and the rocks to cover them and hide them "from the face of him that sitteth on the throne, and from the wrath of the Lamb." They will cry as with one voice, "the great day of his wrath is come; and who shall be able to stand?" (6:15-17)

Yet we read of no repentance, no true turning back to God or trusting His Christ—just an awful realization that they have to face the rejected Lamb, and they cannot escape His wrath. They are like those of whom Jeremiah prophesied who will cry in that day of the fierce anger of the Lord, "The harvest is past, the summer is ended, and we are not saved" (Jeremiah 8:20).

Notice the solemnity of the expression "the wrath of the Lamb." We are not accustomed to couple the thought of wrath, or indignation, with the Lamb, which has always been the accepted symbol of gentleness. But there is a terrible truth involved in it nevertheless.

For if the grace of the Lamb of God is rejected, His indignation and wrath must be faced. It is part of eternal righteousness to do so. God Himself will not, and in accordance with the holiness of His nature can not, have it otherwise. As we read elsewhere, "He cannot deny himself" (2 Timothy 2:13).

> Hear the just law, the judgment of the skies:
> He that hates truth must be the dupe of lies:
> And he who will be cheated to the last,
> Delusions strong as hell must bind him fast.
> —Cowper

For such there can be nothing in reserve but fearfully waiting for judgment and fiery indignation which will devour the adversaries. This judgment will be much worse than that which befell those who despised Moses' law, for they now defy God revealed in grace in the person of His Son. For such there must be the wrath of the Lamb. "Grace like this despised, brings judgment / Measured by the wrath He bore."

But the wrath of God is an even deeper and more intense form of judgment. It will be poured out on the earth from the seven vials (or bowls) of the wrath of God (Revelation 16). The Christ-rejector must abide under this judgment for eternity. It is written, "He that believeth not the Son shall not see life; but the wrath of God abideth on him" (John 3:36). Note the hopelessness of the condition here depicted. Abiding wrath precludes any thought of either annihilation or restoration, and warns us that the results of refusing the matchless grace of God are eternal; for that which *abides* is unending.

This sixth seal brings us to the end of the first part of that last unfulfilled week of the ninth chapter of Daniel. It divides into two parts. The Lord Himself defines the first part as "the beginning of sorrows," while He designates the last part as "the great tribulation." This is introduced for us in the book of Revelation by the breaking of the seventh seal. That will come before us after the great parenthesis of the seventh chapter.

The wrath of *the Lamb* is visited on the nations in the beginning

of sorrows; the wrath of *God* will be their portion in the great tribulation. May He grant, in His mercy, that none who read these words
enter into either the one or the other. Grace is still reigning through
righteousness. A just God waits in lovingkindness to be the justifier
of everyone that believes in Jesus.

CHAPTER SEVEN
THE 144,000 AND THE MULTITUDE OF GENTILES

In the last chapter we were occupied with the first half of the seventieth week of Daniel's prophecy: "the beginning of sorrows" when "the wrath of the Lamb" will be poured out on guilty Christendom and apostate Judaism. All this is yet in the future. Now we find that before the Lord gave John the vision of the opening of the seventh seal (which introduces the great tribulation in all its intensity), He gave him this parenthetic seventh chapter in which are recorded two important visions. In the first, John sees a hundred and forty-four thousand Israelites sealed by an angel. In the second, he beholds a great multitude of Gentiles, led in triumph by the Lamb, taking possession of the millennial earth.

I am sure that many readers have often been perplexed by conflicting theories regarding the hundred and forty-four thousand. The way in which so many unscriptural sects arrogate to themselves this title would be amusing if it were not so sad. The Seventh-Day Adventists apply it to the faithful of their communion, who will be found observing the Jewish sabbath at the Lord's return. They suppose that these will be raptured when the Lord descends and judgment is poured out on the rest of the church. Then we have the followers of Charles Russell (Jehovah's Witnesses) who teach that the hundred and forty-four thousand include only the "overcomers" of their persuasion who continue faithful to the end, following the teaching of the system commonly called "Millennial Dawnism." Another cult also claims that the hundred and forty-four thousand are those who will have their blood so cleansed that they cannot die, but will have immortal life on this earth! There are many other sects whose leaders claim that their own followers will be the hundred and forty-four thousand sealed ones at the time of the end. All of these, however, overlook a very simple fact that, if observed, would save them from their error. The hundred and forty-four thousand are composed of twelve thousand from each tribe of the children of Israel. There is not a Gentile among them, nor is there confusion as to tribe. Whenever I meet people who tell me they belong to the hundred and forty-four thousand, I always ask them, "Which tribe, please?" They are invariably confused for lack of an answer.

The Sealed Israelites (Revelation 7:1-8)

John saw "four angels [four is the world number] standing on the four corners of the earth, holding the four winds of the earth, that the wind should not blow on the earth, nor on the sea, nor on any tree" (1). In Daniel's vision, as recorded in the seventh chapter of his prophecy, he beholds "the four winds of the heaven" striving on the great sea. As a result you have the various world empires coming forth like wild beasts from beneath the restless waves. Here we have the angels holding back these four winds until a certain event takes place. It is very evident that they are restraining the last wild beast from making his appearance. In Revelation 13, the beast with seven heads and ten horns—the Roman Empire in its final form—comes forth from the sea, symbolizing the nations in unrest. This is the great federation of nations which God's Word predicts for the very near future. It is a federation of Satanic origin, which will not be developed until after the church is gone. Even then certain events must transpire before it assumes its final diabolical form.

Verses 2-3 make clear what this event is that must first take place. John saw another angel ascending from the east, having the seal of the living God: "and he cried with a loud voice to the four angels, to whom it was given to hurt the earth and the sea, Saying, Hurt not the earth, neither the sea, nor the trees, till we have sealed the servants of our God in their foreheads" (2-3). The point is that God has chosen a remnant of Israel to inherit the kingdom under the Son of

man, which is so soon to be established. Before the final form of the
Roman Empire is fully developed, these are sealed, marked out for
God's protecting care. So all the power of the beast and all the hatred of his ally the antichrist will not be able to destroy them and
thus prevent the carrying out of God's purpose.

Verses four to eight leave no doubt as to the identity of these
sealed ones. John "heard the number of them which were sealed:
and there were sealed an hundred and forty and four thousand of all
the tribes of the children of Israel." As you go over the list note that
the tribe of Dan is absent. Instead you have two tribes from Joseph—Manasseh and Ephraim. Ephraim, however, bears Joseph's
name. Why is Dan omitted from the twelve and the twelfth made up
in another way? I cannot positively tell you. The rabbis used to say
that the false messiah (the antichrist) would arise from Dan. They
based the supposition on Jacob's words in Genesis 49:17: "Dan shall
be a serpent by the way, an adder in the path, that biteth the horse
heels, so that his rider shall fall backward." We note from the historical record in the book of Judges, that Dan was the first tribe to
go into idolatry. It would not be surprising if Dan would be the
leader in the last great idolatry—the worship of antichrist. But we
may leave this where faith leaves every other difficulty—resting in
the infinite wisdom of God and knowing that He has revealed all
that is necessary for us to know in the present age.

The balance of the chapter brings before us an entirely different
company.

The Gentile Multitude (Revelation 7:9-17)

It seems very strange that some have taught that in this great
multitude we have the raptured church. They have supposed that
the Lord would not come for His church until the middle of the
tribulation period. But a careful study of the passage makes it very
evident that we are gazing here on an earthly, not a heavenly, company. This great multitude embraces the Gentile nations who will
enter into millennial blessing. It is the great ingathering of the coming dispensation. From all nations, and kindreds, and peoples, and
tongues, a vast throng from all parts of the earth will be redeemed

to God by the blood of the Lamb and will enter into the earthly kingdom of our Lord. During the dark days of the great tribulation they will heed the testimony which will be carried to the ends of the earth by Jewish missionaries. These wise among the people will instruct many in righteousness (see Daniel 12). They are identical with the "sheep" of Matthew 25, who are placed on the right hand of the Son of man when He comes in His glory and all His holy angels with Him. They will inherit the kingdom prepared for them from the foundation of the earth.

Verse 14 says these people "came out of great tribulation, and have washed their robes, and made them white in the blood of the Lamb." But nowhere does it say they are taken away to Heaven— quite the contrary. They are in a scene where it is necessary for the Lamb to feed them, lead them, and spread His tabernacle over them. Verse 15 plainly tells us: "Therefore are they before the throne of God, and serve him day and night in his temple"—that is, the millennial temple, which is to be built in the land in that coming day. There will be no day and night in Heaven. The expression can only refer, in this connection, to the temple on earth. Then we read, "He who sits upon the throne will shelter them with his presence" (RSV). The reference is undoubtedly to the Lord's covering His people when He led them through the wilderness. The pillar of cloud by day and fire by night not only guided them through the wilderness but sheltered them from the fierce rays of the desert sun. Thus will He protect and shield His redeemed ones in the age to come.

We are also told that "they shall hunger no more, neither thirst any more; neither shall the sun light on them, nor any heat. For the Lamb which is in the midst of the throne shall feed them, and shall lead them unto living fountains of waters: and God shall wipe away all tears from their eyes" (16-17). It is probably because people have not realized the blessedness of the millennial day that these verses are made to refer to Heaven. But they agree with the predictions of Isaiah and other prophets, in regard to the blessing that the saved nations will enjoy when the Lamb Himself reigns. The struggle for daily bread will be over—they will hunger no more; the often vain effort to quench their thirst will be at an end—they will thirst no more. Even the unpleasant and disagreeable things with which men have been afflicted because of the way sin has jarred God's creation will be at an end. The sun will not light on them, nor any heat.

In that day all the saved of the nations will be able to take up, in the fullest sense, the beautiful words of the Psalmist, which we only feebly enter into now: "The Lord is my shepherd; I shall not want. He maketh me to lie down in green pastures: he leadeth me beside the still waters. He restoreth my soul: he leadeth me in the paths of righteousness for his name's sake" (Psalm 23:1-3).

The church of God will be in a far better scene. While our hope is heavenly, not earthly, we can indeed rejoice to think of the blessing awaiting the earth and its inhabitants. God has promised it and will fulfill all that He has caused to be written by His holy prophets in the sacred Scriptures, for "the scripture cannot be broken" (John 10:35).

What a long, dreary night, with frightful nightmares this world has known, since sin and its attendant evils came in to wreck man's hopes of joy and gladness! But how precious to know that evil will not always have the upper hand. A time is coming when the curse will be lifted. The desert will rejoice and blossom like the rose and even the lower creation will be changed and revert to former habits before sin entered. "The lion shall eat straw like the ox" (Isaiah 11:7). The little child need not fear the most savage of beasts, for they will not hurt nor destroy in that day. Then government will be righteously regulated and abuses of every kind will be stopped. For a thousand glorious years our Lord Himself will reign in righteousness.

I wish to impress on both saved and unsaved this one thing: Whether in dispensations past, in the present age, in the period of judgment, or in that glorious millennial age, every one who is saved at all will be saved through the precious blood of Christ. God has never had any other way of reconciling man to Himself than through the blood of His Son. In Old Testament times, men were saved, if I may say, on credit. The Lord Jesus Christ had already pledged Himself to pay the fearful debt with His own most precious blood. In every dispensation, all who owned their guilt and believed the record God had given were justified by faith on the basis of the work that

Christ was yet to accomplish. That work having now been completed, God has demonstrated His righteousness by passing over these sins done in the days of His forbearance. Now He shows Himself to be just and the justifier of him that believes in Jesus. Dear unsaved one, if you confess your guilt and put your heart's trust in that blessed One, who on Calvary's cross gave Himself for you, then you will be justified and accepted with God in all the value of that precious blood. In the coming hour of tribulation, the hundred and forty-four thousand of Israel and all the Gentiles who receive their message will be saved in exactly the same way; but they will be saved for earth, not for Heaven. To the very end of the millennium, that precious blood will still have the same cleansing effectiveness. The last soul who trusts in Christ will have an unimpeachable standing before the throne of God through its infinite value.

So all blessing for time and eternity rests on the cross of Christ. The reason the nations have missed their way in the past nineteen hundred years, and are struggling in vain for peace and a government in righteousness, is because they have ignored the blood of that cross. There alone, peace was made both in relation to time and eternity.

And now in closing, let me emphasize one thing that I believe needs to be emphasized in these days. I have run across the error in many books on the coming of the Lord that after the rapture of the church there will be a great revival; during this unprecedented spiritual awakening in Christendom, vast numbers of people who have been undecided during the present dispensation of grace will turn to the Lord. It is being widely taught that these will form the great multitude of which we have been speaking. Let me say that I have searched my Bible diligently for any confirmation of such teaching, but I fail to find it. On the contrary, we are distinctly told in 2 Thessalonians 2:10 that God is going to give up those who, during the present age, do not receive the love of the truth that they might be saved. They will be given up to hardness of heart and perversity of spirit. We read in verses 11-12, "And for this cause God shall send them strong delusion, that they should believe a lie: That they all might be damned who believed not the truth, but had pleasure in unrighteousness." Now, there is no intimation here that people who refuse the gospel in this dispensation will have another opportunity to be saved if they are still living when the dispensation of judgment begins. A careful reading of the entire passage will show that the time referred to is when the mystery of iniquity is fully developed and the wicked one revealed—that is, the man of sin. In that age, the Holy Spirit will have been withdrawn. He will go up with the church at the Lord's return to the air.

This is not to say that the Holy Spirit will not act during the tribulation period, but His operations will be similar to His activities in Old Testament times. From Heaven He will influence the hearts of men, opening the eyes of the remnant of Israel, and through them reach an innumerable multitude of Gentiles. But there is no promise that He will operate for blessing on the hearts of those who have had the opportunity to be saved and have refused it. They will be given up to the strong delusion of the last days. They will believe the lie of the antichrist. Consequently they will go into judgment because they deliberately refused the truth when it was offered to them, choosing instead error and sin.

It is a very solemn thing to harden one's heart against God and His message of grace. Pharaoh is the standing example of what strong delusion really means. He hardened himself against the message that Moses brought, and afterwards God Himself confirmed him in his course. Light rejected brings abiding night. Darkness may be natural: in this all are born. It may be willful: in this men deliberately choose darkness in place of light. It may be and often is, judicial: in this men are given up to darkness because of their own perversity. So we read in Jeremiah 13:16, "Give glory to the Lord your God, before he cause darkness, and before your feet stumble upon the dark mountains, and, while ye look for light, he turn it into the shadow of death, and make it gross darkness."

No man need be lost for lack of light. He who will follow the slightest gleam that God gives may be sure of increasing light and light sufficient to lead him to the knowledge of sins forgiven. But, I repeat, light rejected brings night! Therefore, let me plead with anyone who has not accepted God's offer of grace in Christ Jesus. Receive now the gift of His love and be assured of a place with Christ in that coming day. For if the Lord should descend from Heaven to call His church away, you who have heard the gospel and are rejecting it, abiding in your sins, your doom will be eternally sealed.

In the neglected parts of the world where the gospel has not yet been fully proclaimed and the grace of God is as yet unknown, a vast number will receive the message of the Israelite remnant. As they flee from antichrist's persecutions they will proclaim to all the world the gospel of the kingdom. But you will not be numbered among them if the coming of the Lord finds you still unsaved. You will be in exactly the same condition of soul and position of condemnation before God as if you had died in your sins. Jesus said, "When once the master of the house is risen up, and hath shut to the door" (Luke 13:25)—who is there that shall open it? The five foolish virgins, left outside when the Bridegroom came, knocked in vain for admittance later. They picture those who will be on the wrong side of the door that will be closed for all eternity.

Yet, strangely enough, this very parable of the ten virgins has been used by certain teachers to support their unsound theory of a second chance for Christ-rejecters after the Savior calls His church away. These teachers say that the foolish virgins represent persons afterwards gathered in, but who miss the heavenly blessing. Others have based on this parable the equally unscriptural hypothesis that only the more spiritual saints will be caught up at the rapture; the weaker ones will be left behind to be purified during the great tribulation. This is a virtual denial of the truth of the unity of the body of Christ. The weakest member of that body is as dear to the Head as the strongest. All who are Christ's will have their part in the rapture, irrespective of their more or less advanced stage in the Christian life. It is the perfection of the work of redemption that gives anyone the right to claim the promises of God. Salvation is not a reward for service or merit.

CHAPTER EIGHT
THE BREAKING OF THE SEVENTH SEAL

Chapter 8 deals with the breaking of the seventh seal, which opens fully the book of title-deed to this world. This roll was put into the hands of the Lord Jesus by the Father after the church, represented by the glorified elders, was seen around the throne in Heaven (5:6-7).

First let me make a few remarks in regard to the structure of the book of the Revelation. The main body of the book is divided into four sevens. There are the *letters* to the seven churches of Asia; then the seven *seals*; then the seven *trumpets*; and farther on the seven *vials* of the wrath of God. There is something very striking about these last three sevens. First, we have six seals opened, then a parenthesis that takes up chapter seven. In chapter eight, the seventh seal is opened, and the book as a whole is open to view.

This seventh seal includes the seven trumpets. Six trumpets are sounded (8:7–9:21), and again there is a parenthetical portion (10:1–11:14). At the conclusion of this parenthesis the seventh trumpet brings us to the end of all things.

Chronologically, we are as far along when we reach 11:18 as when we reach the great white throne in chapter 20, for the seventh trumpet introduces the world kingdom of our God and His Christ and goes right on to the time when the dead will be judged. So we really have a duplication, in measure, of prophetic truth from this point on. From chapters 4–11 you have truth presented in orderly sequence—a prophetic outline of the things that will take place after the rapture of the church right on to the end of time.

Then, commencing with chapter 12, God seems to turn the roll

over so we may view the other side. He gives us a second view of
the events, especially in relation to Israel. We have details that bring
before us the great actors for good and evil in the last days—the
woman clothed with the sun; the man-child, Christ, who is to rule
the nations with a rod of iron; Michael, the archangel; the dragon,
who is that old serpent the devil; the coming world-confederacy
and its blasphemous head; the lamb-like beast (who I believe is the
antichrist), who looks like a lamb but speaks like a dragon—the
counterfeit of the Lamb of God. There follows a parenthetical portion in chapter 14, which in a very vivid way brings before us the
final issues once more.

Then, in chapters 15–16, we have the vials, or bowls, of the wrath
of God. Once again we have the same structure that has engaged
our attention in connection with the seals and trumpets. We have
six bowls and then a parenthesis. In this instance the parenthesis
occupies only one verse (16:15). Immediately following this, the
seventh bowl of the wrath of God is outpoured bringing us on to the
doom of Babylon, described in detail in chapters 17 and 18. Then in
chapter 19 we have the Lord's descent to the earth, accompanied by
the armies of Heaven, to establish His millennial kingdom and reign
for a thousand years. At the close of this the final judgment takes
place. The heavens and the earth as we now know them, with all the
works of man, will be destroyed. New heavens and a new earth will
be brought in where God will be all in all throughout an eternity of
bliss. The wicked—those who have persistently rejected the Lord
Jesus Christ, both before and after the cross, and the millennial dispensation of righteousness—all who have rejected the message of
God will be cast into the lake of fire.

I have searched the Bible through and through, over and over
again, to find one ray of hope for men and women who leave this
world rejecting Christ. I have never been able to find it. I have looked
into all kinds of theories. I have read hundreds of volumes, some
depicting the annihilation of all the wicked dead promising a second chance after death. But in all these books I have never found
one statement based on the Word of God, to give the slightest hope
to the Christ-rejector. This world is the only place in which God is
offering salvation to Christless men. If you refuse the message of

His grace now, if you deliberately steel your heart against the con-
victing power of the Holy Spirit and you die in your sins, you will
be Christless for all eternity! I think the most awful picture the Bible
gives us of the doom of the lost is in the Epistle of Jude, which
forms such a fitting preface to the book of Revelation. He speaks of
those who make light of God's salvation and who follow after
unrighteousness, as "wandering stars, to whom is reserved the black-
ness of darkness for ever" (Jude 13). I cannot see the least hope for
a Christless soul in that illustration.

When I was a boy in my home in Canada, I remember a period
when night after night a blazing comet appeared in the skies. I heard
older people say that this particular night wonder had not been seen
for something like three hundred years. I asked in amazement where
it had been, and for the first time in my young life I came up against
the wonder of infinite space. I was told that that comet had been
driving on with tremendous velocity millions and millions of miles
away from the sun for one hundred and fifty years. One hundred
and fifty years ago it had gradually begun to come back toward the
sun, and that was why it was then visible. In a few weeks it passed
out of sight, to appear to us no more for another three hundred years.
I can recall wondering what would happen if that comet went off on
a tangent and never came back! This is the appalling picture that
Jude presents in the passage referred to. Those who turn the grace
of God into lasciviousness, those who despise the boundless mercy
He has given through His blessed Son and persist in refusing His
goodness, continuing in their sins, will be driven away from the
Sun of righteousness into outer darkness. They will move on and on
throughout eternity, never to find their way back into the presence
of God. He is giving a little space now for repentance, but the day
of His grace will be over when He rises to shake terribly the earth.
And how are you treating His offer of mercy?

The Seventh Seal (Revelation 8:1-6)

We are told that when the Lamb had opened the seventh seal
there was silence in Heaven for about half an hour. May we not say
it is the calm before the coming storm?—the most awful storm that

will ever break over this poor world. Some of you have lived in regions where thunderstorms are common. No doubt, you have often noted on a hot summer day the clouds suddenly gathering in the sky, becoming heavier and darker every moment. You have heard the thunder reverberating in the skies, peal after peal with increasing intensity. You have observed the lightning flashes. Then suddenly all became still. There seemed to be not even a breath of wind to move the leaves on the trees. Yet an overcast, threatening sky causes the birds to seek shelter, the cattle to move uneasily, and all nature to become expectant. A few moments pass by. Then vivid flashes of lightning cause us to shrink back. Crash after crash follow, and the windows of the heavens seem to be opened—the storm pouring down in a deluge!

We have something similar to this in Revelation 8:1. We saw in chapters 4 and 5 the saints gathered around the throne of God and of the Lamb. We noted that from the throne proceeded thunder and lightning. As the seals were broken, one after another, judgment followed judgment in quick succession on the poor world from which God had gathered out His beloved people. But even the crashing under the sixth seal is not the climax. In Heaven lies the mystery of God's dealing with this world and the judgments yet to fall on it. But when the last seal is broken it will be clear what side God takes in all the affairs of earth. He will judge according to the holiness of His character and the righteousness of His throne. The seventh seal, as we have noted before, introduces the final drama of the great tribulation. No wonder there is silence in Heaven for half an hour before that seal is broken!

It is as though all Heaven is waiting in breathless expectation. We seem to hear the questions: What will the Lamb do next? What will be God's next move toward judging and reclaiming that rebellious world? Verses 2-5 give the answer.

Careful readers of the Bible will connect the seven trumpets with the fall of Jericho. That great city just across the Jordan that barred the progress of the people of Israel into the promised land fell with the blast of God alone. The priests of Israel were given the trumpets of judgment, and for seven days they marched around the city blowing the trumpets. Seven times on the seventh day they did so and at the seventh blast the walls fell down flat. Jericho is a type of this present world in its estrangement from God, and its hatred of God's people. Jericho fell at the sound of seven trumpets.The world, as you and I know it, is going to fall at the sound of the seven trumpets of doom, blown by these angels of judgment (Joshua 6).

The seal is broken, the book is fully unrolled, and the seven angels appear to whom are given seven trumpets. As these angel messengers stand by, waiting one after the other to herald with a trumpet-blast the coming judgments, we are told that another angel came and stood to officiate at the golden altar. He is seen offering incense and therefore is an angel-priest. Who is this angel-priest? I think you will agree that he cannot be a created angel. Scripture never speaks of any created angel offering incense with the prayers of saints to make them acceptable to God. The church of Rome does; but nowhere in the Bible do you get anything of the kind. Throughout the Old Testament the preincarnate Christ is again and again presented as the angel of Jehovah. He was the angel who appeared to Abraham; He was the angel who guided the children of Israel; He was the angel who wrestled with Jacob and put his thigh out of joint by the brook at Peniel; He was the angel who appeared to Moses when the prophet prayed that he might see God; He was the angel who appeared to Joshua to lead the people of Israel against their foes in the land of Canaan; He was the angel of Jehovah again and again revealing Himself throughout the entire dispensation. In the book of Zechariah He is the angel-advocate who stands to plead for Joshua the high priest. So we again find Him in the book of the Revelation presented as an angel-priest who still has a people on earth for whom to plead. They are not members of the church of God, but, as we saw in connection with the fifth seal and chapter 7, they are the hundred and forty-four thousand—a remnant who will be taken out of Israel after the church of God will be called home.

The Word of God is very clear on all this. Romans 11:17 pictures the Gentiles as having been grafted into Israel's olive tree of promise. And the Holy Ghost goes on in that chapter to make it plain that when the Gentile church becomes apostate, God is going to reject it and turn back to Israel. In the tribulation period they will again be grafted into their own olive tree. They will be the witnessing remnant of that awful time and the Lord Jesus will intercede for them in Heaven as He now does for His church. He will not be indifferent to their sorrows in those days of unparalleled tribulation. He will, as the faithful High Priest, bear His people on His heart and on His shoulders, even as Aaron carried the names of the twelve tribes on the breastplate and on the onyx stones set in gold on the shoulder pieces of his ephod (Exodus 28:6-21). So we see Christ pictured by this angel-priest offering incense at the golden altar in the very presence of God.

In this present time the Jews bewail their desolation, and cry out in anguish of heart year after year, "Woe unto us, for we have no Mediator!" But when their eyes are opened and grace begins to operate in their souls they will know the blessedness of priestly intercession on the part of their once-rejected Messiah, whom they will learn to identify with the angel of the covenant of old. They will search their Bibles; they will doubtless read the book of Hebrews; they will study the four Gospels and will see the truth. They will look on Him whom they pierced and will repent and mourn, as described in Zechariah 12:10-4. And God will receive Israel and make her His messenger to the nations. We are not surprised, therefore, when we get this look into glory and see the Lord Jesus as the angel-priest.

He has a golden censer. It is blessed to think that Israel will have such an Intercessor in the coming day? We are told that the smoke of the incense is the prayers of the saints—those suffering saints on the earth. The angel took the censer, filled it with the fire of the altar, and emptied it on the earth. Here is the answer to the cry of His afflicted ones down in that scene of tribulation. The prayers went up to the Father, and judgment came down, "and there were voices, and thunderings, and lightnings, and an earthquake" (8:5).

The Final Storm (Revelation 8:7-13)

I cannot explain fully the symbol in verse 7, but I think I can see a hint of the awful time that is awaiting the people of Christendom who have refused the gospel. Do you remember that the grass is used as a symbol of man (Isaiah 40:6)? Grass trampled beneath the foot is the picture of man in his frailty and weakness. What about the tree? It is another picture of man, but rising up in his pride and independence of God. You remember how Nebuchadnezzar is likened to a great tree and how the rulers in Israel were spoken of as great cedars. John the Baptist said, "Now also the axe is laid unto the root of the trees: therefore every tree which bringeth not forth good fruit is hewn down, and cast into the fire" (Matthew 3:10). Grass is man in his weakness, man in his littleness; the tree is man in his dignity, in his greatness, in his independence—man lifting himself up against God. So the first angel's trumpet distinctly indicates a fiery judgment on that part of the human race that has rejected the gospel now so freely proclaimed. It is an appalling picture, but remember the reality is far worse than the picture!

This is followed in verses 8-9 by another fearful portent. I believe it especially concerns the judgment of the great world-church that has held sway over the consciences of so many people. May I direct your attention to Jeremiah 51:25? There we have the same symbol as is given us in Revelation 8:8—a great mountain cast into the sea. I have already said that every symbol in the book of the Revelation was explained somewhere else in the Bible. In the Old Testament a great mountain burning with fire is the symbol of literal Babylon. In the New Testament this great destroying mountain burning with fire, that is cast into the sea and brought to an end under the judgment of God in this coming day, is evidently spiritual Babylon. Babylon of the Old Testament was the fountainhead of idolatry. Every idolatrous system has had its root in Babylon. Spiritual Babylon is the direct successor of literal Babylon. The direct correlation between the mystic religions of the old Babylon and spiritual Babylon of today is significant. If anyone attempted to make a study of this connection he would be perfectly astonished to find the origin of the ritual services used in "Christian" churches. In the coming day when the second angel's trumpet sounds, Babylon will be cast into the great sea of the nations. That is, in the day of God's wrath the false church will be utterly destroyed by the people she once tyrannized. We will learn more of this when we come to chapter 18.

As the third angel sounded his trumpet a great star fell from

Heaven (8:10-11). Stars in the prophetic scriptures symbolize religious dignitaries. They that turn many to righteousness are to shine as the stars forever and ever. The symbol is used again and again in the Bible for persons occupying places of importance in the spiritual, or religious world, as we say. Here we have a star symbolizing an apostate leader whose influence over man is so great that when he falls the third part of men are poisoned because of his evil influence.

Who is this star? While I do not want to try to prophesy, let me give you a suggestion. Who occupies the highest place in the church in the minds of millions of professing Christian people? Many would say the pope. What if tomorrow the newspapers came out with a headline like this: "The pope declares that Christianity is all a sham, that religion is just a fraud"? Can you imagine the effect that would have? Tens of thousands who would say, "Well, the man we viewed as the head of the church, as infallible, as the authoritative voice on all matters of a religious nature, has denied it all. Now, whom can we trust, and what can we believe?" I do not say that this will definitely happen. I am just giving you a hint of what might be. Do we not see the same thing on a small scale today? When a professing Christian leader gives up what he has once stood for, it has a tremendous influence for evil on people of lesser influence and lesser knowledge. And after the true church is gone, I gather from this symbol that one of the greatest "lights" in the false system left behind will openly apostatize. His teachings will become as wormwood, poisoning and embittering his deluded followers.

The darkness deepens when the fourth trumpet sounds (12-13). Again I do not attempt to tell you exactly what these verses symbolize. But it is evident that light is being rapidly withdrawn. A third of the sky was struck. A third of the moon and stars were darkened. What does it mean? Well, the Lord Jesus said, "If therefore the light that is in thee be darkness, how great is that darkness" (Matthew 6:23). "Light obeyed increaseth light—light resisted bringeth night." Do you know why so many people in Christendom are going into Christian Science, Theosophy, Spiritualism, and the new theology of our times? Do you know why so few people ever get out of these cults? Because of this: They have had the opportunity to receive light from God and they have rejected it. It is written in the Word that "God shall send them strong delusion that they should believe a lie: That they all might be damned who believed not the truth, but had pleasure in unrighteousness" (2 Thessalonians 2:11-12). When God presents His truth to people, responsibility comes with it. When God presents Christ to them, tremendous responsibility is given to them. If you hear the message and reject Christ, do not be surprised if you are caught in one of these unholy ideas of the present day; and perhaps you will never be delivered from it until you wake up in a lost eternity.

Next the three trumpets yet to follow are introduced in a very solemn way. They are distinguished from the four we have already commented on, as "woe" trumpets. They speak of a more intensified form of judgment than any previously portrayed and will be studied in the next chapter. I only desire now to call your attention to the expression, "the inhabiters of the earth" (8:13). We frequently find a similar term in the book of Revelation, "Them that dwell upon the earth." The heaviest judgments fall on these people. They are not merely those that live here on earth, but they form a distinctive class. They are the people who have rejected the heavenly calling. When God offered them full and free salvation through the death of His beloved Son, they turned away from Him. They rejected Christ and chose to follow their worldly desires and love of sin, therefore they became "the inhabiters of the earth."

CHAPTER NINE
THE FIRST AND SECOND TRUMPETS OF WOE

This chapter will examine the fifth and sixth trumpets, known respectively as the first and second *woes*. The added designation of these trumpets implies a solemnity and a fearfulness beyond anything we have previously considered.

The Delusions of the First Woe (Revelation 9:1-12)

Instead of "I saw a star fall from heaven," a better translation would be, "I saw a star *fallen* from heaven." The reference is undoubtedly to that star, symbolizing an apostate leader, referred to under the third trumpet (8:10-11). There we read of a great star that fell from Heaven burning like a lamp. It fell on the third part of the rivers and fountains of waters, poisoning them so that men drinking of them died because the waters were made bitter. Under this fifth trumpet we have the development of the apostasy, of which this leader is evidently the head. He opens the bottomless pit, using a key. In the Gospels, we see the thought of the key when Christ commits to Peter the keys of the kingdom of Heaven; and you will remember our Lord's words to the lawyers, "Ye have taken away the key of knowledge" (Luke 11:52). From these Scriptures it is clear that a key implies a system of teaching and possibly ritual observances connected with it. With this hint we can readily understand what follows.

This arch-apostate, by a system of erroneous teaching and damnable heresies that deny the Lord, opens up the bottomless pit from whence issues a blinding smoke as the smoke of a great furnace. The smoke of the pit is so intense that the sun and air become darkened. It is the strong delusion to which we have previously referred. While it is said in 2 Thessalonians that "God shall send them strong delusion," we here learn that He sends it by permitting this Satanic envoy to delude the nations. Darkening of the sun by means of these Stygian fumes implies that the supreme source of light was blotted out from before men's eyes or minds. Their whole spiritual sky will be made dark by the false system with which they will be deluded. The air is particularly Satan's realm. He is called "the prince of the power of the air" (Ephesians 2:2). The darkening of the air implies the control of this realm by Satanic agencies.

I do not think we will be far wrong if we identify this coming delusion with the occult systems of gnostic origin, so largely prevailing and so rapidly spreading at the present time. These systems, as we have noticed before deny (in any true sense) the personality of God and assert the divinity of humanity. They reproduce, in some form or other, the primeval lie, "Ye shall be as Elohim." This is the very essence of New Thought, Christian Science, Spiritism, Theosophy, and other offshoots of these evil systems. After the restraining power of the Holy Spirit has been removed, they will spread like locusts over all the earth, having tremendous power over the minds of men. This is what the third verse indicates: "And there came out of the smoke locusts upon the earth: and unto them was given power, as the scorpions of the earth have power." Anyone familiar with the locust plagues of the East will understand at once the figure here used. Travelers have told us how the locusts appear in swarms so vast that they seem like great clouds, actually shutting out the sun and filling the whole air. They devour everything before them. Attacking a green field, within a few minutes they leave it as bare as though no vegetation had been there at all. They are the dread of eastern farmers, who are utterly powerless to combat them. They aptly typify or symbolize the spiritual plague of the last days. The symbol of the locusts is coupled with that of the scorpion, because of the torment these evil teachings eventually bring to those who accept them.

It is evident that we do not have any merely literal plague of locusts in view (4-5). Literal locusts would do the very thing which these are commanded not to do. The grass of the earth, green things, trees of all descriptions, are here distinctly protected from their power. Verses 4-5 seem to be an explanation rather than a continuation of the symbol; otherwise we might think of the grass and trees as representing mankind. But it would appear that the apostle here expounds rather than continues the description of his vision, in order that we may not be misled by a literal application. The locusts' power is expended on those men who do not have the seal of God in their foreheads. These are tormented by them for five months, a torment like that of a scorpion when he strikes a man. We have already seen that those bearing the seal of God are the remnant of Israel (7:3-8). These alone in Christendom and Judaism will be preserved from the strong delusion of that day. Our Lord Himself limits Satan's power in the same way; referring to this very period and the plague of false teaching, He says, "If it were possible, they shall deceive the very elect" (Matthew 24:24). Thank God, it is not possible. The seal of the living God in the present dispensation is the indwelling Holy Spirit, given to guide into all truth. In that coming dispensation of judgment the same Holy Spirit will illumine the minds of those who repent in Israel and thus preserve them from this Satanic delusion.

For the rest, so great will be the distress caused by these evil teachings when men fully give themselves up to them, that, "In those days shall men seek death, and shall not find it; and shall desire to die, and death shall flee from them" (verse 6).

Anyone who has ever sought to give spiritual help to persons awakening in measure from the delusions of any Satanic system will understand at once the condition of mind here depicted. I will never forget the almost insane glare of the eye and the hopeless wail in the voice of one poor woman. After having been under spiritualistic influences for a number of years, she at last began dimly to apprehend the dreadful character of the system that had been enslaving her. It was only through much prayer and earnest holding on to God on her behalf that she was delivered. But she told me on one occasion that she had suffered all the torments of the damned during the year and a half when she was seeking deliverance from demon control.

A few years ago I was laboring among the Mormons in Utah. There I learned of a most pitiable case. A family who had accepted the Mormon delusion and emigrated from Great Britain to Utah had practiced the rites of Joseph Smith's abominable system for thirty years. They were at last awakened to the untrustworthiness of it all by the perfidious conduct of certain eminent church leaders. As a result they renounced the entire system and were left without religious convictions of any kind. A few months later the wife and mother was dying. She tossed on her bed in the greatest agony of mind, moaning in her distress and despair, afraid to meet God in her sins. A minister of the gospel was urged by some friends to call and see her, though much against the will of the family. Finally he gained admittance to the dying woman's room. He sought faithfully to present the precious truth of the gospel from God's holy Word and for a time she seemed to listen eagerly. But she turned from him in the end, crying out, "Oh! sir, after one has been fooled by one religion all her life, it is too late to trust another in the hour of death." And so in great agony she passed away, so far as he could tell, into a hopeless eternity.

Oh! I wish that I had the power to impress on men and women everywhere the dreadful responsibility they assume when they tamper with these unholy teachings that already have escaped from the bottomless pit and have darkened the air and blotted out the light of the sun for many souls. No torture can be compared to spiritual torment. The only remedy is that perfect love, displayed in Calvary's cross, which casts out all fear. In the days to which our chapter refers, those who have rejected the grace of God will never again hear that precious gospel. So they are left to cry out in their anguish, seeking death and not finding it.

In verses 7-12 we have a highly symbolic description of this delusion. The shapes of the locusts, we are told, are like horses prepared for battle. This symbolizes their rapid progress and apparently providential irresistibility in obtaining sway over those unprepared to do battle with them. "On their heads were as it were crowns like gold" (9:7)—for apostasy, during that time of delusion, will seem to carry all before it triumphantly, driving from Christendom the last vestige of orthodoxy. Our Lord Jesus asked the solemn question in view of His second advent, "When the Son of man cometh, shall he find faith on the earth?" (Luke 18:8) The "coming of the Son of man" refers not to the rapture, but to the *appearing in glory*. At that time it will, for the moment, seem as though all true faith has been driven from the prophetic earth. Nevertheless by the power of God's Word, a vast company will arise from the distant parts of the world, as we have seen, who will not have bowed the knee to this latter day Baal.

Next we are told "their faces were as the faces of men, And they had hair as the hair of women, and their teeth were as the teeth of lions" (7-8). Three symbols here intermingle, all of which are very evidently found in the cult systems to which we have referred. Faces as of men would seem to imply intelligence, and these evil teachers make a great appeal to human reason. They ridicule the truth of God as a system of cunningly devised fables, while actually they themselves follow clever but illogical theories. Their appeal is to human intelligence—to the mind rather than to the heart and conscience, as Scripture does. Moreover they are characterized by intense seductiveness and attractive fancies, typified by "the hair of women." A woman's hair, we are told in Scripture, is her glory (1 Corinthians 11:15). In the Song of Solomon 7:5 we read, "Thine head upon thee is like Carmel, and the hair of thine head like purple; the king is held in the galleries [tresses]." How many have been turned aside from the path of duty by natural attractions, grossly misused for the purpose of accomplishing unholy ends.

But seductive and apparently rational as these systems are when first presented, they prove at last to have teeth like the teeth of lions, tearing to pieces those who put their trust in them. In the ninth verse we read: "And they had breastplates, as it were breastplates of iron; and the sound of their wings was as the sound of chariots of many

horses running to battle." These iron breastplates destroy all conscience or make them impervious to the shafts of truth, so that the
conscience is never reached. The wings, whose sound is as that of
many chariots rushing to battle, would symbolize the swiftness with
which they conquer those who have turned from the truth and had
pleasure in unrighteousness.

The tenth verse again emphasizes the scorpion-like torment they
produce. "And they had tails like unto scorpions, and there were
stings in their tails: and their power was to hurt men five months."
What a mercy that their power is thus limited. I see no reason why
we should not understand the five months literally. For a very limited time this apostate leader and his emissaries will be permitted to
dominate those who would not have Christ the Lord to reign over
them. In His place, Satan himself is worshiped as Abaddon and
Apollyon. "And they had a king over them, which is the angel of
the bottomless pit, whose name in the Hebrew tongue is Abaddon,
but in the Greek tongue hath his name Apollyon" (11). Satan alone
is the angel of the bottomless pit. So it is made evident at last that
the "God within," to which men are turning today, is no other than
Satan, the great arch-enemy, who has been plotting man's destruction from the very beginning. Self-worshipers are devil-worship-
ers, and in some instances already this has been avowed by the followers of present day apostasy. This then is the first "woe." "One
woe is past; and, behold, there come two woes more hereafter" (12).

The Conflict of the Second Woe (Revelation 9:13-21)

As the sixth angel blew his trumpet a very different sorrow was
loosed on the earth. It seems to be the result, however, of the previous affliction. That is, it shows us what the effect on the world will
be when Satan-worship becomes prevalent everywhere in what was
once called Christendom. It will bring about a tremendous conflict,
setting nation against nation and man against man, until the third
part of men will be destroyed.

I think we have had a remarkable illustration of this in the great
conflict from which we have so lately emerged (World War I). Who
can deny that it was the direct result of rationalistic *Kultur*, and the

denial of the authority of the Word of God? If education without
Christ could save, Germany should have been the most blest nation
on the face of the earth. In that country education seemed to have
reached its highest point—but with what dire results, not only to
that nation but to a large part of the human race! German philoso-
phy had poisoned the world. The colleges and universities of almost every civilized land drank greedily from the poisoned streams
of Teutonic philosophies and infidel hypotheses, and it is only now
that we are beginning to awaken to the baleful effects of such folly.
I have no doubt that Satan himself would have restrained men from
rushing into such bloody conflict had it been possible. What I mean
is this: He was seeking to entrap men with his specious theories and
unholy philosophies, and World War I was an almost unforeseen
result of this. The nations were thrown into confusion by the teachings they had imbibed. The war was like a great explosion which
could no longer be prevented.

These considerations will help us, I think, to understand the second woe. In chapter 7 we saw the four angels restrained from let-
ting loose the four winds of the earth on the great sea of the nations.
In 9:14 a voice from the four horns of the golden altar that is before
God, in response undoubtedly to the angel-priest's intercession in
8:3, cries out to the angel which had the sixth trumpet, "Loose the
four angels which are bound in the great river Euphrates." These
angels are evidently at the present time restraining the great Asiatic
hordes from pouring themselves on the land of Palestine and Europe. The Euphrates formed the eastern limit of the Roman Empire,
and thus was the barrier, as it were, between the East and the West.

We are told that the four angels were prepared, not exactly—as
the King James version reads—"for an hour, and a day, and a month,
and a year," but for "*the* hour, day, month, and year." That is, there
is a definite moment in the mind of God at which this awful power
is to be let loose. Until that hour strikes, not all the evil machinations of men, not all the ambitions of nations, can bring about the
conflict here predicted. But when that hour does strike, no astute
statesman's policy, no treaties, no world federation movements can
prevent the dire catastrophe predicted. Two hundred thousand horse-
men are hurled on the west of Asia and on Europe. They seem like

unearthly warriors, with breastplates of fire, and of jacinth, and brimstone. The horses' heads appear as the heads of lions, because of the unspeakable ferocity of these Asiatic hordes. Fire, and smoke, and brimstone seem to issue from their mouths, telling of the Satanic character of this terrible invasion. The result will be a third part of men killed by the fire, the smoke, and the brimstone, which issue from their mouths. When we recall the millions who have perished as the direct or indirect result of wars and pestilence, we can see how a greater war in the future may well tend to almost depopulate the earth, destroying one-third of the prophetic earth, which is identical with the limits of the old Roman empire.

In verse 19 we read: "For their power is in their mouth, and in their tails: for their tails were like unto serpents, and had heads, and with them they do hurt." Isaiah 9:15 says "The prophet that teacheth lies, he is the tail." This passage helps us to understand both Revelation 9:10 and 19. Whether it be the occult woe of the fifth trumpet or the carnage woe of the sixth trumpet, in each case lying prophets are the leaders in each movement and are responsible for the mental, spiritual, and physical harm accomplished.

It is a solemn thing to realize that even judgments such as these will have no effect in leading men back to God and to repentance. Punishment does not of itself lead men to repentance, so we are told in verses 20-21: "The rest of the men which were not killed by these plagues yet repented not of the works of their hands, that they should not worship devils, and idols of gold, and silver, and brass, and stone, and of wood: which neither can see, nor hear, nor walk: Neither repented they of their murders, nor of their sorceries, nor of their fornication, nor of their thefts." This is in accordance with the general testimony of Scripture, which nowhere intimates that punishment produces penitence. The Universalist teachers deny this and insist that all punishment, whether in time or eternity, will result in the final salvation of the delinquent. They teach that eventually all men will learn by judgment if they refused to learn by grace, and will turn to God for salvation. But both here and later in this same book of Revelation we find that the heaviest judgments of God, falling on guilty men, do not soften stony, rebellious hearts. Rather men become hardened in their sins and are more blasphemous and

God-defiant when judgment is poured out on them.

In eternity, God will not permit open defiance of His will. Our Lord Jesus tells us that in Hell there will be not only "weeping" because of suffering, but "gnashing of teeth." This phrase expresses not open opposition but the angry defiance of the heart of man, which will be filled with hatred to God but be powerless to openly oppose His government. If the cross of Christ with its marvelous exhibition of holy love will not reconcile men to God, punishment will never avail to win their hearts.

CHAPTER TEN
EATING THE LITTLE OPENED BOOK

In this chapter we are given the first part of the parenthetical portion that comes in between the sixth and seventh trumpets (11:15). We have already noticed that there are similar parentheses between the sixth and seventh seals and the sixth and seventh vials. It is an evidence of divine order not to be overlooked. The seventh trumpet ushers in the millennial kingdom and goes right on to the close of the course of time and the establishment of the great white throne for the judgment of the wicked dead. But before these final events are brought to our attention, we are given fuller instruction regarding God's plan for Israel in connection with these future events.

This tenth chapter contains truth largely of a moral character, therefore one is likely to pass over it without very careful attention. It does not seem, at first sight, to have to do with any of the great movements we have been considering in connection with either Israel or the Gentiles. In the first chapter of the book of Daniel we have set before us, in the history of the three Hebrew youths who refused to be defiled with the king's meat, the necessary moral condition for spiritual instruction. So in this tenth chapter we find the Lord dealing in a very special way with His beloved apostle John, in order that he may be the better prepared to unfold the great mysteries lying in the rest of the book of Revelation. And in the Lord's preparation of His servant John, we get great moral principles that should speak to our own hearts. If grasped correctly these principles better prepare us to serve the living and true God while we wait for His Son from Heaven.

The Angel of the Covenant (Revelation 10:1-7)

The mighty angel can surely be no other than that same glorious angel of the covenant whom we saw standing at the golden altar officiating as the angel-priest of the heavenly sanctuary (8:3-5). Of no created angel could such glorious things be said as those John wrote in connection with this wondrous being.

The reason our Lord is brought before us in this angelic character is that in this portion of the book of Revelation we are dealing largely with Israel, the earthly people, before their Messiah has been revealed to them. Therefore it is only natural that He should take the same position that He had with them in Old Testament times. They will receive a fuller revelation when He descends in glory. They will behold the marks of His passion and cry out in amazement, " What are those wounds in thy hands?" Then He will answer, "Those with which I was wounded in the house of my friends." At last the full truth will burst on them that the crucified Nazarene and the angel of the covenant are identical. "They shall look upon me whom they have pierced, and they shall mourn for him as one mourneth for his only son,…as one that is in bitterness for his first-born" (Zephaniah 12:10). This will be the true day of atonement for Judah and Jerusalem. They will afflict their souls as they realize the enormity of their sin in rejecting their divine Savior. The merits of His atoning work will be applied to their hearts and consciences. Then will they be able to cry out in the full assurance of faith, "He was wounded for our transgressions, he was bruised for our iniquities: the chastisement of our peace was upon him; and with his stripes we are healed" (Isaiah 53:5). But until that moment of His full unveiling, He is to them the angel of the covenant—an uncreated angel.

He comes down out of Heaven, clothed not merely with a cloud, but *the* cloud, as it should read; the cloud is the symbol of the divine glory. The cloud is the chariot in which He led His people of old through the wilderness all the way from Egypt to the land of promise. We are expressly told that in that cloud was the angel of the covenant (Exodus 14:19). It is the uncreated cloud of glory that dwelt between the cherubim above the mercy-seat in the tabernacle

(Leviticus 16:2). When Solomon built the temple and dedicated it to Jehovah, He came in the cloud, dwelling in it as His house (1 Kings 8:10-13). Nearly five centuries later, when Ezekiel was called on to declare the desolation of that once holy house, he beheld the cloud lifted up from the most holy place. It tarried a moment over the door of the sanctuary, then departed and hung above the city wall as though loath to give up the place where His glory had so long been manifested (Ezekiel 10). Slowly the cloud moved over to the adjoining mountain on the east, the mount of Olives, and then up into the heavens (11:23-25).

Thus the visible representation of Jehovah's presence had disappeared from Israel because of their sins. That cloud never returned to the land of Palestine until our Lord Jesus Christ went up into the holy mount, which we commonly call the mount of transfiguration. There Peter, James, and John had a vision of the coming kingdom— "the power and coming of our Lord Jesus Christ" (2 Peter 1:16). There they saw Him transfigured and talking with Moses and Elijah— Moses representing the saints who have died and will be raised again at our Lord's return, and Elijah picturing those who will be caught up at Christ's coming, without dying. Peter, overwhelmed by such an abundant revelation and not knowing what to say cried, "Lord, it is good for us to be here:...let us make here three tabernacles; one for thee, and one for Moses, and one for Elias" (Matthew 17:4). And while he was speaking, "behold, a bright cloud overshadowed them" (5). This was the Father's way of showing them that He would have no mortal man, however holy and devoted, put on a level with His beloved Son. After Christ had died on the cross and was raised from the dead by omnipotent power, He led His disciples out to the mount of Olives near Bethany. With hands lifted up in blessing, he was parted from them, and they watched Him going up until the cloud received Him out of their sight. When He returns again we will behold Him on the cloud and every eye will see Him (Acts 1:9-11). So here, when John wrote, "I saw another mighty angel...clothed with a cloud," we may understand at once that this angel can be no creature; He is Himself the Creator of all things, our Lord Jesus Christ, clothed with the sign of the divine majesty.

Next we observe that the rainbow which we saw in chapter 4

around the throne of God, is now seen wrapped, as it were, around the head of this mighty angel. It seems to speak of His coming to confirm the covenant made with Noah after the world had been destroyed by a flood. Another evidence that it is a divine person who is here brought before us, is found in the next clause: "His face was as it were the sun" (10:1). It is the same face that Saul of Tarsus saw when he was marching along the Damascus road, his heart filled with hatred against the Lord Jesus and burning with rage against His followers. Struck down, he saw a light above the brightness of the sun and in that glorious light beheld the once-crucified Christ of God. He heard Him ask in tenderest accents, "Saul, Saul, why persecutest thou me?" (Acts 9:4) When He comes again it will be as the Sun of righteousness.

"His feet," we are told, were "as pillars of fire," thus linking Him with the same wondrous Being described in chapter one. There we read that "his feet [were] like unto fine brass, as if they burned in a furnace." We also read a similar description in Daniel 7.

We are told next that He had in His hand "a little book open" (10:2). There have been various speculations as to what this book might be. It seems to me it could be no other than the same book we had before us previously (Revelation 5:1). It is the title deed to the earth, the seals of which have been broken, one after the other, until the entire scroll is seen unrolled. The Lord descends with all the evidences of divine majesty and with this title deed in His hand He sets His right foot on the sea and His left foot on the earth, as indicative of taking possession of His own inheritance. As Man on earth, He had redeemed that inheritance with His own precious blood.

His voice is the voice of the conqueror: "He cried ... as when a lion roareth" (3); for the angel and the Lion of Judah's tribe are one and the same. When He had cried, seven thunders uttered their voices. The thunder, we have noticed before, speaks of judgment. John said, "When the seven thunders had uttered their voices, I was about to write: and I heard a voice from heaven saying unto me, Seal up those things which the seven thunders uttered, and write them not" (4). As Mediator of the new covenant He seals up the utterance of the seven thunders. It is not necessary for us to know *what* they uttered. They represent judgment due to wayward man, but He Himself has borne the judgment and those who trust in Him need never know its dreadful secrets.

> Let us love, and sing, and wonder,
> Let us praise the Saviour's name;
> He has hushed the law's loud thunder,
> He has quenched Mount Sinai's flame.
> He has bought us with His blood;
> He has brought us home to God

Have you ever noticed how inquisitive people often are in regard to those things that the wisdom of God has purposely kept from them? In the Old Testament dispensation the law was hidden in the ark, covered with the mercyseat; yet the men of Bethshemesh foolishly looked into the ark and were killed in judgment (1 Samuel 6:19). So there are things hidden from the people of God in all dispensations, which He would have them leave with Himself. "The secret things belong unto the Lord our God: but those things which are revealed belong unto us and to our children" (Deuteronomy 29:29). It is only too natural for man to pass over the precious revealed truth that would be for his sanctification and blessing. Instead he occupies himself with hidden things, which are not given him now to know. If it had been for his blessing to know, God would have revealed these hidden things. I am often asked, "What do you suppose was written in the flying roll of Zechariah's vision?" I only know what the Word has said. I am also asked, "What were the unspeakable things Paul heard when caught up into the third heaven?" If Paul could not utter them, how could we? And so many have puzzled over the things spoken by the seven thunders, but faith rests in the fact that John was commanded not to write them.

It is important to notice the difference between the last clause of verse 6, as found in the King James version and in any critical translation. Instead of reading, "That there should be time no longer," read, "That there should be no longer delay." Because of the erroneous translation given in our generally correct and excellent English version, many have been misled into supposing that this vision brings us to the end of time. However, the context makes it very plain that such is not the case. The vision is distinctly a premillennial one. The point is that the hour of accomplishment has almost struck, and God will not delay the completion of His plans and the fulfillment of His promises. "A short work will the Lord make upon the earth" (Romans 9:28). The angel swears by Him that liveth for ever and ever (that is, by Jehovah Himself, the Creator of all things) that nothing will cause any more delay. In the days when the seventh angel sounds his trumpet, the mystery of God—that is, the mystery of God's long tolerance of evil—will be finished. Everything will then be made plain. The mystery of retribution—the mystery of predestination—the mystery of the great struggle between light and darkness and good and evil—all will be explained then. There will be no more secrets in God's ways and dealings, and man will need no longer question; the dispensations of faith will have come to an end, and the dispensation of sight will have dawned. Are you often troubled by questions as to God's purpose, His counsels, His judgments, His apparently strange dealings with you and with the world? To the man who has not the secret of the Lord, His ways may seem contradictory. Learn from this Scripture to wait in patience until God Himself makes all clear in the days of the voice of the seventh angel.

The Little Scroll (Revelation 10:8-11)

In the second part of the chapter we are occupied with a very different line of things. We are now to read of an experience the apostle John had that God would have every student of His Word undergo.

What are we to understand by verses 8-10? You will recall that a similar experience was given to the prophet Ezekiel (Ezekiel 3). He too was called on to "eat the book." And the lesson in both instances is the same. It is only as we feed on and digest the Word of God that we ourselves are nourished and built up in the truth of our most holy faith. Only then are we in a right condition of soul to use that Word for the help and instruction of others. David said, "Thy word have I hid in mine heart, that I might not sin against thee" (Psalm 119:11). And again, "Thou desirest truth in the inward parts: and in the hidden part thou shalt make me to know wisdom" (Psalm 51:6). This, I take it, is what John's experience illustrates. He was commanded to eat the little book that was in the angel's hand—that is, to meditate on it and to make it thoroughly his own.

Someone has said that in these busy days of ours meditation is a lost art. Would to God it were restored and His people were more given to feed on His truth. For it is not only that God would have John and Ezekiel eat the book, He wants you to eat it likewise. He has given it to you who believe on His Son, to be the food of your own souls, to make you fit to serve Him in this world. And remember this is just as true of the prophetic books as of every portion of the Word of God. In both the instances cited it is particularly the prophetic word that is in view. Lay hold of dispensational truth, of prophetic teaching, in this very practical way and it will have a most beneficial effect on your inner man.

John said that when the book was in his mouth it was very sweet, but when he had eaten it his inward parts were made bitter. This is most instructive. There is no sweeter portion in all Scripture than that which God has revealed concerning the manifestation of His blessed Son. Prophetic truth is generally sweet and attractive to those whose interest is just being awakened in it. But if followed up, if the book is really eaten, it leads to self-judgment and to separation from evil, and this will always be bitter. There is not one of us who readily takes the place that God's Word would put him in during this period of Christ's rejection. And so the point here is that God's truth makes demands on people. You who are following these studies with me will soon find this out, if you have not already done so. If you conscientiously undertake to walk in the truth revealed, you too will know something of its bitterness. You cannot enjoy things that you used to enjoy if you receive the prophetic testimony and walk in the power of what is revealed there. As the great divine program unfolds before your mind, it may be very interesting, and in this sense the book is sweet. But as great divine principles enter your hearts, and you realize more and more the call to strangership in this Satan-controlled world, the truth becomes bitter indeed, and it makes demands on you. It is not always the sweet things that are best for us; we need the bitter as well as the sweet. Every soul who has walked in the truth as God has revealed it to him, has finally found the blessedness of obedience. "To obey is better than sacrifice, and to hearken than the fat of rams" (1 Samuel 15:22).

It is a very sad thing indeed when truth is simply held in the intellect, with no particular bearing on the life. In speaking of the second coming of the Lord, the apostle John wrote, "Every man that hath this hope in him, purifieth himself, even as he is pure" (1 John 3:3). It is a truth that should affect the believer at every angle of his life. Anyone who truly believes that Christ will return cannot afterwards live for self or for the world. If one professes to hold the second coming of Christ and yet lives like the world, he demonstrates that whatever he may hold mentally, the truth of the Lord's coming does not hold him. That truth believed makes carnal Christians spiritual; it makes worldly people heavenly; it makes covetous people generous; it makes careless people earnest. And so I want to be very frank with you. If you do not desire to let this truth have its sway over your lives, it might be better to cease studying this book of the Revelation right here. For all God's truth has been made known for the obedience of faith. I am certain that these truths are going to change the lives of some people completely, or they will harden them in their waywardness and be the means of searing their consciences as with a hot iron.

After the apostle had eaten the book, the angel said to him, "Thou must prophesy again before many peoples, and nations, and tongues, and kings" (11). This is of importance in connection with the further opening up of the book. This verse does not mean that John was to go to other peoples and nations to prophesy. Rather he is to prophesy in regard to these nations, to the same servants of God to whom he has already been giving the word. The point is that when the seventh trumpet sounds (11:7) the present outline of prophecy comes to a close; for as previously mentioned, the seventh trumpet carries us right on to the great day of judgment at the end of time. But in the last verse of the eleventh chapter (which properly belongs to chapter 12) John begins once more to prophesy concerning nations, and kings, and tongues, and people. This second great outline culminates in the new heaven and new earth. You will remember that the roll which was seen in the hand of Him that sat on the throne, the seals of which were broken by the Lamb, was written on two sides (5:1). As the book was unrolled, John could see clearly what was written on the inside, and I understand this to be the outline we have already had before us. But beginning with chapter 12, the roll is, so to speak, reversed, and we see what was written on the other side. God confirms the former outline and fills in details there omitted, so that we have a clearer and fuller understanding of the great events yet to take place in the world where our Lord was crucified.

If this is clearly seen, the book becomes plain. Otherwise there is confusion. There are those who endeavor to make everything chronological with their scheme of interpretation. The trumpets not only follow the seals, which is quite correct, but these interpreters go on to make the vials, or bowls of wrath, follow the trumpets. This necessarily puts the twelfth chapter and the rapture of the manchild far over into the seventieth week. Yet, as we will see when we reach that point, chapter 12 and chapter 4 fit together chronologically. As when God gave Pharaoh two dreams (the one confirming the other) so here the message is duplicated that we may know the certainty of the words of truth wherein we are being instructed.

CHAPTER ELEVEN
TWO WITNESSES AND THE SEVENTH TRUMPET

In the first thirteen verses of Revelation 11 we have the remainder of the parenthesis which began in chapter 10. When reading this portion the careful student of the Word of God will be reminded of the passages relating the measuring of Jerusalem in Zechariah 2 and the measuring of the millennial temple in Ezekiel 40. We also read of the measuring of the holy city, the new Jerusalem, in Revelation 21.

The Two Witnesses (Revelation 11:1-13)

The vision in the opening verses of chapter 11 clearly involves Jerusalem and the future temple in the last days. I think we may say that throughout the Bible when God speaks of measuring anything the thought is implied that He is marking it off as that which belongs to Himself. When one purchases a piece of ground or is about to take possession of a property, it is a very common thing to measure it and mark off its lines.

In Zechariah 2 we are told that the prophet beheld a man with a measuring line in his hand, to whom he put the question, "Whither goest thou?" The answer was, "To measure Jerusalem, to see what is the breadth thereof, and what is the length thereof" (Zechariah 2:2). And in the fourth verse the angel who is interpreting the visions for Zechariah said to another angel, "Run, speak to this young man, saying, Jerusalem shall be inhabited as towns without walls for the multitude of men and cattle therein: For I, saith the Lord, will be unto her a wall of fire round about, and will be the glory in the midst of her" (4-5). Then, in the balance of the chapter, we have a very distinct prophecy of the future deliverance of God's earthly people from all their foes. They will be brought from the land of the north and from all parts of the world where they have been carried in the days of their captivity. This will not be fully accomplished until the Lord Jesus Himself has appeared in glory, for we read, "Thus saith the Lord of hosts; *After the glory* hath he sent me unto the nations which spoiled you: for he that toucheth you toucheth the apple of his eye. For, behold, I will shake mine hand upon them, and they shall be a spoil to their servants: and ye shall know that the Lord of hosts hath sent me" (8-9, italics added). The daughter of Zion is then called on to rejoice because Jehovah Himself will dwell in the midst of her. "And many nations shall be joined to the Lord in that day, and shall be my people" (11). He will dwell in the midst of them, and they will know that the Lord of hosts has sent His prophet to them. "And the Lord shall inherit Judah his portion in the holy land, and shall choose Jerusalem again," (12) says the Word of God.

Clearly, it is this very restoration that God had in mind when He gave John the vision of Revelation 11. The angel called on him to "Rise, and measure the temple of God, and the altar, and them that worship therein" (11:1). That is, once more God acknowledges a witnessing company, a worshiping people in Jerusalem. Observe that this is in the days of the great tribulation before the complete fulfillment of Zechariah's prophecy, for the glory will not yet have appeared. Therefore John is instructed not to measure the court which is outside the temple; for it is still to be given to the Gentiles, "and the holy city shall they tread under foot forty and two months" (2). This will be the last three and a half years of the final seven that compose Daniel's seventieth week; we have seen that this seventieth week has not yet been fulfilled, nor can be until Jerusalem and the people of the Jews are again acknowledged by God as His own.

It is very evident that already God is overruling events with a view to this restoration. The marvelous deliverance of Jerusalem in December 1917, when the Turkish flag was hauled down after practically 1260 years of misrule and oppression, and the banners of the Allies raised in its place, was preparing the way for this very thing. It is well known that General Allenby (later Lord Allenby), to whom God gave this great victory over the Turkish army, was instructed in the truth of the second coming of our Lord Jesus Christ. When General Allenby received from the Turkish governor of Jerusalem the surrender of the holy city it was indeed a most important event, filled with greater meaning than millions dreamed of. This event was clearly ordered of God in view of the promised restoration of Israel to the land. It was one of His hidden purposes when He permitted the World War. The surrender of the holy city, without the firing of a shot, as the airplanes of the allied forces circled over the ancient capital of the land of Palestine, was undoubtedly in answer to the prayers of thousands of the people of God. It would be unbearable to think of the representative of a so-called Christian nation shelling the city where our Savior taught and died, and which must ever be sacred in the eyes of both Jew and Christian. When the armies of the Allies led by Allenby entered through the Jaffa gate, Arab, Jew, and Christian alike recognized the fact that the hour had struck for God to open the way for the fulfillment of many prophecies of bygone ages, as recorded in His Word. It was undoubtedly the turning-point of the entire conflict, for eleven months afterwards the armistice was signed.

Zionism has taken on new and remarkable vigor, and money has poured into its coffers to transplant the poor of the flock from the lands of the north and the country where they have suffered so much, to their own ancient patrimony. Their hopes are high, their jubilation great, but Scripture makes it very plain that they have before them the bitterest experiences they have ever known, and these to be endured right in their own land. For God declared that from the days of Titus, Jerusalem would be "trodden down of the Gentiles, until the times of the Gentiles be fulfilled" (Luke 21:24).

The expression, "the times of the Gentiles," refers to the entire period of Gentile supremacy. It began when God gave Judah into the hand of Nebuchadnezzar, king of Babylon and will continue on to the time when the Stone from Heaven will strike the image on its feet; that is, when the Lord Jesus Christ, at His second coming in judgment, will destroy all Gentile dominion, and His own kingdom will supersede every other.

The last three and a half years, designated in Revelation 11:2 so definitely as 42 months, will be the worst of all this period of Gentile treading-down. The tribulation of those days will be so dreadful, our Lord has told us, that unless they are shortened, no flesh would be saved. And the center of all this tribulation will be the land of Palestine itself. But during this time and immediately preceding it, God will not leave Himself without witness (3-4).

It seems clear to me that the 1260 days of verse 3 refers to the first half of the week. During this time God will have a witnessing remnant in Jerusalem testifying to the near coming of the kingdom. They will call on all Israel to repent in view of that time of the restitution of all things spoken of by the prophets.

I do not know that we need limit the witnesses to two individuals. Two is the number of testimony, and we need to remember that we are dealing here with symbols, not necessarily with the literal personalities. Therefore the two witnesses might well symbolize the witnessing remnant of Judah as a whole. But I would not be dogmatic as to this, for it might be the mind of God to send two individuals, as here described, to herald the near coming of His Son. The fourth verse again links the prophecy with the book of Zechariah: "And two olive trees by it, one upon the right side of the bowl, and the other upon the left side thereof" (4:3). There, the two olive trees are priesthood and prophetic testimony, keeping the candlestick shining for God. In Revelation the olive trees are said to be two candlesticks, but the thought is the same. It is worship and testimony in that time when Jacob's trouble is just beginning.

These witnesses are immortal until their work is done, for, we are told that "if any man will hurt them, fire proceedeth out of their mouth, and devoureth their enemies: and if any man will hurt them, he must in this manner be killed" (Revelation 11:5). That is, if any man desires to hurt the witnesses he is cut off in judgment.

We next learn that "these have power to shut heaven, that it rain not in the days of their prophecy: and have power over waters to turn them to blood, and to smite the earth with all plagues, as often as they will" (6). It is a testimony in the power and spirit both of

Elijah and of Moses. Therefore, some have drawn the conclusion that the two witnesses would be Moses and Elijah sent back to earth before the coming of the Lord Jesus Christ. I admit the possibility of this, though it does not seem probable to me. John the Baptist came in the spirit and power of Elijah (Luke 1:17); to those who would receive it, he was Elijah which was to come. So these witnesses, whether literally two, or symbolizing a much larger company, will be in the spirit and power both of the prophet who came to restore Israel to the true God and the great prophet who first led them out of Egypt.

Nothing can interfere with their witnessing until they have finished their testimony. Then "the beast that ascendeth out of the bottomless pit [of whom we will learn more in chapter 13] shall make war against them, and shall overcome them, and kill them" (7). They will be the objects of the bitter enmity of the vile head of the coming revived Roman empire, or western federation of nations, who will not tolerate any worship but that which is offered to himself. He, therefore, will destroy them, "and their dead bodies shall lie in the street of the great city, which spiritually is called Sodom and Egypt, where also our Lord was crucified" (8). Jerusalem will fall into apostasy, culminating in the worship of the antichrist and the beast. God's holy city will sink at last to the level of Sodom, from which only Lot was saved, and Egypt, out of which Israel was delivered by Jehovah. Through the unbelieving Jews "the name of God is blasphemed among the Gentiles" (Romans 2:24); by them the Lord of glory was crucified and wrath will come on them to the uttermost.

In verses 9-10 we have the sad picture of joy among the nations because this last testimony for God on earth has been destroyed. We see the whole apostate world—Christendom and Judaism alike—congratulating one another that there is no longer any voice raised to call in question their apostasy and wicked ways. In the present time of our Lord's rejection and His session at God's right hand Christendom, in the very manner depicted in these verses, pretends to observe Christ's coming to earth. Having crucified the Lord of glory, the nations join in celebrating what is called "His birthday," sending gifts one to another. In that coming day, in the same way, they will make merry and show their delight because the last voice on His behalf has been silenced. They will rejoice over the dead bodies of His witnesses. What a solemn scene it will be—civilized peoples rejoicing in that awful day when the wrath of God is just about to be poured out in all its fullness on that guilty world. For three and a half days it will seem as though Satan were triumphant and everything that is of God overthrown!

Verses 11-12 picture another rapture—another cohort of the first resurrection—taking place in the midst of that final week. These martyrs, who had sealed their testimony with their blood, are raised in power and caught up to be with their still rejected Lord. Like Himself, they will ascend to Heaven in a cloud, but unlike their Master, their enemies will see them. And it would seem as though this visible rapture will have some effect on those remaining in Jerusalem, for in verse 13 we learn, "The same hour was there a great earthquake, and the tenth part of the city fell, and in the earthquake were slain of men seven thousand: and the remnant were affrighted, and gave glory to the God of heaven." Observe He is still the God of heaven, but in a little while He will be revealed as the God of the whole earth, as verse 4 has already intimated. This is the first time that we read of any people during that period of tribulation giving glory to God, but whether this implies any true turning of heart to Himself on the part of some, I dare not attempt to say. All that this Scripture says is that "the remnant were affrighted," and this in itself does not necessarily imply that there is any true repentance.

The Seventh Trumpet (Revelation 11:14-19)

With this great earthquake the second woe is past, and we are told, "Behold, the third woe cometh quickly" (14). This third woe is none other than the seventh and last of the trumpets, which ushers in the world kingdom of our God and His Christ. It is a calamity only to His enemies, but a cause of great rejoicing to all who love His name, in view of creation's deliverance from bondage to sin.

Verses 15-18 complete the present prophetic series (verse 19 properly belongs to chapter 12). The seventh angel's trumpet brings in Christ's long waited for and glorious kingdom. And on its proclamation, the saints in Heaven, as symbolized by the four and twenty elders, will fall before God on their faces. They will worship Him and give Him thanks—He, the everlasting Jehovah—because He has taken to Himself His great power to reign.

The eighteenth verse covers the entire millennium and carries us on to the judgment of the wicked dead, to the end of time. All judgment has been committed to the Lord Jesus Christ. And we need to remember that the entire millennium is a period of judgment: first, judgment on the angry nations when the wrath of God is poured out on them at the beginning of the millennium; judgment for His own servants who will be rewarded in that glorious kingdom according to their faithfulness during Christ's rejection; judgment on the wicked dead who, at the great white throne, will answer for the deeds done in the body and be dealt with accordingly. Those who have arrogated to themselves the right to judge and destroy others will then be judged and destroyed themselves when the great moral governor of the universe, who has kept Himself hidden so long, will be fully revealed. If you will refer to the chart, you will see that the seventh angel's trumpet brings us to the end of the first prophetic outline. That is, chapter 11:18 carries us as far along chronologically as chapter 20:11-15.

And now may I emphasize the importance of being prepared for the near coming of the Lord Jesus Christ, in view of the remarkable manner in which Palestine, the Jews, the nations of Christendom, and the professed church of God are even now being prepared for the very experiences we have been attempting to describe? These things are not "cunningly devised fables" (2 Peter 1:16) but stern realities. Anyone who has his eyes opened and understands something of the teaching of the prophetic word, can see clearly that we are near the end of the present dispensation.

I remember on one occasion speaking in the city of San Jose, California before a group of over forty ministers, on the second advent of our Lord. Many of them ridiculed the idea—only four declared themselves as believing in it. Most of them were noncommittal, having no definite convictions either for or against my theme. One dear old minister seemed to resent the thought of the Lord's

coming as a future thing. He declared that, to him, Christ came when
he had been converted to God some forty years previously. But I
was invited to return a week later. For an hour and a half we had a
most animated debate on the subject. Finally one clergyman declared that he thought the personal coming of the Lord Jesus was an
absolute absurdity. He did not believe He existed as a distinct personality, clothed with a resurrected body; His resurrection was entirely spiritual, and to quote his own words, "He only exists today
as part of the all-pervading spirit of the universe. Therefore, I believe, my brethren, in no apocalyptic coming of Jesus. I never expect to see Him in a body, but I believe in the ever-coming Christ.
He is coming in the clouds, but they are not literal clouds. He comes
in the clouds of affliction, in the political clouds, in the war clouds,
in the clouds of sorrow and distress, but a personal premillennial
advent is, in my judgment, an utter impossibility."

This brought to his feet the minister who had somewhat opposed
me at the previous meeting. He cried in distress, "Do I understand,
Doctor, that I shall never see my Lord who saved me by His death
upon the cross?" "I think not," was the reply. "Have I then," exclaimed the other, "been wrong all these years as I have sung,

> I shall know Him, I shall know Him,
> As redeemed by His side I shall stand;
> I shall know Him, I shall know Him
> By the print of the nails in His hand?"

"Oh!" replied the other, "that's all very well as poetical license,
but I don't think you should take it literally."

"Brethren," cried the aged minister, as the tears burst from his
eyes, "I take back what I said last week. I find I agree with this
brother, who has been speaking to us on the coming of the Lord, far
more than I thought I did. I look to see the personal coming of my
Savior. I shall never be satisfied until I behold the King in His beauty.
But I have always supposed He would not come until the day of
judgment; but as I think it over, it seems to me that, after all, that is
what my brother believes; only he thinks the day of judgment will
be a thousand years long. And Doctor," he said, turning to the min-

ister who had presented such unscriptural and unholy views, "I am afraid, if there are many in the church like you, it will take a thousand years to put things right."

My friends, this is indeed what I would impress on you and what the seventh angel's trumpet so clearly intimates. The day of judgment will be a thousand years long. The judgment seat of Christ takes place in the heavens immediately after the rapture of the church. The judgment of the living nations referred to in Matthew 25 will take place on the earth when the Son of man will come in His glory, and all His holy angels with Him, to establish His kingdom over all the world. That thousand years will be the reign of righteousness. He will rule all nations with a rod of iron and judge unsparingly everything that ventures to lift itself up against His authority—all that refuse to be subject to His dominion. And at the close He will judge all the wicked dead, who will be raised for that very purpose, and cast into the lake of fire because they have rejected His grace. And in view of all this, I plead with you who are out of Christ, "Agree with thine adversary quickly, whilst thou art in the way with him" (Matthew 5:25). In other words, come to God in Christ Jesus now and have your case settled out of court. For if you first meet God in that solemn hour of judgment, you will be forever beyond the reach of mercy.

For all who trust in the Lord Jesus now, there will be no judgment in that solemn day. For He has said, "Verily, verily, I say unto you, He that heareth my word, and believeth on him that sent me, hath everlasting life, and shall not come into condemnation, but is passed from death unto life" (John 5:24). How sweet and precious the promise here given to every believer in the Lord Jesus Christ! Observe that all believers possess eternal life *now*. It is not that they are looking forward to receiving eternal life in the day of judgment, or at the coming of the Lord—though they will enter into life then; that is, they will become participants in that scene where eternal life is fully revealed. But they have that life now by virtue of having received Christ, for "he that hath the Son hath life" (1 John 5:12). Therefore they will not come into judgment, but they will be called to appear at the judgment seat of Christ to give an account of their service for the Lord. Since His grace saved them they will never be called into judgment for their sins. Their sins have already been judged on the person of the Lord Jesus Christ when He died on Calvary's cross where He bore the condemnation of all who would put their trust in Him. Such have already passed out of death unto life and enjoy even now the guarantee of the coming glory.

CHAPTER TWELVE
THE WOMAN AND THE MAN-CHILD

With this chapter we begin our study of a very distinct part of the book of Revelation embracing chapters 12, 13, and 14, which form a connected outline of events. Chapters 12-13, as noted on the chart, bring before us "the great actors for good and evil in the last days" (Walter Scott). Chapter 14 gives us the consummation—the Lamb on mount Zion, returned to bless the remnant of Israel, and through them the world, and the final judgments relating to the preparation for the actual setting up of the kingdom.

I think I may say without exaggeration that I have read or carefully examined several hundred books purporting to expound the Revelation. I have learned to view this twelfth chapter as the crucial test in regard to the correct prophetic outline. If the interpreters are wrong as to the woman and the man-child, it necessarily follows that they will be wrong as to many things connected with them. Therefore I ask your particular attention as we endeavor to see what light Scripture itself throws on this remarkable vision.

As indicated in the previous chapter we should begin to read from verse 19 of chapter eleven, as this is the commencement of the third great division of the book of Revelation.

It may be well here to draw attention to the several "openings" in their order. In chapter 4:1, we read, "A door was opened in heaven," which introduces the second division of the book. This division reveals the saints in Heaven around the throne of God and the judgments that follow the taking of the seven-sealed book.

In chapter 11:19 we read, "The temple of God was opened in

heaven," and in the temple was seen the ark of the covenant, which at once calls to mind God's covenant with His earthly people Israel. The lightnings, voices, thunderings, earthquake, and great hail that followed the opening of the temple illustrate fearful judgments to be poured out on the prophetic earth. Yet the ark shows that God will remember His covenant with Israel and preserve the remnant safely through it all.

In chapter 15:5 this thought is intensified in connection with the coming forth of the seven angels that have the seven last plagues. There we read, "After that I looked, and, behold, the temple of the tabernacle of the testimony in heaven was opened," and from that temple the seven angels went forth. The fact that the testimony is thus mentioned, again emphasizes God's protecting care of His earthly people.

The fourth "opening" is in chapter 19:11. "And I saw heaven opened, and behold a white horse; and he that sat upon him was called Faithful and True, and in righteousness he doth judge and make war." The chapter goes on to describe, in highly symbolic form, the Lord's appearing in open judgment. These four openings are of deep significance and lead to a greater understanding of the Book. The first we have already considered. The second will occupy this as well as the following two chapters. The third introduces the seven last plagues, in which is filled up the wrath of God. And the fourth ushers in the glorious millennial kingdom.

The Woman and the Dragon (Revelation 12:1-6)

In the first six verses we are shown a divinely given picture, in which God is throwing His own white light on events that otherwise would be incomprehensible to His creatures. A woman appears, arrayed with the sun, the moon beneath her feet, and on her head a crown of twelve stars. She cries out in pain of childbirth until she delivers a man-child. And this man-child is distinctly said to be the one who is to rule all the nations with a rod of iron. The woman has a terrible, vindictive adversary—a great red dragon, who is described as having seven heads and ten horns, and on his heads seven diadems. Notice that the word rendered "crown" in the King

James version is not the word we have already had before us in this book—the crowns on the heads of the elders in Heaven (4:4). Theirs was a victor's *wreath*, but the dragon wears the imperial *diadem*. His is a reigning crown, for he is "the prince of this world," acting, as we will see shortly, through the Roman empire. His tail, we are told, "drew a third part of the stars of heaven, and did cast them down to the earth."

In the vision John saw him standing before the woman, waiting for her deliverance so that he might devour her child immediately upon its birth. But he was thwarted in his malignant intentions, for the child was caught up to God and to His throne. The woman, the mother, then fled into the wilderness, where God Himself had prepared a place for her, that she might be kept in security and nourished for 1,260 days.

First of all, who or what are we to understand this woman to represent? Many tell us she is the church. Others insist that she represents some system of teaching. Roman Catholic expositors have seen in her the virgin Mary and suppose the whole scene to depict her assumption into Heaven and her glory as its queen.

There have been individuals down through the centuries who have arrogated the vision to themselves. For instance, Johanna Southcott (1750-1814) gave herself out as the bride of Christ and deceived many. Or Mrs. Mary Baker Patterson Glover Eddy, who very modestly conceived and gave forth the thought that the woman was a highly symbolic picture of herself and the man-child represented that which she brought forth—Christian Science; whereas, the dragon was "mortal mind" endeavoring to destroy her new religion! We need not waste our time with such theories.

The first view I mentioned—that the woman represents the church—is one that needs careful examination. In doing this, let us first inquire who or what does the man-child symbolize? If we allow Scripture itself to answer, we find there is a person and a company of people answering to this description. In Psalm 2 Jehovah says to Messiah, "Thou art my Son; this day have I begotten thee. Ask of me, and I shall give thee the [nations] for thine inheritance, and the uttermost parts of the earth for thy possession. Thou shalt break them with a rod of iron; thou shalt dash them in pieces like a potter's vessel" (7-9). This, clearly enough, is our Lord Jesus Christ, who is soon to reign over all the earth. Undoubtedly He is primarily the man-child who is to rule the nations with a rod of iron and the special object of Satan's malignity. But we have already seen, in Revelation 2:26-28, that when He reigns He will not reign alone for His promise to the faithful overcomers in the church period is: "And he that overcometh, and keepeth my works unto the end, to him will I give power over the nations: and he shall rule them with a rod of iron; as the vessels of a potter shall they be broken to shivers: even as I received of my Father. And I will give him the morning star." Is there then any incongruity in understanding the man-child to represent both Christ Jesus our Lord and His church? Surely not, for He is the Head of the body, the church, which is the fullness, or completion, of Himself. So the title "The Christ" is applied to both Head and body viewed as one in 1 Corinthians 12:12 where we read, "For as the body is one, and hath many members, and all the members of that one body, being many, are one body: so also is Christ"; literally it reads, "the Christ." We may then, on the authority of Scripture itself, safely affirm that the man-child represents the one new Man who is to rule the nations with a rod of iron—Christ, the Head, and the church, His body. If this be so, then it is impossible that the woman should symbolize the church.

But there are those who tell us that only the strong spiritual members of the church are designated in Scripture as overcomers. The woman pictures the church as a whole, whereas the man-child symbolizes the overcoming part of the church. They say this part will be raptured prior to the great tribulation, while the rest of the church will be purified through that time of trouble. But Scripture definitely determines the untruthfulness of this contention, for we are told distinctly, "This is the victory that overcometh the world, even our faith. Who is he that overcometh the world, but he that believeth that Jesus is the Son of God?" (1 John 5:4-5) An overcomer is one who has personal faith in Christ, and every believer in this sense overcomes. Those who do not are proven not to have real faith and are simply professors, not possessors. This theory denies the unity of the body of Christ; it fails to recognize the intimate relation existing between the Head and all the members.

But who then is this star-crowned, sun-robed woman, who has the moon beneath her feet? First, let me ask, "Is there any other place in Scripture where we have the sun, moon, and twelve stars brought together in a similar way?" You will at once recall Joseph's dream in which he saw the sun, moon, and eleven stars making obeisance to him. He himself was the twelfth star. His father rightly saw in this a picture of all Israel with its twelve tribes. And this was a hint worth considering. But, again, we are distinctly told concerning our Lord Jesus that it was of Israel "as concerning the flesh Christ came" (Romans 9:5). And it is of Israel that Isaiah was singing when he exclaimed, "Unto us a child is born, unto us a son is given: and the government shall be upon his shoulder: and his name shall be called Wonderful, Counsellor, The mighty God, The everlasting Father, The Prince of Peace" (Isaiah 9:6). *Israel* is the mother of whom, as concerning the flesh, Christ came. The church did not give birth to Christ. He founded the church. He, as the last Adam, slept in death that the church might be taken from His wounded side. But He did come from Israel. Over and over again in the Old Testament that nation is depicted as being in the anguish of childbirth, waiting for His appearing. Look at Micah 5:2 and Isaiah 66:7-8. By a comparison of these Scriptures with the one before us we see that "before [Israel] travailed, she brought forth." That is, Christ Himself personally was actually born before the time of her great period of anguish in the days of the coming tribulation. But during that time of trouble He will be born in the consciousness of the nation, and they will realize that He belongs to them—that He is Israel's Son.

The twelve stars on her head may well speak of her twelve patriarchs and her twelve tribes. The moon beneath her feet symbolizes the reflected glory of the old covenant. While the sun, in which she is enwrapped, tells of the new covenant glory in which she appears before God. At Christ's actual birth, Satan put into operation the power of the Roman empire through Herod, its puppet in Jerusalem, to seek His destruction. But He was preserved from Herod's efforts when the young children of Bethlehem were destroyed. Though crucified by a Roman governor and by Roman authority, He was raised from the dead by the glory of the Father and caught up to God and to His throne.

We have seen that the man-child symbolizes both Head and body—the complete Christ. Therefore, as in other prophecies, the entire present dispensation is passed over in silence. The church is represented in its Head, caught up with Christ. For immediately after this, Satan, again acting through the Roman empire which is to be revived in the last days, turns on the woman Israel and seeks to vent his wrath and indignation against her. But God prepares a place for her, and she is hidden in the wilderness—possibly the wilderness of the peoples, as Ezekiel 20:35 so graphically puts it. There she will be protected during the 1260 days, which, as we have already seen, appear to refer to the first half of the seventieth week—"the beginning of sorrows."

The Great conflict (Revelation 12:7-12)

Our attention is turned from earth to Heaven where we are shown a future great conflict to occur in the heavenly places. A third actor in these stirring scenes is now introduced; it is Michael, the leader of the heavenly hosts. But he is no stranger to the reverent student of the Word of God. We have already made his acquaintance in the book of Daniel. We know him as the great angelic prince, the archangel, who is particularly charged with the care of Daniel's people (Daniel 12:1). Daniel's people, we have seen, are symbolized by the woman whom we have been considering. When our Lord Jesus Christ returns for His church, we are told that the voice of the archangel will be heard from Heaven, together with the shout of the Lord and the trump of God. Michael's voice will awaken, or call together, all those of Israel who have died in the past dispensation and who will have their part in the first resurrection. Together with the church and the saints of previous ages, they will enter into the Father's house.

Their passage through the air and enthronement in glory would seem to be the signal for the driving out of Satan and his hosts from the upper air, where they have been permitted to maintain their hold during the past five thousand years. Satan is called the prince of the power of the air (Ephesians 2:2). Believers are told that their conflict is with wicked spirits in heavenly places (Ephesians 6:12). These evil hosts are continually endeavoring, by deception, to keep Christians from enjoying their present portion in Christ, but when the church is caught up, the evil forces will be ignominiously driven from what we might call the "outer court of Heaven" and cast down on the earth. The great dragon, the energizing spirit of the old Roman empire, and the one who is to be the energizing spirit of the same empire when revived, will be cast down. In verse 9, that there may be no possibility of mistake, he is distinctly designated as "that old serpent, called the Devil, and Satan, [the deceiver of] the whole world."

When he and his accursed followers are hurled from the heavens, a voice of praise is heard above. This voice celebrates the full salvation of God's redeemed and the establishment in power of the kingdom of our God and the authority of His Christ because "the accuser of our brethren is cast down, which accused them before our God day and night." This is no new thought. Satan appeared as the accuser in the days of Job, accusing that righteous man before the Lord. Zechariah also, in vision, saw him accusing Joshua, the high priest. He has been permitted by God to act as the great prosecuting attorney, if I may so put it, at the high court of the universe. But no charge that he has ever been able to bring against those redeemed to God by the precious blood of Christ has ever stood because that infinite sacrifice has fully availed to meet them all. Well may we sing:

> I hear the accuser roar
> Of ills that I have done;
> I know them all, and thousands more,
> Jehovah findeth none.

Or, as a verse of another beautiful hymn puts it:

> Though the restless foe accuses,
> Sins recounting like a flood;
> Every charge our God refuses—
> Christ has answered with His blood.

Christ is our advocate, and it is Satan's malicious accusations that call for His constant advocacy on our behalf. As a result of this, the Holy Spirit applies to the hearts of the saints on earth the truth of God in divine power, practically cleansing their ways. And so it is said, "They overcame him by the blood of the Lamb, and by the word of their testimony; and they loved not their lives unto the death" (11).

Satan's casting down will be the signal then for great rejoicing in Heaven, where the Old and New Testament saints will have been caught up. It will be the signal also of great sorrow on the earth, because the devil will have come down in great wrath, knowing that his time is short. He has always been the hater of all who belong to Christ so he will seek for any on earth who confess His name in that day to destroy them completely. This is what is brought before us in verses 13-17.

The Woman is Sustained (Revelation 12:13-17)

The explanation of these verses is plain in view of what we have already discovered. The dragon will at once turn all his energies against Israel, but God has pledged Himself to preserve her through the great tribulation. And so, there were given to the woman two wings of a great eagle for a specific purpose: "that she might fly into the wilderness, into her place, where she is nourished for a time, and times, and half a time, from the face of the serpent." *A time* indicates a year; *times*, two years; and *half a time*, six months. All this comprises the last three and a half years of the tribulation period and is the same time period as the forty-two months of the previous chapter. As to the expression "two wings of a great eagle," God said in regard to Israel, "I bare you on eagles' wings, and brought you unto myself" (Exodus 19:4). God delivered Israel from Egypt and cared for them in the wilderness. In that coming day, He will deliver them from the wrath of the dragon and protect them in the wilderness of the peoples. Afterwards, they will come up from that wilderness in great numbers to dwell in their own land.

In vain the serpent casts water as of a great river out of his mouth, hoping that he might cause her to be carried away by the stream. He

would seek to ruin her by that which emanates from his mouth—
evil teachings, I take it, in contrast to the water of life given by our
Lord Jesus Christ. We may get the idea of this if we recall the fact
that many Jews have been carried away by that Satanic flood from
the mouth of the dragon known as Christian Science. So in the days
of the great tribulation, Satan will try to swamp and destroy Israel
as a nation by the evil teachings he will spread through the world.
But even the earth itself will help the woman, opening its mouth
and swallowing up the river which the dragon casts out. That is,
Israel will be driven out among all the nations, as I take it. Israel
will be so shocked and horrified by the evil results of these Satanic
teachings that they will themselves be preserved from them. Just as
the captivity in Babylon, the fountain-head of idolatry, cured Judah
of her own idolatrous tendencies for a period of time, so Israel's
experiences among the Gentiles in the last days will be used by God
to preserve her from the evil river in which the dragon would drown
her. Unable to destroy the nation as such, he makes a special effort
to ruin the rest of her offspring, or the remnant that keep the commandments of God and the testimony of Jesus. These, I take it, are
those who remain in the land, as pictured by the two witnesses.
There they maintain a testimony for God against all the persecutions of the antichrist. The next chapter will tell us how the devil
will seek to destroy this remnant.

CHAPTER THIRTEEN
THE TWO BEASTS

The Coming Federation of Nations (Revelation 13:1-10)

A federation of nations! How much is this phrase on the lips of politicians and persons interested in national affairs at the present time (1919)! It was far otherwise but a few years ago. When teachers of prophecy declared that the Word of God predicted just such a federation as men are now deeply interested in, they were met with ridicule. It was openly declared that these teachers were dreamers, giving in to foolish imaginations, and proclaiming something that could never be fulfilled. But World War I and new conditions have changed the viewpoint of these cavillers considerably in the last few years. Now there are those who hold the confederacy of nations as the one solution to the difficulties confronting statesmen everywhere. Many consider this alliance will be the panacea for all reconstruction perils. Just what will come out of it all, while the church still remains on earth, one would not attempt to prophesy. But after the church is gone there will indeed be a great confederacy of the nations that have sprung out of the old Roman empire. It will be Satanic in origin and character, and will in fact be the devil's last card, if I may borrow such an expression, before he is obliged to admit his complete defeat. This is the subject of the first ten verses of Revelation 13.

In the last chapter we were noticing that the enmity of Satan will be turned against God's earthly people (Israel) in a special manner, after the church has been caught up to meet the Lord in the air. In this chapter we will see just what form that enmity will take. And in properly placing this passage, we need to remember that this portion of Revelation has in view a time of solemn and momentous import—the time between the first resurrection and translation of the saints at the rapture and the glorious appearing of the Lord Jesus Christ. This chapter encompasses the time before Christ returns as the long-looked-for Messiah of Israel, who will sit on the throne of His father David and rule over all the earth in righteousness. If there is confusion as to this, nothing will be clear.

It is not hard to imagine something of the condition in which this world will be found after all real Christians have been snatched away to be with the Lord; especially when we realize that many in high places—rulers, governors, and other political leaders, are at heart Christian men. Perhaps, I should not say *many* compared with those who are unsaved and indifferent to the claims of Christ for Scripture tells us that "not many mighty, not many noble, are called" (1 Corinthians 1:26). Lady Huntington was a devoted woman who lived in the days of Whitefield and the Wesleys and was such a help in spreading the gospel. She used to say that she was just going to Heaven by an "M." Had the verse been "Not *any* noble," there would have been no hope for her, but the "M" took her in.

But certainly there are some in high places who truly know the Lord and would be caught away with the church at His coming. Their removal would be like the breaking of a dike, permitting the rushing waters of anarchy to sweep over every land. Think how evil will then be intensified. What frightful lengths unsaved men will go to in their efforts to bring about a millennium without Christ. Whether carnal men realize it or not, the true Christians are the light of the world and the salt of the earth. Let every Christian suddenly be taken away from this world, and you will have gross darkness covering the earth. With the preservative power of righteousness gone, the masses of men will be given up to corruption and violence. Read the account of the days before the flood, and you will have some sense of the chaotic condition that will prevail. Even now we see lawlessness spreading everywhere in the world. And back of all this is a Satanic effort to destroy all faith in God and His Word, and to substitute in its place evil systems that can only result in eternal ruin to those who follow them.

In our day, though the enemy comes in like a flood, the Spirit of God is here to lift up a standard against him. The Word of God tells us that the mystery of lawlessness does already work, but during this dispensation the Holy Spirit hinders the full development of evil. When He is taken out of the world—that is, when the Holy Spirit takes the church up to meet the Lord in the air—then the last hindrance to the power of evil will be gone. There will no longer be any restraint on the machinations of the devil. In Heaven the saints will be presented before the judgment seat of Christ. As we have seen, for the last time Satan will appear as the prosecuting attorney against them before God, as he has done for so many centuries. But he will be utterly cast out of Heaven and will come down to the earth with great wrath because he knows that his time is short. Only in Israel will he find a testimony for God in that day, so he will turn all his malice against that people. He will undertake to work for their ruin through human government when it has utterly cast off God.

In Daniel 2 we are told that Nebuchadnezzar had a dream of a great image, which depicts "the times of the Gentiles." This term refers to the period during which the Jews are scattered among the Gentiles, the times in which the nations hold authority over the land of Palestine. These Gentile times began with Nebuchadnezzar, who is represented by the head of gold. Following this comes the rule of the Medes and Persians, depicted by the silver breast and arms. That, in turn, was succeeded by the Greco-Macedonian empire, set forth by the bronze torso of the image. The last world-empire is the kingdom of iron, the Roman. But Daniel goes on to show that the Roman empire would take on a very peculiar form in the time of the end. In the feet of the image you have an attempt to amalgamate that which cannot be amalgamated, iron and clay. It is a picture of man's attempt to amalgamate the iron of imperialism with the potter's clay of social democracy.

It is impossible to mix imperialism and democracy. The one must, of necessity, destroy the other. And this Scripture which we now have before us, makes it plain that in the end the imperial power is going to triumph in measure. Men will grow weary of the constant conflict, which has been so prolonged; for, whatever optimistic statesmen still may say, God's Word shows that the confusion will grow worse and worse. And we need not be surprised if, even before the church is taken away, instead of raising armies to make

the world safe *for* democracy, it may become necessary to con-
script the young manhood of our nation in an attempt to save the
world *from* democracy. The people will soon attempt to take everything into their own hands, thus jeopardizing all property rights.
This is a condition which cannot forever be tolerated. Out of it all
will rise, after the church has been caught up to meet the Lord, one
man who will combine in himself the statesmanship of a Caesar,
the military genius of a Napoleon, and the personal attractiveness
of a Chesterfield. This man will head a combination of ten powers,
formed, as before mentioned, from the nations that have sprung out
of the old Roman empire. When they have cast off all allegiance to
God and His Word, through this confederacy he will, for a time at
least, dominate the world.

As already intimated, Daniel pictures this final phase of things
by the ten toes of the image. Of old, the Roman empire was divided
into the eastern and western parts, which is symbolized by the two
legs of the great image, but united under one central authority until
disintegration began.

In Daniel 7 we read of the times of the Gentiles pictured in a
different way. The man of God had a vision in which he saw nothing beautiful or grand, but the four great empires were represented
as four ravenous beasts, waiting to spring on each other. These beasts
were so dreadful that nothing on earth fully satisfies the description
of the wild creatures there depicted. The Babylonian empire was
symbolized by a lion with the wings of an eagle—a hybrid, formed
from a beast of the earth and fowls of the air. The Medo-Persian
dominion appeared as a bear, lifting itself up on one side. It had
between its teeth three ribs dripping with blood, representing probably the three chief cities of the Babylonian empire that were sacked
by the Medes and Persians under Cyrus. The Grecian, or Alexandrian
empire, was pictured as a leopard with four heads and four wings of
a bird on his back. The four heads, of course, depicted the fourfold
division of this Greco-Macedonian empire after Alexander's death.
Finally, Daniel wrote that the fourth beast was dreadful and terrible. It had great iron teeth and broke in pieces and devoured all
that came in its way. He gave no exact description of it, however he
added that it had ten horns.

That last beast clearly answers to the iron legs of the image, the Roman power. The ten horns are the ten toes, which illustrate it in its final form. I think there can be no doubt whatever that it is this last dreadful beast which is fully delineated for us in our present chapter. It is the Roman power which was in existence when the Lord was born and was responsible for His death upon the cross. The Jews had no power at all unless it were ratified by Pilate, as representing Caesar. Therefore the Roman empire, of which Pontius Pilate was the official representative, crucified the Lord of glory. It is true that Pilate simply gave the sentence called for by the Jews, and therefore they are held responsible for killing their Messiah. But the Roman procurator must face that clause, repeated over and over again through the centuries in the recitation of the Apostles' Creed: "He was crucified under Pontius Pilate." Pilate can never get away from that. It will stand against his record forever.

We have already seen in Revelation 12, that the great red dragon, having seven heads and ten horns, represents Rome energized by Satan seeking to destroy the man-child. Here, in chapter 13, we have Rome in the time of the end. The empire revived, summoned from the sea of the nations by the devil himself. Verse one should read, according to the best manuscripts, "*He* stood upon the sand of the sea," that is, Satan, the dragon. And it is he who summons the wild beast to rise up out of the waters, "having seven heads and ten horns, and upon his horns ten crowns, and upon his heads the name of blasphemy." This is imperial Rome revived, as the ten crowns declare.

After the death of the Lord Jesus Christ the Roman empire continued in existence for something like 500 years, though divided into the eastern and western parts, which until the end of its history held together more or less loosely. It was finally destroyed by the invaders from the north and the east. But though the empire as such was broken in pieces, nevertheless Roman principles prevailed throughout the great part of Europe and became the basis of the civilization which we now know. Our American system of jurisprudence is founded on that of Rome. In World War I the Allies, including America, were all representatives of the old Roman empire, with the exception, of course, of Japan, China, and other heathen nations. On the other side we saw the very same powers joined together (the Goths, Vandals, and Huns), who, in the fourth, fifth, and sixth centuries, hurled themselves upon the Roman empire and destroyed it. It was a most singular thing surely, and almost unexplainable for those who do not read their Bibles, that in the twentieth century the same great divisions were maintained as in the closing days of Roman domination. But we may see from this how readily that Roman empire will be revived through a great international movement—a confederation of all the Latin or Latinized nations. One of the great agencies which shall have much to do in bringing this about will be the Roman Catholic church, whose power is increasing continually, even in the very lands where the Reformation, at one time, would have made this impossible.

It was the boast of the Roman conquerors that they never destroyed a civilization; they absorbed into their own great commonwealth everything that was best of the various nations which they subjugated. And we cannot but be reminded of this as we read the second verse: "And the beast which I saw was like unto a leopard, and his feet were as the feet of a bear, and his mouth as the mouth of a lion: and the dragon gave him his power, and his seat, and great authority." Observe how, in these few words we have a distinct illustration of the fact that the last phase of the Roman empire will be linked up with all that has gone before. In Rome you have the leopard of Greece, the bear of Persia, and the lion of Babylon. Thus you have incorporated into this last great confederacy the chief elements of every civilization that has left a great mark on the world. Everything that man has been able to build up and has learned to value throughout the centuries, will be headed up in this final federation of nations.

For it is not Rome as existing in John's day merely which is in view, but Rome as it will exist in the closing days of the dispensation. This is plain from the third verse, if rightly understood: "And I saw one of his heads as it were wounded to death; and his deadly wound was healed: and all the world wondered after the beast." We will find help in understanding the heads if we turn to Revelation 17:8-13. There we are told that the same beast is in view. In those brief words, we have a synopsis of the whole history of the Roman empire. For something like 900 years it was the greatest earthly power. But a time came when it could be truly said "the beast is not." It had been destroyed; its imperial head had been wounded to death. For centuries no man unenlightened by the Word of God would have been bold enough to have predicted the return of imperial power to that fallen dominion; but Scripture had declared that it would come to pass. While statesmen and carnal theorists have rejected what seemed to them a ridiculous assumption, students of prophecy, guided by the Spirit of God, have for nearly a century taught that the nations into which the Roman empire had been divided will again come together under one head. Today only a bold man would deny the likelihood of this very thing. But when statesmen talk of a coming world federation, how little they realize who it is who is going to bring this about. The beast is to ascend out of the abyss for it is Satanic power that will bring into existence what is here pictured. It will be the devil's last effort to make men believe that they do not need God's Christ, that they can have peace and security while the Prince of Peace is rejected. But God will ruin all their plans, for He has said, "I will overturn, overturn, overturn, ...until he come whose right it is" (Ezekiel 21:27).

But now notice two interpretations of the seven heads. We are told they are seven *mountains*, on which the woman sits, and they "are seven *kings*: five are fallen, and one is, and the other is not yet come; and when he cometh, he must continue a short space. And the beast that was, and is not, even he is the eighth, and is of the seven, and goeth into perdition" (Revelation 17:10-11).

The seven mountains have generally been taken as meaning the seven hills on which the imperial city is built. I am inclined to think this is correct, even though some would refuse the idea from the fact that the hills themselves are not in any sense mountainous in character. But the very fact that it was the delight of the Romans to speak of their capital as the seven-hilled city, would naturally bring this city to mind to any who read John's description.

As to the second interpretation, a king is the familiar symbol for a form of government. Livy, the Roman historian, showed us that Rome had passed through five very distinct forms of government prior to John's day. The sixth, which was in existence in John's time, was the imperial. That was the form which was destroyed, and I am persuaded that this was the head wounded to death (13:3). But that deadly wound is to be healed, for the imperial form is to be restored, but under altogether different conditions, making it distinctly the seventh. For ten nations, all banding themselves together, will elect one of their number as the head of the confederacy. This man is distinctly called the beast. It reminds us of Louis XIV, who said, "I am the State." This beast will exercise authority as the elected head for only a short time before throwing off all restraint (as did Napoleon, elected as first consul, and later declaring himself emperor), thus bringing about the eighth form, which derives from the seventh.

So spectacular will be his coup d'état that men will be thrilled with admiration at his masterly genius. Accepting the principle that nothing but an imperial form of government can give them settled and continuous peace, they will readily acknowledge his pretensions. In doing so they will worship the dragon that gave power to the beast and do homage to the beast himself, saying, "Who is like unto the beast; who is able to make war with him?" (4) I think God has given us a wonderful illustration of this very thing in the history of Napoleon Bonaparte, as mentioned above. Think of this Corsican, utterly insignificant, first coming into notice as a second lieutenant in the revolutionary army. Suddenly, after the bloody reign of terror, he emerged from his former obscure place, and became the central figure of the world in that day. Elected by an overwhelming majority as first consul of France, he proclaimed himself imperator, dazzling all France and the world for a time, and ended his course on the isle of St. Helena.

One greater than Napoleon will yet arise out of the chaotic conditions that will prevail in Europe after the church has been taken home. He will be a man of marvelous appearance and transcendent ability, wholly given up to Satan. He will be the great civil leader of the last days—the man who will have the final word in all matters, religious as well. All the civilized earth will wonder after him and do homage to him and his hidden master, the devil. In his pride and his folly he will speak great and blasphemous things against God. He will doubtless consider himself the man of destiny whom no

power, human or divine, can overthrow. But the God whom he denies has limited his control, for power will be given him only "to
continue forty and two months"; that is, for three and a half years,
the last half of Daniel's seventieth week, he will be in authority
over the prophetic earth. During that time he will open his mouth in
blasphemy against God and blaspheme His name and His tabernacle and all that dwell in Heaven, namely, the saints who will have
been caught up at the rapture. He will make war with the faithful in
God's restored Israel and overcome these saints on earth, power
being given him over all countries, and tongues, and nations.

This then is the manner in which the dragon will attempt the
destruction of the remnant of the woman's seed. His effort will be
to completely root out everything that is of God in the earth. In
order to do this he will have a trusty lieutenant dwelling in the land
of Palestine itself, who will uphold him in all his nefarious plans.
The rest of chapter 13 (verses 11-18) deals with this assistant.

The days of the beast are the days referred to by our Lord Jesus
Christ when He said that if it were possible the very elect would be
deceived. But, thank God, He will preserve His own, even in that
dreadful day. So we learn from verse 8 that none will be deceived
by him nor do homage to him, but those "whose names are not
written in the book of life...from the foundation of the world." How
solemn is the challenge of verses 9 and 10 of the 13th chapter: "If
any man have an ear, let him hear. He that leadeth into captivity
shall go into captivity: he that killeth with the sword must be killed
with the sword. Here is the patience and the faith of the saints."
These will be the days of the great tribulation, which, in all its intensity, will be directed against Israel. But the Lord will be watching over His little flock. Scattered as they will be among the heathen, He will be to them a little sanctuary in every place that they
may wander.

Only those who have exchanged the heavenly hope for an earthly
one will be deceived by this great leader. He is the coming man for
whom the world is waiting. Mistaken and blinded statesmen will
hail him as the head of the nations, the one who will solve the problems—social, political, and economic—that are now disturbing the
world. How blessed to be warned by God Himself of all these things

beforehand, that we may walk apart from everything that savors of that day of reproach and blasphemy. And when it actually comes, who can question the value of this present scripture for the guidance and consolation of God's earthly people Israel. Otherwise they might well be in despair at the apparent defeat of righteousness and the triumph of iniquity.

But "the triumphing of the wicked is short," (Job 20:5) and "the man of the earth" will be destroyed in due time. Faith will have its reward when the Lord appears from Heaven to take vengeance on all who dare lift up their bloody hands against His afflicted people. "Here is the patience and the faith of the saints."

The Personal Antichrist (Revelation 13:11-18)

The world is waiting for an authoritative religious leader. In an age of doubt and uncertainty men are longing for one who can speak a final word on all the ethical, religious, and political questions which today trouble so many. Instructed Christians know that God has already spoken authoritatively in the person of His Son and revealed His mind in His holy Word. But they, too, are looking for a coming One, even the coming of the Lord Jesus Christ from glory to establish Heaven's authority and power on the earth. He will descend from Heaven and with all His glorified saints will reign over the earth for a thousand years of peace and blessing. However, the coming man for whom unbelievers look is one whom they expect to be born on the earth—a man of the earth, therefore not the Lord from Heaven. This expectation is to have its fulfillment in "the man of sin," the personal antichrist, the false messiah, who will soon be revealed. In fact, it is a solemn consideration that he may already be in this world—perhaps a baby—possibly a precocious youth—possibly a man of affairs! But he will not be made known until after the church of the firstborn has been raptured at the presence of the Lord.

The remarkable thing is that many who are waiting expectantly for the antichrist imagine they are looking for a reincarnation of Christ Himself. They profess to wait for a savior and expect him to appear on earth, born after the course of nature. Theosophists and others are expectantly waiting for a great world-teacher. They are really preparing the world for the advent of the man of sin, the son of perdition.

To be forewarned is to be forearmed. God's holy Word has predicted the coming of this false one and has clearly shown what will lead up to his revelation. No Spirit-taught Bible student can fail to observe the shadow of the antichrist falling across many pages of prophecy. "Ye have heard," wrote the apostle John, "that antichrist shall come" (1 John 2:18). The only question that troubles many has to do with the identification of the person or thing referred to. Is the antichrist a person or a system? Many weighty names could be quoted in favor of either view, but, in order that our faith may not stand in the wisdom of men, but in the power of God in this matter as in all else, we desire to be guided by the written Word.

Before turning to a number of definite Scriptures, let me remind you of this blessed fact: Christ is a person—a glorified, holy, all-powerful person—one of the eternal Trinity. He has taken humanity into union with deity through being born of a virgin on earth, where He humbled Himself as man to the death of the cross. Logically one would expect that the antichrist would also be a man, a definite personality, opposed to the Lord Jesus Christ, yet claiming to be all that He was—usurping the place of Christ. But we would not forget that there is in the world a body united to Christ of which He is the glorified Head. There is also a great apostate system opposed to this divine one. This system falsely claims to be the spouse of Christ and the only authorized custodian of the mysteries of God. Is this system the antichrist, or is it rather Babylon the great, the antichurch? I think we will see as we go on that the latter view is the correct one.

The prophetic Scriptures outline two great religious deceptions: a false Christ and a false church. But the one is not to be confused with the other. The antichrist will be a *man*, as the Christ of God is a Man. Babylon is a vast organized *system*, even as the church of God is a divine organization. But the one is a Satanic counterfeit of the other. When the voice of prophecy speaks of the antichrist, the masculine pronoun *he* is used. When it speaks of the false church it uses either the neuter or the feminine, *it* or *she*. There is good reason for this. The antichrist is the final head of the apostate system that bears the same relationship to him, in an outward way, that the church does to Christ. Ever since the primeval promise of the seed of the woman who was to bruise the serpent's head (Genesis 3:15), men have looked and longed for a deliverer to arise from among themselves. Such an expectation was grounded on Scripture and was fulfilled in the birth of Christ. But since He has been rejected, this expectation has become a perversion of the truth. The God-sent deliverer, "the woman's seed," has been caught up to God and to His throne. It is the *serpent's* seed who is coming (the *anti*-Christ), and they who wait for him realize it not! The serpent has for millenniums been the symbol of esoteric religion, which stands for wisdom. The coming one will claim to be the wisdom of God. Esoteric religion, I may say, is the religion *par excellence* of the antichrist.

A man then is being awaited. His advent draws near. He will come at last when the restraining power, the Holy Spirit, has returned to the heavens. This coming one is the grand monarch of the new humanity cult. He is the coming leader or Mahdi of the Muslims. He is the long-expected last incarnation of Vishnu waited for by the Brahmins; the coming Montezuma of the Aztecs; the false messiah of the apostate Jews; the great master of all sects of Yogis; the ultimate man of the evolutionists; the *Ubermensch* of Nietzsche, the Hun philosopher, whose ravings prepared the way for World War I. He will be a Satan-controlled, God-defying, conscienceless, almost superhuman man—an individual whose appearing will mean the consummation of the present apostasy, and the full deification of humanity to his bewildered dupes. Thus the world will turn away from the Christ of God and stretch out eager hands to welcome the coming man of sin. And, depend on it, he will be on time! God's Word has declared his advent as surely as it predicts the second coming of the Lord Jesus Christ from glory.

Meanwhile the great antichurch (the evil system that is a counterfeit of the true church for which Christ died) is casting overboard every truth of Scripture. This antichurch follows the lies that will prepare them to receive "the liar" of whom 1 John 2:22 speaks—the antichrist. "All liars, shall have their part in the lake which burneth with fire and brimstone" is the unalterable decree of the God of truth (Revelation 21:8).

The most complete description of antichrist is found in Daniel 11:36-45. Notice that in these verses it is predicted that a king will arise in Jerusalem who will be an utter atheist. Yet evidently, he will be a Jew; for it is distinctly said of him that "neither shall he regard the God of his fathers, nor the desire of women" (Daniel 11:37). The expression "the God of his fathers " can mean nothing else than the God of Abraham, Isaac, and Jacob. It is frequently so used in Scripture. The expression "the desire of women" is recognized by both Jewish and Christian expositors as referring to the messiah. This point is, I think, very important, for the antichrist could not be the false messiah if he were not a Jew. Otherwise he would have no claim on the allegiance of Israel. He will be a great Jewish leader who will seem, at first, to be a wonderful lover of his people and will establish them in their own land. But he will soon throw off all restraint, exalt himself, and will magnify himself against every god. He will speak marvelous things against the God of gods during the last three and a half years of Daniel's seventieth week. Notice how this passage in Daniel connects so intimately with the portion we are considering in Revelation 13. In verse 11 we read: "I beheld another beast coming up out of the earth; and he had two horns like a lamb, and he spake as a dragon." Observe he does not arise from the Gentile nations (depicted by the sea) as does the first beast. He comes up out of the earth, or land—that is, the land of Palestine, the very same land in which the king (Daniel 11) is to be revealed. He had "two horns like a lamb," for he seems at first to have both the meekness and strength of the Lamb of God, but his dragon-like speech betrays him. It is the speech of self-exaltation, which indicates that his condemnation is the same as that of his master, the devil, who fell through pride.

Daniel wrote that though the willful king will not regard any supernatural god, he will honor one who is called "the god of forces" (11:38). Evidently he is a man, for the king pays tribute to him: "a god whom his fathers knew not shall he honor with gold, and silver, and precious stones, and pleasant things." This mighty one will be the backer of the antichrist. In return for his protection, he will cause Palestine to submit to his authority and pay tribute to him. Thus "a strange god...he shall acknowledge and increase with glory: and he shall cause them to rule over many, and shall divide the land for gain" (11:39). This relationship is also implied in Revelation 13:12: "And he exerciseth all the power of the first beast before him, and causeth the earth and them which dwell therein to worship the first beast, whose deadly wound was healed." He is the vicegerent of the first beast. This first beast, whom the world recognizes as a god (in the sense in which it recognized the Caesars of old as gods) is the master whom he enriches with Jewish wealth.

Verses 12-14 tell us that antichrist is not only a crafty politician, but a wonder-worker as well. The striking account of the lawless one in 2 Thessalonians 2:3-12 agrees with this description. Those verses are a prediction of the coming of the atheist king of Daniel 11 and the wonder-worker of Revelation 13.

One of the signs of the times in our own days is the unhealthy craving for marvels and wonders, which is so prevalent in many places. It is a most dangerous condition of mind, and Christians should beware of anything of the kind. We are too near the end of the dispensation to expect divine miracles in any number, but Satanic signs and wonders will increase as we draw nearer the end. When the antichrist himself appears, he will give men all the marvels for which they long—only to deceive them and lead them to accept his ungodly pretensions.

Just exactly what is meant by the "image" of the beast (13:14), I do not pretend to say. I have no doubt it is linked with our Lord's warning as to the abomination of desolation that is to be set up in the holy place (Matthew 24:15). At any rate, it will be the culmination of the apostasy, and will be the signal for all believing Jews, who in that day of great persecution cleave to the Lord, to flee from Jerusalem and hide themselves in distant parts among the nations until the appearing of the Messiah Himself. We are told that the lamblike beast will give life to the image. It will speak "and cause that as many as would not worship the image of the beast should be killed" (13:15). A great society will be formed of apostate Jews and apostate Gentiles, which will be patterned somewhat after our present day labor unions and oath-bound organizations. This is intimated in verses 16-17: "And he causeth all, both small and great, rich and poor, free and bond, to receive a mark in their right hand, or in their foreheads: and that no man might buy or sell, save he that had the mark, or the name of the beast, or the number of his name." Christians in this present time should keep themselves from all such worldly associations and unequal yokes.

Our Lord Jesus told the Jews of His day, "I am come in my Father's name, and ye receive me not; if another shall come in his own name, him ye will receive" (John 5:43). He was speaking of this awful person whom we have seen portrayed in these various Scriptures. With them we might also link Zechariah 11:16-17:

> For, lo, I will raise up a shepherd in the land, [note that, he will arise in the land of Palestine] which shall not visit those that be cut off, neither shall seek the young one, nor heal that that is broken, nor feed that that standeth still: but he shall eat the flesh of the fat, and tear their claws in pieces. Woe to the idol shepherd that leaveth the flock! the sword shall be upon his arm, and upon his right eye: his arm shall be clean dried up, and his right eye shall be utterly darkened.

This idol shepherd is put in contrast to the Good Shepherd whom Zechariah was to represent, who was sold for thirty pieces of silver (11:12). This part of the prophecy has been literally fulfilled, and we may be certain that the rest will all come to pass in due time.

For this idol shepherd the Jews are even now waiting, though they little realize it. At a Zionist congress, some years before World War I, Max Nordau declared, according to the published reports, "We are ready to welcome any man as our Messiah who will lead us back to our own land and establish us there in prosperity." Max Nordau was a so-called reformed Jew, who gave up the Messianic hope as set forth in the holy Scriptures. When Dr. Mosinsohn, of the Hebrew College of Jaffa, was touring America in the interests of the same Zionist movement, I had the privilege of hearing him give an address at the University of California. In the course of his remarks he said, "Think of all the great religious leaders who have come out of the East. Moses arose in the East, Buddha, Confucius, Jesus and Mohammed all arose in the East. And we say to you people of the West, with confidence, that if you will restore the Jew to his ancestral home it will not be long until we will give you another great religious leader who will perhaps transcend all who have gone before." A Christian physician and I, who had gone to the lecture together, looked at one another in amazement. We felt that we were listening to a John-the-Baptist of the antichrist, so startling was the announcement. And with the light that the prophetic word throws upon the now very near future, who can doubt that this Hebrew leader's declaration will indeed seem to an unbelieving world to be fulfilled in the willful one who is to be raised up in the land of Palestine, and who will be acknowledged by apostate Judaism and apostate Christendom alike as the Christ—the coming man. Toward this awful end all modern cults and isms are tending, and when the personal presence of the Holy Spirit has been withdrawn from the earth, his manifestation will not long be withheld.

I know that many have considered the papacy to be the fulfill-ment of the prophecies we have been considering; and I do not wonder at this, for that unholy system is one of the most amazing counterfeits of what is of God that the world has ever seen. But it certainly does not meet all the requirements of the case; though it is undoubtedly one of the "many antichrists" of which the apostle John writes, when forewarning us of the antichrist whose coming is still future.

I would direct your attention to six things predicted of this false one which have never been true of the papacy and are never likely to be.

First: The antichrist must be a Jew, otherwise he would not be acknowledged by Israel as their messiah.

Second: He is to rise up in the land of Palestine, not in Italy; in Jerusalem, not in Rome.

Third: He is to be subject to and in league with the civil power; he will not dominate it as the papacy did for centuries.

Fourth: He is to be acknowledged by the mass of the Jews as their king and religious leader. It is well-known that the Jews have never conceded to the pretensions of the popes.

Fifth: He is to be the patron of Israel, whereas the Catholic church has ever been their persecutor.

Sixth: He is not to be revealed until after the hindering Holy

Spirit is removed. That will only be when He goes up with the church at the return of the Lord Jesus Christ for His people, before the hour of judgment strikes for this godless world where the Word of God, the Christ of God, the Spirit of God, and the church of God have all been rejected.

There are other systems equally anti-christian as the papacy, but none of them answer to the above requirements. Therefore none of them are to be confused with the personal antichrist who is yet to arise and delude for a time those "who refused the love of the truth that they might be saved." The many antichrists are preparing the way for this incarnation of iniquity.The avidity with which men and women drink in their evil teachings may give us some idea of how easy a thing it will be for the false Messiah to establish his claims.

Some would ridicule the thought of vast numbers responding to such monstrous pretensions. But we need to remember that God Himself is going "to give them up" in retributive judgment "to believe *the* lie," because they would not have His truth. (In the original version of 2 Thessalonians 2:11 it is the definite article "*the* lie"—not "a lie" as in the King James version.) In our own day, how easily deceivers, not to speak of Rome itself, have been able to enslave the minds and consciences of vast multitudes of people who refuse the simple truth of the Word of God. All this is taking place with the Holy Spirit still in the world, waiting to guide into all truth every honest soul who is willing to be led by Him and taught through the Word. How much easier it will be for error to assert itself when He is no longer here!

I know that many of you will be anxious to have me attempt to expound verse 18 and tell you plainly what is meant by its mystic number. All I can say is that *six* is the number of *man*, and *three* of *manifestation*. In these three sixes I see the full revelation of what is in the heart of man—man's last effort to attain to divinity and deity, to rob God of His glory and to exalt himself. But, undoubtedly, when the antichrist actually appears and the first beast is seen, the meaning will be so plain that every one who turns to God in that day will be warned thereby to "have no fellowship with the unfruitful works of darkness" (Ephesians 5:11). But they will cleave to the

Lord all the more earnestly because they know that the end has drawn so near. Guesses as to the meaning of 666 have been innumerable; I will not add another.

In closing, I would again remind my readers, that time for us also is flying quickly by. If any of you are unsaved, it is well for you to remember that mercy's day is quickly gone. Gospel light already seems to be vanishing from the earth; the darkening apostasy is making rapid strides; a famine for hearing the Word of the Lord will soon be here. Oh, that now, in this day of grace, men would heed the testimony of the Scripture of truth, receive the virgin-born Son of God as Savior and Lord, and spurn the lies of every antichrist. "Oh earth, earth, earth, hear the word of the Lord! / Hear, and your soul shall live"

"He that heareth my word, and believeth on him that sent me, hath everlasting life, and shall not come into condemnation; but is passed from death unto life" (John 5:24).

CHAPTER FOURTEEN

THE HARVEST AND VINTAGE

R evelation 14 forms a distinct section of the book. It consists of one vision divided into six parts and evidently has to do with the closing up of the great tribulation and the introduction of the kingdom. It is as though God would give to John, and to us, a heartening view of the consummation, before describing in detail the closing trials that will occupy the last half of the tribulation period.

The Lamb on Mount Sion (Revelation 14:1-5)

Verses 1-5 present a beautiful little prophetic picture, quite complete in itself. It sets forth that which is to take place after the desolations of Israel are ended. The glory will dawn in the land where Jesus lived and died and rose again, and to which He is coming back in person.

Observe, to begin with, that mount Sion is on the earth. The vision has to do with the return of the Lamb to the city that once rejected Him. It is common for Bible readers to spiritualize the various localities mentioned in the Bible. Thus Jerusalem, mount Sion, and Israel are all made to mean the church, or possibly even Heaven itself, whereas they have no such application. When God says Israel, He means Israel. When He speaks of Jerusalem He does not intend us to understand that either Heaven or the church is in view. Mount Sion is that mount Zion which David first set apart to God, and is a distinct locality to this day in the land of Palestine, within the limits of the city of Jerusalem. It is a place on earth, not in Heaven, and there the Lord Jesus Christ is going to gather the Israelite remnant to Himself when He comes to set up His kingdom. For, although many have taught the contrary, I believe that the 144,000 of this chapter are the very same as the sealed 144,000 of Revelation 7. In the earlier chapter John saw them sealed before the great tribulation began; God had pledged Himself to protect them. No matter how vindictively their enemies might assail them, He had set His own mark on them. He had promised to bring them safely through those tempestuous and difficult days. Now, in chapter 14, we see that same company gathered about the Lamb on mount Sion, the firstfruits of the kingdom age.

The Lord reveals His Father's name to them. The seal of the living God on their foreheads is, in fact, this blessed revelation. They know God as Father and rejoice in His protecting care and tender love. In Heaven there are those who rejoice with them in a very special way. These are distinguished from the elders who represent, as we have already seen, the entire priestly company caught up at the rapture. But as the great tribulation goes on, Jewish believers, who will be martyred because of their faith, will also join that heavenly throng. So we are told that John heard "a voice from heaven, as the voice of many waters, and as the voice of a great thunder: and I heard the voice of harpers harping with their harps" (2). These sing, "as it were a new song before the throne, and before the [living ones] and the elders: and no man could learn that song but the hundred and forty and four thousand, which were redeemed from the earth" (3). These in Heaven and those on earth will have passed through the same experiences in measure. There will be a sympathetic cord struck, to which both respond. The new song here, as elsewhere, is the song of redemption.

The company on mount Sion are next described as undefiled, a virgin band who have kept themselves from the prevalent uncleanness in those fearful days. It is to be their hallowed privilege to follow the Lamb wherever He goes. They are described as being "redeemed from among men, being the firstfruits unto God and to the Lamb" (4). Thus we have a firstfruits of the kingdom age, even as our Lord Himself is described as the firstfruits of the present dispensation and His church, associated with Him, is "a kind of firstfruits of his creatures" (James 1:18).

The portion of this special company is the blessing of Psalm 32 pronounced upon the man in whom is no guile and the blessing that our Lord pronounced upon Nathanael (John 1:47). A guileless man is not a sinless man; he is one who has nothing to hide. When sin is all confessed and judged in the presence of God, guile is absent. And so this guileless company are described as without fault before the throne of God. They certainly do not appear there in any righteousness of their own, but saved by the same precious blood that today makes faultless every believer in our Lord Jesus Christ.

The Everlasting Gospel (Revelation 14:6-7)

This everlasting gospel is not to be distinguished from the gospel that has been proclaimed throughout the centuries. In truth, the very fact that it is called "everlasting" shows that it is identical with the gospel as proclaimed from the beginning. It is the good news of all the ages that God is sovereign, and man's happiness consists in recognizing His authority. In the present dispensation, the full truth of the gospel of the grace of God is added to this blessed fact. The gospel of the kingdom is but another aspect of this same news from Heaven, emphasizing particularly the lordship of Christ. There can only be one gospel, for the apostle tells us, " Though we, or an angel from heaven, preach any other gospel unto you than that which we have preached unto you, let him be accursed" (Galatians 1:8). But that one gospel has different phases. In the Epistle to the Galatians Paul speaks of "the gospel of the circumcision" and the "gospel of the uncircumcision"—the same gospel, but presented in one way to the Jews and another to the Gentiles. When the Lord was here on earth ministering, as also was John the Baptist, they preached the gospel of the kingdom. But men rejected the kingdom, and so, for the time being, the kingdom is in abeyance. This is the day of the church.

The Son of man is compared to a man who has gone into a far country to receive for himself a kingdom and to return. When the word is given by the Father He will descend to take the kingdom, to be proclaimed as King of kings and Lord of lords. Throughout the present dispensation He is taking Jews and Gentiles who believe on

His name and uniting them into the one body, the church. After the church has gone, there will not be a Christian left on earth. Then God is going to commence again to work among the Jews and He will send them out to preach the gospel of the kingdom unto the ends of the earth. Finally, we have the very last phase of that gospel immediately preceding His coming. It is the final call for the guilty nations to prostrate themselves in the dust and pay homage to their Creator. It is mercy indeed that in that hour of judgment, before the last blow falls, the call will still go forth to men everywhere to acknowledge the claims of the omnipotent One whose mercies have been rejected so long. In this chapter however we do not hear of any response. But Scripture elsewhere warrants the thought that many who had never previously heard and rejected the gospel will in that day open their hearts to the message and repent and thus be led to welcome the King.

Babylon (Revelation 14:8)

Babylon is more fully described for us in chapters 17–18, but we have to defer any detailed exposition of this subject until a later chapter. I will say that just as Babylon of old was the fountainhead of idolatry, so is mystic Babylon today the mother of all false religious teaching in Christianity. In the time of the end it will be headed up in one great false church. That worldly church, which has proved so unworthy and false to her Lord, is to be utterly destroyed. I have no doubt that all over the world there will then be scenes with men crying, "No God; no church."

I know that many religious leaders at the present time are very enthusiastic about what they call "the reunion of Christendom" but that reunion will simply be a great federation of Christless churches. They will form the most powerful religious association that has ever been known in this world—Catholic, Greek, Protestant, and all other systems united into one—after the true believers have gone. For a time, this great institution will dominate everything until men will say at last, "What is the use of a church like this; why not destroy the whole thing and be done with it once and for all?" So they will destroy it throughout the world, as they once destroyed it in France and in Russia.

Would that professed preachers of the gospel realized, before it is too late, that when men take up religion in which there is no real conversion and which has no place for the work of the Holy Spirit, the whole thing will soon go on the rocks. In spite of the latitudinarianism of the times in which we live, it is still blessedly true that when faithful men preach the genuine old-time gospel of the grace of God in power, people are willing to go and hear. Speaking generally, even unsaved men and women have more respect for the old, old story of redeeming love than they have for modern shams. When a man comes to the place where he no longer believes in the Bible, in the blood of Christ, in regeneration, he says to himself, "Why am I paying money to keep up the church. I had better pay it to a lodge or a club. I can get more out of something like that than I can get out of the church." Have you ever noticed that Unitarianism has never been a financial success? Therefore when a preacher, in one of our orthodox churches no longer believes in orthodoxy, you will observe that generally he holds on to his position in the orthodox institution as long as he can. Loaves and fishes are more common there, after all, than in the heretical systems that are languishing all about us. And so we can understand how it will be in the great tribulation. Babylon, for a while, will dominate everything. The head of the nations will be the head of the church. The antichrist will be supreme in religious matters; but when Babylon falls, what a tremendous shake up there is going to be!

The Third Angel's Message (Revelation 14:9-12)

The angel's solemn message declared that those who turn away from the true God, reject His Word, and instead worship the beast and his image will have to drink the very dregs of the cup of God's wrath.

The Seventh-Day Adventists tell us that the third angel's message is the sabbath message. They teach that worshiping the beast and receiving his mark consists in recognizing the holiness of the first day of the week. Who can conceive of a God of love and grace pouring out His wrath on men because, with earnest desire to glorify Him, they keep the resurrection day? All is perfectly clear when one realizes that the judgment pronounced in these verses is the doom of apostasy. In retributive judgment, God will press the cup of His wrath to the lips of those who have refused the cup of salvation. Nor is there any evidence that that judgment will come to an end, for verse 11 distinctly says, "the smoke of their torment ascendeth up for ever and ever: and they have no rest day nor night, who worship the beast and his image, and whosoever receiveth the mark of his name."

It will indeed require courage of a very high order to stand up against that apostate condition and firmly hold to the truth of God as then revealed. And so we are told in verse 12, "Here is the patience of the saints: here are they that keep the commandments of God, and the faith of Jesus." This supports what we have been pointing out that these converts will be Jewish believers. They keep the Old Testament commandments of God and yet the faith of Jesus as declared in the New. Their part is not in the body of Christ. That glorious truth of the present dispensation is not for them. But they will have learned, at last, that Jesus is the promised Messiah. He was rejected by their nation when He came in grace, but He is coming again in mighty power. So they will bring forth fruits befitting repentance, demonstrated by their pious, godly lives and desire to glorify the One their nation rejected.

You have often heard verse 13 used in connection with funerals in the present dispensation. I do not question that it may be so used with blessing, but its full application refers to a coming day. Notice that little word *henceforth*. A voice from Heaven said, "Blessed are the dead which die in the Lord from henceforth: Yea, saith the Spirit, that they may rest from their labors; and their works do follow them." The point, I take it, is this: the darkest part of the great tribulation is still before them. The storm clouds, heavy with judgment, may break at any moment, but immediately following, the kingdom is to be set up. Those who pass through the tribulation will enter into the kingdom on earth. Those who die during its course will have their part in the heavenly kingdom, and so a special blessing will be theirs. In other words, from that point on it will really be better to die than to live. They will rest from their labors, be spared further tribulation on the earth, and will have their place with their Lord in Heaven. This place will be far better than the highest place in the kingdom here on earth, glorious as that will be.

And now let me press a question on my readers, whether saved or unsaved. You also must leave this world shortly. What kind of works are going to follow you? If saved, what have you been doing for the Lord? If unsaved, then I beg you remember that your sins will follow after you—those sins you have been trying to forget; those sins from which you have fled; those sins for which you fool-ishly thought you could atone by effort of your own. When you stand up, at last, poor, and naked, and miserable, before the great white throne, you will find all your sins there. They will grab onto you like the hell-hounds that they really are and drag you down to the lake of fire. Do not turn away from this solemn truth. The blood of Christ alone can wash you from all those sins. Then, as a believer in the Lord Jesus, you can live for Him in this world and your works will follow you to Heaven, for all that is done for Christ will abide for eternity.

The Solemn Harvest (Revelation 14:14-16)

You will remember that our Lord Jesus spoke about the harvest. He declared that it is the end of the age, the time when the wicked are going to be separated from the just. He is going to gather the wheat into His garner, but burn up the tares with fire unquenchable (Matthew 13:37-42). This is what you have here; it is discriminat-ing judgment. The earth is reaped. The Son of man will claim for Himself everything that is of God. All that is contrary will be given up to judgment. Observe that it is the Son of man who sits on the cloud and directs the reapers. All judgment is committed to the Son. The One who once hung on Calvary's cross is the same blessed person who is coming to execute judgment. This is, I take it, the same in nature as the judgment in Matthew 25. It is premillennial and not postmillennial, like the judgment of the great white throne.

Jesus is coming back to the world that crucified Him. He is going to gather for His kingdom, out of all nations, those who have heeded His message and cared for His messengers. But all who have heard His gospel and rejected it will be given up to judgment.

The Vintage (Revelation 14:17-20)

The vintage is very different from the harvest. The harvest, as we have just seen, is discriminatory, while the vintage is unsparing judgment.

The vintage has to do with the vine—the vine of the earth—and this vine is apostate Israel. We are familiar with the figure as used in regard to Israel in the Old Testament. Isaiah used it, and in Hosea we hear the Lord saying, "Israel is an empty vine, he bringeth forth fruit unto himself" (10:1). The same figure is used in Psalm 80 and 81. When our Lord was here He could say, "I am the true vine" (10:1). He was the only one in Israel bearing good fruit. All who accept His message become branches in the living vine. By and by, the vine is going to be replanted in Palestine. In fact, we may go further and say, the vine is being replanted in Palestine. The Jews are going back to their own land; it stirs one's soul as Scripture is being fulfilled before our eyes. They are being replanted in their own vineyard, but replanted for what? For the vintage of the wrath of God. A remnant will be gathered out, separated to the Lord, but the rest will be given up to unsparing judgment in the time of Jacob's trouble. Fleshly Israel, the vine of the earth, can produce no fruit for God. But in that day of great distress, the clusters of the vine of the earth will be cast into the great winepress of the wrath of God. And we are told the winepress was trodden outside the city. Blood came out of the winepress, rising as high as the horse bridles for 1,600 furlongs. This is said to be the actual length of the land of Palestine. The picture is that of the entire land drenched in blood up to the horse bridles. What will the reality be? O Lord, how long?

Thank God, there are brighter things ahead. In fact, the best days for Israel and the whole earth lie beyond that awful scene of wrath and carnage. But we need to remember that the people of the Jews brought their judgment on their own heads by refusing the Prince of

Peace when He came in grace to deliver them. In Pilate's judgment hall they cried, "His blood be on us, and on our children" (Matthew 27:25). The centuries bear witness how dreadfully this fearful imprecation has been answered by a just God. The scene depicted in these closing verses of Revelation 14 shows that a more dreadful fulfillment is yet in the future. Immanuel's land, once stained with His own precious blood, will be red with the gore of those who reject Him. Even in that day when their own Scriptures will be so marvelously fulfilled before their very eyes, they will still refuse Him and instead assent to the unholy claims of the antichrist. Of old, they chose Barabbas in place of Jesus which is called Christ. Unchanged in spirit to the very end, they will prefer the "son of perdition" to the Son of God, and thus bring upon themselves swift destruction.

CHAPTER FIFTEEN
GLORIFIED ISRAEL

Revelation 15–16 form one connected vision depicting the final scenes of the dispensation of judgment, which occupies a large portion of the content of the book of Revelation. We need to remember that the Revelation is primarily a book of judgment. While it may seem very pessimistic to be occupied with so many fearful scenes, all is bright at the end. The book does not close until the new heavens and new earth are brought in, where righteousness will dwell throughout a blissful eternity. Therefore I need not apologize for continually bringing before you picture after picture of God's judicial dealings with the prophetic earth. He has given us these revelations out of kindness to us. We may be warned by them to avoid what lies ahead of this guilty world and to shun every form of the apostasy which He is so soon coming to judge.

The Glorified Witnesses (Revelation 15:1-5)

In the last chapter we noticed that there was one particular company of saints in Heaven who responded in a very noticeable manner to the 144,000 Israelites standing on mount Sion. In the fifteenth chapter the scene is changed. The prophet sees what is going on in Heaven, and this company at once comes before his vision (1-3).

The redeemed company standing on the sea of glass with the harps of God is not to be confused with the church of the present dispensation. We are told that they sing the song of Moses the servant of God and the song of the Lamb. Clearly then, they are Israelites. They are singing the song of Moses, which is the celebration of Jehovah's victory over Israel's foes, and the song of the Lamb, which is the song of redemption. They are those who have been slain by the servants of the last great apostate power, but who have been raised from the dead and raptured during the tribulation period. Perhaps they are the two witnesses of chapter 11. But they are at least like them in that they have been faithful witnesses on earth and because of their witness-bearing have been put to death. They are seen as raised from the dead and caught up to God and to His throne. Like the elders, they have in their hands the harps of God and are a worshiping company.

These are said to stand on the sea of glass, which is here represented as mingled with fire (2). The sea of glass, as pointed out previously, corresponds to the brass sea in Solomon's temple and the brass laver in the court of the tabernacle. It is an illustration of the Word of God needed for cleansing on earth; in Heaven it is crystallized, a glassy sea on which the glorified saints take their stand to praise Him who has redeemed them to Himself and made them forever clean. The glass is seen as mingled with fire because of the fiery trial through which these martyrs have passed.

I would observe that the rendering "King of saints" (KJV) at the close of verse 3 is generally recognized as faulty. The better manuscripts read "nations" though some have "ages" in place of "saints." Nowhere is the Lord spoken of as "King of saints." He is, however, "King of the nations" and the "Ruler of the ages." These glorified witnesses to His saving power praise and adore Him for His justice and truth. They recognize the righteousness of His ways and the holiness of His person. Because of this, all nations will come and worship before Him in the day that His judgments are displayed. Observe, it is not the grace of God that will bring the nations to own His authority and worship before Him. It is "when [his] judgments are in the earth, [that] the inhabitants of the world will learn righteousness" (Isaiah 26:9). Nowhere does Scripture teach the conversion of the world through the preaching of the gospel in this dispensation. Eventually, the world will be converted, but only after the unbelieving portion has been purged out by judgment. The remnant left for the kingdom will give glory to the God of Heaven.

In the fifth verse we have another of the "openings" of this marvelous book. We read, "And after that I looked, and, behold, the temple of the tabernacle of the testimony in heaven was opened."

The mention of the tabernacle of the testimony brings Israel again before us. It reminds us that these judgments carry out God's covenant with His ancient people Israel, when the nations that have oppressed them must be punished. "Jerusalem [is] a burdensome stone for all people: all that burden themselves with it shall be cut in pieces, though all the people of the earth be gathered together against it" (Zechariah 12:3). Therefore the nations who have vented their hatred on Israel cannot escape the wrath of God.

The Seven Angels (Revelation 15:6-8)

The seven angels are to complete the wrath of God. They introduce and close His final visitations in judgment on the Gentiles. Then the many prophecies of retribution in Scripture will be fulfilled. "It is a righteous thing," said the apostle Paul, "to recompense tribulation to them that trouble you" (2 Thessalonians 1:6). If this could be said in regard to saints of the church period, how much more in regard to Israel. Many people have been troubled with what are called the imprecatory Psalms. They cannot understand David calling down the judgment of God on His enemies, or Israel's prayer for the overthrow and destruction of all their foes. But in the righteous government of God, those nations that have oppressed and sought the destruction of His people must be visited with the fierceness of His wrath.

Joseph Cook told how at the beginning of the Civil War, a gentleman was in conversation with a minister of the gospel. He was objecting to the imprecatory Psalms because they did not seem to him to be in harmony with the spirit of Christianity. As they talked together a newspaper was brought in, and the minister read, "The federal army is marching upon Richmond." "Good," exclaimed the other, "I hope they will destroy it." "That," cried the preacher, "is an imprecatory psalm." The point is that it is thoroughly in keeping with God's mind to desire the triumph of righteousness and the overthrow of what is iniquitous.

God's glory is at stake. His righteousness demands the punishment of iniquity, both in this world and in that which is to come. He does not apologize for dealing thus with unrighteousness, nor do His servants need to apologize for Him.

Verse 8 indicates that when the seven angels are about to come forth to execute their awful mission, it will be one of intense concern in Heaven. The temple is seen filled with smoke from the glory of God and from His power. Man, though redeemed, is represented as standing outside in awe, awaiting developments.

CHAPTER SIXTEEN

THE VIALS OF THE WRATH OF GOD

T he seven vials (more properly, bowls) of the wrath of God are all included in the judgments of the last half of the great tribulation. They show the intensive character that these judgments will take as the end draws on. It seems to me the series covers just a very brief period at the close of the last half of Daniel's seventh week. The pouring out of the bowls depicts the judgments that will fall on the kingdom of the beast and the antichrist's sphere of authority at the very end of the great tribulation.

The First and Second Bowls (Revelation 16:1-3)

As this chapter opens a great voice out of the temple is heard saying to the seven angels, "Go your ways, and pour out [empty] the [bowls] of the wrath of God upon the earth" (1). As in the case of the seven trumpets and the seven seals, I cannot tell you just how much we are to take as symbolic and how much as literal in this septenary series of judgments. We know that the book of Revelation is a book of symbols. Yet there may be a great deal more in it that is literal than many of us suppose. The literal judgments may be intimately linked with the symbolical. No one reading this chapter carefully can fail to observe how intimately the results of the bowls of wrath are linked with the plagues that fell on Egypt preparatory to Israel's deliverance. God is again about to deliver His people for the last time. The outpouring of these bowls depicts, in large measure, the woes that were visited on the kingdom of Pharaoh. But descriptions perhaps must be taken symbolically rather than literally; or perhaps both interpretations coalesce.

In verse 2 we read, "And the first went, and poured out his vial upon the earth; and there fell a noisome and grievous sore upon the men which had the mark of the beast, and upon them which worshiped his image." This answers to the plague in Egypt where God inflicted man and beast with boils and sores. It perhaps symbolizes a spiritual plague on those who have received the mark of the beast and worship his image. This plague will cause as great an annoyance as the physical suffering that would follow such a grievous sore on the bodies of men. Notice that the sphere of this plague is the earth and it answers to the first trumpet of Revelation 8. But it is very evident that while the sphere is the same, the judgment is more intense.

In the same way the second angel's bowl links with the second angel's trumpet which affected the sea. But again we have greater intensity, for in verse 3 we read, "And the second angel poured out his vial upon the sea; and it became as the blood of a dead man; and every living soul died in the sea." What a scene of death and desolation, whether we think of it as physical or spiritual or both. "All they that hate me," says Wisdom in the book of Proverbs, "love death" (8:36). And so death is the portion for those who have refused the life that is in Christ Jesus.

The Third and Fourth Bowls (Revelation 16:4-9)

The third angel's trumpet affected the rivers and fountains of waters. In verse 4 we read that the very sources of life are destroyed, as in the plague that fell on Egypt when the river itself became blood. In verses 5-7 God's righteousness in thus dealing with those who had slaughtered His servants is fully attested. Every right-thinking person will add his "Amen," for God is righteous in all His ways, whether in grace or in judgment.

The fourth angel's bowl is poured out on the sun, even as at the sounding of the fourth trumpet the third part of the sun was struck (8:12). But again we have greater intensity in the judgment than in the trumpet series. "Power was given unto him to scorch men with fire. And men were scorched with great heat, and blasphemed the name of God, which hath power over these plagues: and they

repented not to give him glory" (16:8-9). The sun is the supreme
source of light. This implies that that which should have been for
man's comfort becomes a curse instead and the means of his bitter
suffering. But, though their anguish is so great, men are not brought
to repentance by punishment. God's name is blasphemed, and His
creatures refuse to give Him glory. This is a solemn consideration
for those who teach that punishment is really only chastisement and
is always corrective.

The Fifth Bowl (Revelation 16:10-11)

The next section intensifies this in a remarkable way. The fifth
angel empties his bowl on the seat of the beast, striking the center
of the last great confederation and filling his kingdom with darkness. Then we read that "they gnawed their tongues for pain, and
blasphemed the God of heaven because of their pains and their sores,
and repented not of their deeds" (10-11). Darkness and anguish do
not tend to soften men's hearts or lead them to confess their sins.
Their very suffering stirs them up to blaspheme God more. So in
the outer darkness of a lost eternity, our Lord has told us there will
be weeping and wailing because of suffering endured. But there
will also be the gnashing of teeth, which implies rage and indignation against God. With permanency of character he who rejects Christ
is guilty of eternal sin and eternal punishment necessarily follows.

At the sounding of the fifth angel's trumpet, we were told the
bottomless pit was opened, "and there arose a smoke out of the pit,
as the smoke of a great furnace; and the sun and the air were darkened by reason of the smoke of the pit" (9:2). This explains the
darkness that fills the kingdom of the beast when the fifth angel's
bowl of wrath is poured on the seat of the beast. It is judicial darkness brought about by demoniacal delusions.

The Sixth Bowl (Revelation 16:12-16)

We now come to the bowl of the sixth angel, which was very
much on the minds of people during the past years of bloody warfare. Again and again the question was raised whether World War I

was the Armageddon conflict predicted in the Bible. Teachers instructed by the Word have invariably assured anxious questioners that while that war may have set the stage for Armageddon, it cannot be that great conflict itself. Armageddon is a definite locality in the land of Palestine. The word means "the mountain of Megiddo." It refers to the mountain that overlooks the valley of Esdraelon—the great plain of Jezreel in the northern part of the land of Palestine. Napoleon Bonaparte said this plain would make an ideal battleground for all the armies of the world. There, the last great battle is to be fought, just before the appearing of the Lord in glory.

The great river Euphrates was formerly the eastern boundary of the Roman empire and later of the Turkish dominion. Thus, I believe, the sixth angel's vial of wrath poured out on the Euphrates speaks of the destruction of that latter power. Luther said, "When the Turk is driven out of Europe, then comes the day of judgment." And, in a certain sense, this will undoubtedly be true—not the day of judgment for the wicked dead, but the day of judgment for the living nations. The Turk is an intruder in Europe, the enemy of both God and man; but I am convinced that his hold on Constantinople and the surrounding country is very nearly ended. God will drive the Ottoman empire from Europe and punish that nation. (Since the above was written the Ottoman empire has fallen). The cry of martyred Armenia, and of other peoples who have suffered fearfully from these Asiatic hordes, will be answered by the destruction of the nation that brought such havoc. It is very evident, I think, that God is already beginning to bring this to pass. If you have a map of Europe of one hundred years ago, notice the place that the Turkish empire then had and compare it with a map of the present day, and see how much of its territory has been wrested from it.

I am convinced that it will not be long before Turkey is driven out of Europe altogether. Then, according to the book of Daniel, it will "plant the tabernacles of [its] palace between the seas in the glorious holy mountain; yet [it] shall come to [its] end, and none shall help [it]" (11:45). Driven into Asia Minor, it will finally, I take it, attempt to establish itself in the land of Palestine. And this will arouse not only the European powers in the league of the ten kingdoms, but it will stir up the eastern and northern nations besides.

Turkey will, if I understand the prophetic scheme aright, be backed in the last days by Russia, and possibly by Germany too, in opposition to western confederation. Both these great powers will be anxious to hold the land of Palestine, which is admittedly the key to the so-called Eastern question. But the activity of these European nations will arouse the races of the far East, for when the Euphrates is dried up, we are told it is "that the way of the kings of the east might be prepared" (Revelation 16:12).

Who are the kings of the east? Various theories have been suggested. Some consider they may be the so-called lost ten tribes of Israel returning to their land, or perhaps the dominions of Persia, Afghanistan, and so on. It is significant that the word rendered "the east" is really "the sun-rising." Is it only a coincidence that for at least a millennium Japan has been known as "the kingdom of the rising sun"? May not the Mongolian races, possibly allied with India be the kings of the east depicted in Revelation 16 as coming in conflict with the powers of the west? Thus the whole world will be thrown into bloody warfare, and all nations be gathered together against Jerusalem to battle.

This great world-conflict will be the direct result of the working of demons, for we are told that three unclean frog-like spirits came out of the mouths of the dragon, the beast, and the false prophet. These demons will work miracles, visiting the kingdoms of the earth (that is the prophetic earth) and of the whole world (that is, the nations outside the prophetic earth) "to gather them to the battle of that great day of God Almighty" (16:14). This will be the great and final Armageddon conflict—the place where they will meet one another in an attempt to settle the final issues.

Notice that there is a parenthetical statement in verse 15. It comes in just before the close of this section, thus preceding the seventh bowl. It is the voice of the Lord Himself, "Behold, I come as a thief. Blessed is he that watcheth, and keepeth his garments, lest he walk naked, and they see his shame." The time of His appearing is very close. Those who look for His coming should be watching and keeping their garments undefiled, lest they be put to shame before the ungodly. The undefiled are those who keep themselves from all fellowship with the Satan-inspired movements of the last days. They will walk with God in holy separation from the abounding iniquity, as directed by His Word. The voice is for us as well as for the saints in a future day.

The Seventh Bowl (Revelation 16:17-21)

The seventh angel's bowl poured out into the air indicates the utter destruction of every spiritual and religious institution that man has built up apart from God. It is the absolute overthrow of civilization and the complete wreck of all man's hopes to bring in even livable conditions in this world, while rejecting the Lord Jesus Christ. The scene is one of anarchy and confusion. Despite the signs of divine wrath resting on the souls of men, they still blaspheme God and give no sign of repentance.

Let me remind you that the church of God is to be caught up before these scenes take place on the earth. We are looking for the Lord Jesus Christ, who is our Savior from the coming wrath. Do you know Him? If not, I plead with you in the light of all we have had before us, "Flee from the wrath to come" (Matthew 3:7).

CHAPTER SEVENTEEN
BABYLON: ITS CHARACTER AND DOOM

(PART ONE)

This chapter addresses a theme, the wonder of which grows on me every time I speak of it, namely the mystery of iniquity in its final form: Babylon the great. This vast system of error is so like Christianity in some respects that thousands of apparently spiritually-minded people have not been able to distinguish it from Christianity. Yet, when tested by the Word of God this system is seen to be a counterfeit of that church which God has purchased with the blood of His own Son.

Although we have heard of Babylon's fall twice in this book, we have not learned to what city or system it referred. But the chapter now before us is entirely devoted to that interesting and solemn subject. A careful study of what is revealed here should free us from all doubt or perplexity as to the identification of Babylon.

Chapters 17–18 form another of the great parentheses of the book of Revelation. Chronologically chapter 19 immediately follows chapter 16. But before going on with the direct order of events, John is taken aside as it were to see this remarkable vision of the false church, before he beholds the union of the true church with the Lamb in glory.

The Vision (Revelation 17:1-6)

The beast in verse 3 is the same as that of Revelation 13 and is therefore the Roman empire. It is the empire as a whole, but with the last phase especially emphasized. The woman (verses 3-6) is a religious system, that dominates the civil power, at least for a time. The name on her forehead should easily enable us to identify her. But in order to do that we will do well to go back to the Old Testament, and see what is there revealed concerning literal Babylon; the one will surely throw light on the other. We have also the added instruction of secular history that supplies us with some very important facts in this connection. It throws a flood of light on the succession of spiritual Babylon of the apocalypse to literal Babylon of the Old Testament.

As we go back into the dim twilight of history with Scripture, we learn that the founder of Bab-El, or Babylon, was Nimrod. We read of his unholy achievements in the tenth chapter of Genesis. He was the arch-apostate of the patriarchal age. He is described as "a mighty hunter before the Lord"—the rabbis called him "a hunter of the souls of men." Going out from the presence of the Lord, he impiously sought to gather a multitude around himself. In defiance of the express command of God to spread abroad on the face of the earth, he persuaded his associates and followers to join together in "building a city and a tower which should reach unto heaven." They were not building a tower to climb up into the skies to escape another possible flood. It was to be a tower of renown, rising to a great height and recognized as a temple or rallying center for those who did not walk in obedience to the word of the Lord. With all the effrontery of our modern apostates, they called their city and tower *Bab-El*, the gate of God; but it was soon changed by divine judgment into Babel, confusion. It bore the stamp of unreality from the first, for we are told "they had brick for stone, and slime had they for mortar." Throughout the ages an imitation of that which is real and true has characterized Babylon.

Nimrod, or Nimroud-bar-Cush as he is called on the monuments, was a grandson of Ham, the unworthy son of Noah. Ham's character is revealed in his exposure of his father's shame (Genesis 9:22).

We know that Noah had brought through the flood the revelation of the true God. He was a preacher of righteousness, and his utterances on more than one occasion show that he had the prophetic gift. Ham on the other hand seems to have been all too readily affected by the apostasy that brought the flood. He shows no evidence of self-judgment, but the very opposite. His name, as spelled out upon Egyptian monuments, is *Khem*. This name agrees with the literal sound of the Hebrew word rendered Ham in our Bibles. It means "swarthy, darkened," or, more literally, "the sun-burnt." And the name indicates the state of the man's soul. For a sunburned person is one who is darkened by light from heaven. Ham had been granted wonderful mercies; he was saved from the flood because of his father's faith. But he abused his privileges and "turn[ed] the grace of our God into lasciviousness" (Jude 4). He was actually darkened by the burning rays of the light that God caused to shine on his soul. Thus his conscience became seared as with a hot iron, and he became the founder of a race that departed from the living God. He led the way into idolatry, worshiping and serving the creature more than the Creator.

We know something of what this means. We speak of people today who have become hardened to the gospel. They too have been darkened by the light, and they are often the ring-leaders in apostasy: "If therefore the light that is in thee be darkness, how great is that darkness" (Matthew 6:23). There are many who used to listen with tears in their eyes to the story of the matchless grace of God as revealed in the cross of Christ. Now they are unmoved however tenderly that story is told. They have become hardened in their sins, and their seared consciences no longer feel the Spirit's breath. It is a most dangerous thing to trifle with light from Heaven.

Ham became darkened by the light. We know his failure and sin. But when Noah had recovered himself and knew what his son had done to him he pronounced, by the spirit of prophecy, a curse on Canaan, not on Ham. Do you wonder at that? I did until I saw that God had already pronounced a blessing on all three sons of Noah—Shem, Ham, and Japheth. So Noah passed over his unworthy son and uttered a curse on Canaan, who we can well believe was, as we say, "a chip off the old block." Ham begat a son named Cush, "the black one," and he became the father of Nimrod, the apostate leader of his generation (Genesis 10:6-8).

Ancient lore now comes to our assistance and tells us that the wife of Nimroud-bar-Cush was the infamous Semiramis the first. She is reputed to have been the foundress of the Babylonian mysteries and the first high-priestess of idolatry. Thus Babylon became the fountainhead of idolatry and the mother of every heathen and pagan system in the world. The mystery-religion that was originated there spread in various forms throughout the whole earth and is still with us today. It is identical with the mystery of iniquity which was at work in Paul's day (2 Thessalonians 2:7). It will have its fullest development when the Holy Spirit has departed and the Babylon of the apocalypse gains control.

Building on the primeval promise of the woman's seed who was to come, Semiramis bore a son whom she declared was miraculously conceived! When she presented him to the people, he was hailed as the promised deliverer. This was Tammuz, whose worship Ezekiel protested against in the days of the captivity (Ezekiel 8:13-14). Thus was introduced the mystery of the mother and the child, a form of idolatry that is older than any other known to man. The rites of this worship were secret. Only the initiated were permitted to know its mysteries. It was Satan's effort to delude mankind with an imitation so like the truth of God that they would not know the true seed of the woman when He came in the fullness of time. To this Justin Martyr bears definite witness.

From Babylon this mystery-religion spread to all the surrounding nations as the years went on and the world was populated by the descendants of Noah. Everywhere the symbols were the same, and everywhere the cult of the mother and the child became the popular system. Their worship was celebrated with the most disgusting and immoral practices. The image of the queen of Heaven with the babe in her arms was seen everywhere, though the names might differ as languages differed. It became the mystery-religion of Phoenicia, and was carried to the ends of the earth by the Phoenicians. Ashtoreth and Tammuz, the mother and child of these hardy adventurers, became Isis and Horus in Egypt, Aphrodite and Eros in Greece, Venus and Cupid in Italy, and bore many other names in more distant places. Within one thousand years Babylonianism had become the religion of a world that had rejected the divine revelation.

Linked with this central mystery were countless lesser mysteries; the hidden meaning was known only to the initiates, but the outward forms were practised by all the people. Among these were the doctrines of purgatorial purification after death; salvation by countless sacraments such as priestly absolution; sprinkling with holy water; the offering of cakes to the queen of Heaven as mentioned in the book of Jeremiah (7:18; 44:19); dedication of virgins to the gods, which was literally sanctified prostitution; weeping for Tammuz for a period of 40 days prior to the great festival of Istar, who was said to have received her son back from the dead (it was taught that Tammuz was slain by a wild boar and afterwards brought back to life). To him the egg was sacred, depicting the mystery of his resurrection. His chosen symbol, the evergreen, was set up in honor of his birth at the winter solstice. At this time a boar's head was eaten in memory of his conflict and a yule-log burned with many mysterious observances. The sign of the cross was sacred to Tammuz, as symbolizing the life-giving principle and as the first letter of his name. It is represented on vast numbers of the most ancient altars and temples and did not, as many have supposed, originate with Christianity.

The patriarch Abraham was separated from this mystery-religion by the divine call. The nation that sprang from him had constant conflict with this same evil cult, until Jezebel, a Phoenician princess. Under her authority this cult was grafted onto what was left of the religion of Israel in the northern kingdom in the day of Ahab and was the cause of their captivity at the last. Judah was polluted by it, for Baal worship was but the Canaanitish form of the Babylonian mysteries. Only by being sent into captivity to Babylon itself did Judah become cured of her fondness for idolatry. Baal was the sun god, the life-giving one, identical with Tammuz.

When Christ came into this world the mystery of iniquity was in control everywhere, except where the truth of God as revealed in the Old Testament was known. Thus, when the early Christians set out on the great task of carrying the gospel to the ends of the earth, they found themselves everywhere confronted by this system in one form or another. Although Babylon as a city had long been but a memory, her mysteries had not died with her. When the city and temples were destroyed, the high priest fled with a company of initiates and their sacred vessels and images to Pergamos, where the symbol of the serpent was set up as the emblem of the hidden wisdom. From there, they afterwards crossed the sea and emigrated to Italy, where they settled in the Etruscan plain. There the ancient cult was propagated under the name of the Etruscan Mysteries, and eventually Rome became the headquarters of Babylonianism. The chief priests wore mitres shaped like the head of a fish in honor of Dagon, the fish-god, the lord of life—another form of the Tammuz mystery, as developed among Israel's old enemies, the Philistines. The chief priest when established in Rome took the title *pontifex maximus*, and this was imprinted on his mitre. Julius Caesar, like all young Romans of good family, was an initiate. When he became the head of the state, he was elected pontifex maximus. This title was held henceforth by all the Roman emperors down to Constantine the Great, who was, at the same time, head of the church and high priest of the heathen! The title was afterwards conferred on the bishops of Rome and is borne by the pope today. This declares the pope to be, not the successor of the fisherman-apostle Peter, but the direct successor of the high priest of the Babylonian mysteries. He is the servant of the fishgod Dagon, for whom he wears, like his idolatrous predecessors, the fisherman's ring.

During the early centuries of the church's history, the mystery of iniquity worked with astounding effect. Babylonian practices and teachings had been largely absorbed by that which bore the name of the church of Christ. The truth of the Holy Scriptures on many points had been wholly obscured, while idolatrous practices had been foisted on the people as Christian sacraments. Heathen philosophies took the place of gospel instruction. Thus was developed that amazing system which for a thousand years dominated Europe until the great Reformation of the sixteenth century brought in a measure of deliverance.

This vision of the woman drunk with the blood of the saints filled the apostle with amazement (17:6). It seemed incredible that the glorious movement with which he had been identified for a

generation should ever become so perverted as to become the mother
of harlots and of every abomination, and should even become the
slaughterer of the saints of God. But her bloody history during the
dark days of persecution bears awful witness to the truth of the
vision. The angel, however, goes on to show that the future has
more marvelous things in store than we should otherwise have dared
to imagine. No past period of Rome's history fully answers to what
is brought before us in the rest of the chapter.

We hear a great deal about the desirability of church-federation.
But men seem to forget, or never to have known, that it is God
Himself who has torn Christendom apart because of her unfaithful-
ness and apostasy. We are told that it would be an excellent thing if
the different denominations of Protestants could be united in one
great body, and then join hands with the Catholic church. It is pointed
out that such a vast united church could dominate the world. Besides it would make for such increased efficiency and would sim-
plify the financial problems which have so troubled and perplexed
our boards and officials for so long. But we need to remember that
such a union as this would not be the body of Christ at all. It would
simply be a worldly confederacy of saved and unsaved—just great
Babylon over again. The body of Christ remains undivided in spite
of Christendom's unhappy schisms, for it is composed of all truly
saved people who have by the Spirit's baptism been made one in
Christ. While outward unity is desirable, it would not be a blessing
if it were at the expense of the truth.

The Interpretation of the Vision (Revelation 17:7-18).

We have already seen in our study of the thirteenth chapter that
the beast depicts the Roman empire as revived in a Satan-inspired
league of nations after the church dispensation is over. This will be
very different than any league that may be formed in our times while
the church is still here. The federation of the future will be utterly
godless and God-defiant. When that league is formed it will be only
natural that a confederacy of all religious systems be worked out,
and this too will be satanic in character. It will be a union of Christless
professors, inheriting all the human and demoniacal mysteries of

Babylon. In other words all sects will be swallowed up in the one distinctively Babylonish system that has always maintained the cult of the mother and the child. This system will dominate the civil power for the first part of the tribulation period. Thus the woman will be in the saddle again and ride the beast! He who has eyes to see and a heart to understand can readily discern the preparations now in progress with this very end in view.

From verses 9-11 we learn the identity of the city where Babylon has her seat. We also learn that when the final form of the empire appears she will attain the position of preeminence that she has sought so long. Only Rome answers to the description given. Previously we saw that the eighth head, who is of the seven, is the last great world-ruler who will dominate the league of nations in the time of the end. His capital will be the so-called eternal city.

It would seem however from verses 12-14 that the other ten kings act in fullest harmony with the beast. This completely nullifies the theory that the vision refers to any past history of the nations into which the Roman empire was divided. Never have they thus acted in unison, but Europe has been a scene of conflicting nations and warring powers since the break-up of the empire itself. We must look to the future for a time when the ten kings will receive power one hour with the beast. Then they will impiously make war with the Lamb only to be overcome by Him who is King of kings and Lord of lords.

The similitude of the waters is explained for us in verse 15: "The waters which thou sawest, where the whore sitteth, are peoples, and multitudes, and nations, and tongues." Babylon has ruled over all nations in the past, deceiving them with the wine of her fornication. She will bear rule again over all nations, until wearied with her blandishments, the world, whose favor she courted, will spurn her at last (16-18).

There is no mistaking the identity of the woman. Pagan Rome was the lineal successor of Babylon. Papal Rome absorbed the Babylonian mysteries; and the Rome of the beast in the last days will be the seat of the revived satanic system that began with Nimrod and his infamous consort Semiramis. From that day to the present, that system has been opposed to everything that is of God. It changed the truth of God into a lie, worshiping and serving the creature more than the Creator.

Ancient Babylon was the mother of idolatry. In Jeremiah 50:38 we read, "It is the land of graven images, and they are mad upon their idols." It was she who taught the nations to substitute idolatry for spiritual worship. Today one-third of Christendom has followed her in the adoration of images, and another third worships icons or pictures. There can be no question as to the Babylonish origin of these abominations. Nothing of the kind was known in the churches of God until the heathen mysteries were grafted unto Christianity. The images of the mother and child that are enshrined in Rome's temples are only different in name to the images worshiped in the temples of Semiramis, Ashtoreth, Isis, and other so called "queens of heaven." In many instances the old idols were simply renamed and adored as before. In southern Europe there is a statue of Apollo, the sun-god, identical with Tammuz and Baal. This statue is worshiped by deluded Romanists as St. Apollos; the S was carved on the pedestal later than the original name!

The mother of the Lord Jesus Christ assumed no such place among the early Christians as she has now been given in Rome's mysteries. She is seen as a lowly worshiper and as joining with others in prayer in Acts 2, the last mention of her in Scripture. The Bible gives no hint of the fable of her assumption and crowning as queen of Heaven. It is Babylonianism pure and simple.

The word of the Lord to His people of old is most instructive for us now in the light of all we have been going over.

> Flee out of the midst of Babylon, and deliver every man his soul: be not cut off in her iniquity; for this is the time of the Lord's vengeance; he will render unto her a recompense. Babylon hath been a golden cup in the Lord's hand, that made all the earth drunken: the nations have drunken of her wine; therefore the nations are mad. Babylon is suddenly fallen and destroyed: howl for her; take balm for her pain, if so be she may be healed. We would have healed Babylon, but she is not

healed: forsake her, and let us go every one to his own country: for her judgment reacheth unto heaven, and is lifted up even to the skies (Jeremiah 51: 6-9).

It is a lamentable fact that Babylon's principles and practices are rapidly but surely pervading the churches that escaped from Rome at the time of the Reformation. We may see evidences of it in the wide use of high-sounding ecclesiastical titles, once unknown in the reformed churches. It is also seen in the revival of holy days and church feasts such as Lent, Good Friday, Easter, and Christ's Mass, or as it is generally written, Christmas. I quite admit that some of these festivals if divested of any ecclesiastical character may be observed in innocence in the home. But when they are turned into church festivals they certainly come under the condemnation of Galatians 4:9-11, where the Holy Spirit warns against the observance of days and months and times and seasons. All of them, and many more that might be added, are Babylonish in their origin. At one time they were linked with the Ashtoreth and Tammuz mystery-worship. Through Rome they have come down to us. We do well to remember that Babylon is a mother, with daughters who are likely to partake of their mother's characteristics; it is written, "As is the mother, so is her daughter" (Ezekiel 16:44). Therefore it behooves all who love the Lord and desire His approbation to "depart from iniquity," and seek to "follow righteousness, faith, charity, and peace, with them that call on the Lord out of a pure heart" (2 Timothy 2:22).

We will have a fuller account of Babylon's doom in our next chapter. To those who desire to make a fuller investigation of Babylonianism, I commend Alexander Hislop's monumental work, *The Two Babylons*, to which I am indebted for many of the above facts.

CHAPTER EIGHTEEN
BABYLON: ITS CHARACTER AND DOOM

(PART TWO)

In the previous chapter I sought to identify the Babylon of the apocalypse. I tried to show just how it was linked with Babylon of the Old Testament, the literal city in the land of the Chaldeans on the plain of Shinar. This chapter will give more details as to its unholy character and its awful doom. We also will get a better idea of the incredible way in which its principles have permeated civilization, affecting the entire civil and commercial fabric of the age in which we live. All of these principles must be destroyed in order to prepare the way for a higher and happier condition of society to be ushered in at the Lord's return.

The Fall of Babylon (Revelation 18:1-10)

The opening verses of chapter 18 synchronize with the second angel's message in Revelation 14:8 and introduce the judgment of the seventh vial as foretold in chapter 16:19. Babylon will therefore continue up to the very end of the tribulation period. Its destruction by the beast and his ten kings will be a last frantic effort to rid themselves of this dreadful incubus, just before they are destroyed by the appearing of the Lord in glory. The antichrist will be the pretended incarnation of the woman's seed and will be accepted as such by apostate Christendom and apostate Judaism. Thus Satan's masterpiece will seem to carry all before it until the true seed of the woman appears from Heaven. He will descend with all His holy ones, to the consternation of His enemies and the joy of His suffering saints, the persecuted remnant of Israel and those from among the nations who will receive their testimony in that day. These are not people who in this present dispensation of grace have refused the message of the gospel; it is only those to whom that message will not have gone until after the rapture of the church. Second Thessalonians 2 bears a clear and convincing testimony to this distinction.

The description of fallen Babylon as the habitation of demons, the hold of evil spirits, and a cage of unclean birds is a most graphic one (18:2). It strikingly depicts the horrible end of the apostasy. That which professes to be the spouse of Christ, and which issues its often blasphemous decrees as under the direction of the Spirit of God, is seen to be but a Satan-inspired and demon-directed system. Every unholy thing flourishes in this system, and evil men can find shelter and are protected in the promulgation of their evil doctrines and practices. The papacy has fully answered to this in the past, and its character remains unchanged to this present hour. It would be practically impossible to find a viler history than that of the medieval popes and their emissaries. It was a Roman Catholic writer who said of this period, "The annals of the church are the annals of hell."

The proverb, "The corruption of the best thing is the worst of corruptions" is strikingly illustrated in the history of the church. It seems almost impossible to believe that the church to which the apostle Paul addressed his Epistles could, in a few centuries, degenerate into the Roman church as now known. But this is the mystery of Babylon, as we have already seen. It is even more amazing that the Reformation churches, once delivered from this vile system, should now hopefully look for reconciliation with it, so readily forgetting its dreadful past and overlooking its present wicked pretensions! We in America, and our brethren in Britain, see Rome at its best, for men do not readily do in the light what they will do in the dark. But as it has been said, "Character is what a man is in the dark"; we may test this system by the same principle. If you want to know the true character of Catholicism, go to the lands where the light of Reformation has barely penetrated. Look at the countries south of us, the great Latin American republics, where the papacy has controlled and poisoned the morals of the people for centuries. There you will see the results of Babylonianism unchecked by enlightened Christianity. What a horrible cesspool of iniquity it is. There idolatry reigns in most abhorrent form. The gospel is a proscribed teaching, which would be absolutely prohibited if the church had full power as it did before.

In the Old Testament, idolatry is branded as spiritual fornication. In the New Testament it is the unhallowed union of the church and the world. We see both in this evil system today. Who is so unblushingly idolatrous as Rome? Subtly she is enlarging her sphere of influence and will continue until the scarlet woman again rides the beast—until the church dominates the state. By devious ways she seeks to "make America catholic," and undo the work of the Reformation in England.

Commercialism has always flourished under the patronage of the popes. This is another powerful weapon that Rome knows well how to use. Commerce is the goddess of the present feverish age, and to her everything must be sacrificed. The Babylon of the future is not only a great church, but a great commercial system as well. Men will finally turn to her for the solution of the problems that now perplex them. While she is the professed enemy of socialism, she delights to be regarded as the patron of the working classes on the one hand and the protector of capital on the other. She has a veritable genius for the commercial. "In Rome," cried Luther, "they sell everything. They would sell the Father, and sell the Son, and sell the Holy Ghost." The stamp of simony is on her brow and all who would glorify God should avoid her principles and flee from "the error of Balaam."

The call of verse 4, if I understand it correctly, is not merely a warning to saints in a coming day who may be in danger of being deceived by her. It is also a message for all who even now discern her true character. Separation from evil is imperative for all who would have the Lord's approval. This was the call heard by the reformers of the sixteenth century. But, unfortunately, many who are supposed to be their successors have returned in spirit to that

which their fathers left behind. There is many a Babylonish garment today hidden in Protestant tents or even displayed on Protestant shoulders. How else are we to account for the widespread return to principles and practices once abhorrent to those whose boast
it was that the Bible and the Bible alone is the religion of Protestants. The Bible is losing its hold on the consciences of the people
because its inspiration and authority is being so widely denied by
those who have solemnly sworn to teach it and defend it. We need
not wonder that Babylonish ways and teachings are coming into
vogue again. Men want something stable, something infallible; and
if they cannot have the infallible Word of the living God they will
turn to a professedly infallible church.

But the hour of God's judgment draws on swiftly. He will not be
a silent spectator of all these abominations forever. Soon He will
pour out the bowls of His wrath on spiritual Babylon as He did of
old on the city of idolatry on the Euphrates. "For her sins have
reached unto heaven, and God hath remembered her iniquities" (5).
Then will go forth the sentence recorded in verses 6-7.

A comparison of the prophecies of Isaiah and Jeremiah in regard
to the fall of ancient Babylon will show how plainly the doom of
the spiritual counterpart is prefigured there. In several instances the
same identical figures are used. This has led some commentators to
suppose that the doom of the literal city was not final. So it is taught
by some that Babylon is to be rebuilt on her ancient site. She is to
flourish for a few years as the religious and commercial metropolis
of the world, only to be destroyed for the final time at or immediately preceding the Lord's second coming. These teachers generally agree in making this restored Babylon the seat of the antichrist.
As a rule, they identify him with the future world emperor. But I
think we have already shown that a careful comparison of the Old
and New Testament Scriptures on these subjects make this view
untenable. The city of old has fallen to rise no more. The system
that succeeded it is to be judged by God and destroyed as literally
as her predecessor, according to verse 8.

Although God will use the ten kings and the beast to bring this
about, they will themselves bewail her fall, when they find to their
horror that the whole fabric of civilization is falling with her (9-10).

Something like this was seen in the days of the French Revolution and has been seen in measure in more recent history. With the destruction of the church, no matter how corrupt, came the breaking up of all social barriers. A flood of anarchy and violence seemed likely to involve the entire nation in ruin. Even Napoleon I saw the necessity of re-establishing the church—though largely shorn of its power—on the ground that a poor religion is better than none at all in holding the masses in restraint.

We can readily understand therefore how Babylon's fall will send a thrill of horror through all who have been linked in any way with her. Her fall will cause the kings of the earth who have enjoyed her favor to bewail her and lament for her when they see the smoke of her burning. Standing afar off, they cry, "Alas, alas that great city Babylon, that mighty city! for in one hour is thy judgment come" (10). It would seem that, coincident with the fall of the system, comes the fall of the city where she has had her seat. By some act of God, perhaps such as a great earthquake, it will be forever destroyed. That proud and haughty capital which has borne the title of "the eternal city" for two millenniums is surely doomed because of her impiety and hateful pride. It is a well-known fact that all southern Italy is of a peculiarly volcanic character. The very soil seems to be "stored with fire," to use a Scriptural phrase which is applied in 2 Peter 3:7 (literal rendering) to the heavens and earth as a whole. In a very remarkable manner this is true of the vicinity of Rome, and it may yet prove to be the means of its complete destruction. In such a case the phrase "the smoke of her burning" may be far more literal than some have supposed.

The Lament of the Merchants (Revelation 18:11-19)

These verses present a magnificent elegy and deserve more careful consideration than our limited space will permit. They picture the destruction of the great commercial system that men are building up with such painstaking care and which some fondly view as the panacea for all the disturbances that have wrought such distress among the nations. How often was it said before the outbreak of World War I that labor would not fight and that capital dare not. It claimed that there was too much at stake; but how false have all such predictions proved. We may however be assured that when it is over, for a time a tremendous effort will be exerted to build up a financial system that will be world-embracive and that will unite the nations in the bonds of commercial self-interest. We know that all such schemes are doomed to disappointment, for the prophetic word has clearly foretold its failure. There can be no lasting peace until the Prince of Peace becomes the governor among the nations.

And so we are permitted in this present portion of our book to stand by, as it were, and look on as Babylon falls and to hear her merchants bewailing her doom and their own tremendous losses. As her merchandise is tabulated, now with none to buy, we notice among the precious things mentioned are the bodies and souls of men—not merely "slaves," as in the King James version. And this is the awful thing about Babylon. She has made merchandise of the bodies and souls of her dupes. Turning away from the rich grace revealed in the gospel, they have tried to purchase what God was freely offering. In the end they find that they have sold their souls to a cruel and avaricious system that is conscienceless and remorse- less as the grave. How fearful must be the accounting at the judg- ment bar of God of those responsible for such terrible deceptions!

The Final End of Babylon the Great (Revelation 18:20-24)

No wonder Babylon's fall brings joy in Heaven, though it in- volves the earth-dwellers in selfish sorrow. "Rejoice over her, thou heaven, and ye holy apostles and prophets; for God hath avenged you on her" (20). She had shed their blood like water, but the ven- geance of God, though it seems to slumber long, will awaken at last. Every upright soul will justify God when He visits her in His wrath and indignation with the judgments symbolized in these verses.

The figure used in Jeremiah 51:63-64 is repeated in Revelation 18:21. A mighty angel is seen casting a great stone into the sea. This stone, like a tremendous millstone, is a fitting symbol of that mysterious power which had crushed the nations and ground the saints of God beneath it for so long.

How solemn are the angel's words in verses 21-23. How solemnly do they contrast with the lamentations of the merchants of the earth, whose only grief is that no man buys their merchandise any more.

It is the destruction of the greatest schemes and works of man, to make way for that which has been in the mind of God and promised through His prophets from the beginning of the world. Cain went out from the presence of the Lord and built a city after the murder of his brother Abel. This was the beginning of man's boasted civilization. All the arts and sciences had their origin there. There were artificers in brass and iron. Trade and barter, the pursuit of the unrighteous mammon began there. Those who handled the harp and the organ also dwelt there. Music charmed the weary sons of Cain as they sought to make themselves happy and this world attractive apart from God.

The Lord blotted all this out in the deluge, but it is evident that Ham, Noah's son, had learned the same ways. The world as an ordered system of things, apart from God, had a new beginning in his family. We have seen that Nimrod built a city and a tower, and it became the mother-city from which others went out and built a civilization, godless and selfish. That system eventually crucified the Lord of glory. His accusation was written above Him in Hebrew, the language of religion; Greek, the language of culture; and Latin, the language of world-politics—the world, as such, arrayed against God and His Christ. And this is the world which is to reach its culmination in Babylon the great. The greatest geniuses that earth has ever produced will preside over it, only to be judged by God because of its inveterate enmity to everything holy and its constant rejection of His Son. Its downfall will prepare the way for the establishment of the kingdom of God and the reign of righteousness and peace, for which humanity has sighed so long. Man's city must fall to give place to the city of God which will stand forever. Therefore the joy in Heaven at Babylon's destruction.

"And in her"—that is, in Babylon—"was found the blood of prophets, and of saints, and of all that were slain upon the earth" (24). This closing verse of chapter 18 should make it clear that while Rome is the inheritor of the mysteries of ancient Babylon, it also is a world-inclusive system of apostasy. This, and this alone, fully

meets the requirements of this last verse. When God makes inquisi-
tion for blood, He finds it all shed by Babylon the great. For, if man
had not gone out from the presence of the Lord, this earth would
never have been stained with human blood; brotherhood and righteousness would have prevailed everywhere. Babylon therefore is
guilty of all the corruption and violence that have darkened the history of the human race; it caused the death of the Christ of God
Himself. May grace be given to all to whom this message comes to
"flee out of the midst of Babylon, and deliver every man his soul"
(Jeremiah 51:6).

CHAPTER NINETEEN
THE TWO SUPPERS

In the opening verses of Revelation 19 we are given another look into Heaven and permitted to note the exultation caused by the judgment of the great harlot.

Rejoicing of the Saints (Revelation 19:1-5)

All the redeemed of every age, who when on earth knew something of this awful power of iniquity, will then rejoice that the harlot is forever overthrown. This is the last time the twenty-four elders are seen in the book. The symbol changes in the next section, and the bride, the Lamb's wife, takes their place. The elders represent the heavenly saints as a worshiping company of holy and royal priests. But when the harlot-church is off the scene, the true bride appears and the elders are never again mentioned. It is noteworthy that in their final appearance (19:4), as in their first in chapter 4, they are seen in the attitude of worship. They adore the Lamb as Creator and Redeemer in chapter 4. Here they adore God as moral governor of the universe and for the display of His righteous judgment.

In response to their note of praise comes a voice from the throne itself, saying, "Praise our God, all ye his servants, and ye that fear him, both small and great" (5). This concludes the solemn and soul-stirring portion, in which the character and doom of the great mystery of Babylon have been so vividly portrayed. Happier scenes lie before us. But these scenes could only be introduced by the judgment of that which had so grievously departed from the living God. Happy will it be for us if we learn to judge, not only the unclean system we have been considering, but every tendency in ourselves to partake of its spirit.

Next we are to be occupied with two opposite scenes: one of which is to take place very shortly in Heaven and the other on earth. Both are called suppers. The one is the marriage supper of the Lamb. The other is the great supper of God. The first is all joy and gladness. The second is a scene of deepest gloom and anguish. The marriage supper of the Lamb ushers in the fullness of glory for the heavenly saints. The great supper of God concludes the series of judgments that are to fall on the prophetic earth. It opens the way for the establishment of the long-waited-for kingdom of God.

When I use the term *the prophetic earth*, I refer to the Roman earth—that is, to that portion of the world which lies within what were once the confines of the Roman empire. It also includes that part of the world where Babylon will dominate at the time of the end. As I understand it, the heathen nations that have not yet taken professedly Christian ground will not be included in the scene on which God's heaviest judgments will fall. Although necessarily all the world will suffer in measure when Christendom and Judaism are visited by the fires of His wrath. "The day of God's red heavens" will be worldwide, but its intensity will be on the prophetic earth.

The Marriage Supper of the Lamb (Revelation 9:6-10)

In verses 6-7 John revealed that following the final end of Babylon the hour for the heavenly nuptials will have struck. But who is the bride, or the wife of the Lamb, mentioned here for the first time? Is this special dignity the portion of Israel or is it that of the church of the present dispensation? Both views have been advocated by godly and able teachers; one should perhaps speak with diffidence when dwelling on a contoversial theme.

In the Old Testament Israel certainly is the wife of Jehovah. Is this the same thing as "the bride, the Lamb's wife"? Are there not revealed in these two expressions two different glories—the one to be displayed on earth, the other in Heaven? It seems very plain to me that the marriage supper of the Lamb takes place in Heaven just before the Lamb descends with all His saints to take His great power and reign. When He reigns His bride will reign with Him. And this is certainly the church, which He has called out of the world for that very purpose. There will be other heavenly saints, but these are distinguished for us from the bride.

It also seems clear that there is a very real difference between the wife of Jehovah and the heavenly bride of the Lamb, the incarnate Son. The wife of Jehovah, now set aside for her sins, will be acknowledged by God as His own in the day of her repentance. The bride of Christ, now espoused as a pure virgin to her absent Lord, is waiting for her marriage nuptials until He calls her home. But some have objected to this view, to use their own words, as a kind of spiritual polygamy. My answer would be that where we are only speaking in figures the objection does not apply. The church which is His body is distinctly identified with His wife in Ephesians 5:30-32, otherwise the figures used in that passage become meaningless. So it seems plain that we are warranted in viewing Israel as the earthly bride and the church as the heavenly bride. Both are dear to His heart. He purchased them with His precious blood, but each has a special character of her own.

The marriage supper of the Lamb is the time of displayed glory, when the results of the judgment seat of Christ will be fully exhibited in the saints. That event itself, as we have seen, takes place immediately after the rapture of the church. The Lord's word is clear as to this: "Behold, I come quickly, and my reward is with me, to give every man according as his work shall be" (Revelation 22:12). But the full manifestation of the saints in the same glory with their Head and Lord, their heavenly Bridegroom, can only be after the false church has been exposed and judged. Then the Lamb's marriage day will come. And so we are told, concerning the Bride, that "to her was granted that she should be arrayed in fine linen, clean and white: for the fine linen is the righteousness of saints" (19:8). It is well known to students of the original text that the word rendered "righteousness" in this verse is in the plural and should therefore be translated "righteousnesses" or "righteous acts." It is not imputed righteousness that is here in view, nor the believer being made the righteousness of God in Christ. It is that which we have already seen in connection with the elders: the fine linen illustrates the righteous acts of the saints themselves, right-doing while here on earth.

The judgment seat of Christ will expose these acts, which will form the wedding garment of the bride on her nuptial day.

In the light of this Scripture we may well be exercised as to our own ways. Are you, dear fellow believer, preparing any fine linen for that coming day? You are familiar with the thought of the prospective bride's hope chest. How interested the engaged girl is in filling that chest in view of her wedding day. May I say that we too have a spiritual hope chest to fill? Everything that is really done for Christ is something added to that bridal chest. Some of us, I am afraid, will have rather a poor supply. The wedding garments are to be prepared here on earth, as the Spirit of God Himself works in us to will and to do of His good pleasure. Let us not be neglectful of this for the time is short, and the night is coming when no man can work. It is true that even our very best deeds, our most devoted service, all need to be washed and made white in the blood of the Lamb. He will not fail to value correctly and to richly reward everything that was for His own glory in our lives. But all that is done for self, all that springs from unholy motives, will disappear in that day. That which was the result of His Spirit working within us will abide forever. It will be to His praise and glory and for our own eternal joy as we see what pleasure we have given Him.

In verse 9 we are shown a group who are certainly to be distinguished from the bride. These are all friends of the Bridegroom who rejoice in His joy and share in His gladness. I understand them to be the Old Testament saints and the tribulation saints, who, though they form no part of the church, share in the heavenly glory. These are pictured as the guests at the wedding who participate in the general gladness of the occasion and whose presence adds to the happiness of the bride and Groom. Thus we have a scene of unalloyed delight and holy, unending gladness, for sin will never enter there to destroy that hallowed joy.

So ravished and enraptured was John's heart as this vision passed before him that he fell down to worship at the feet of the angel who showed him these things. He was rebuked for his grave mistake by the glorious messenger, who cried, "See thou do it not: I am thy fellowservant, and of thy brethren that have the testimony of Jesus: worship God: for the testimony of Jesus is the spirit of prophecy"

(10). Our Lord Himself, because He was God, received worship and blessed the worshiper, as in the case of Thomas when he was convinced of His resurrection (John 20:28). But the angel scrupulously refused what belongs to deity alone.

But the rapidly changing prophetic pictures hurry us on. So we ask what will follow the marriage supper of the Lamb?

The Rider on the White Horse (Revelation 19:11-16)

In verse 11 we read of the last of the wondrous "openings" in this book of Revelation. How the heart thrills and the pulses bound as we read this description of the descending Christ of God and His saints! It is the coming of the Lord to the earth with His redeemed; before we saw His coming to the air to rapture them to Himself.

You will remember that we read of a rider on a white horse when the first seal was broken; but that one did not come from Heaven. He went forth on the earth and was of the earth, and his plans were doomed to disappointment (6:1-2). The rider of this chapter comes from Heaven and His plans will never miscarry. And right here is the safety of the Christian. He knows that no future earth-born man can ever be the Christ for whom the Word has taught him to wait. Jesus came once in lowly guise, born of a virgin; He comes again, descending from Heaven. All who come in any other way saying "I am Christ" are deceivers and antichrists. "As it is appointed unto men once to die, but after this the judgment: so Christ was once offered to bear the sins of many; and unto them that look for him shall he appear the second time without sin [or, apart from sin, having nothing to do with the sin-question] unto salvation" (Hebrews 9:27-28). This is the appearing that is depicted here. It is the coming of the Son of God to take vengeance on His enemies and to deliver His earthly people, who will be looking for Him with longing hearts and eager, anxious eyes.

The description of the descending Lord is most striking. He rides a white horse as the Prince of Peace. He is called Faithful and True, as in the message to the church in Laodicea (Revelation 3:14). He comes to execute righteous judgment and thus to establish the divine authority over all the earth. His eyes as a flame of fire, as in the vision of the Son of man in the midst of the lampstands, tell of His readiness to detect and deal with all iniquity. The many diadems on His head proclaim His authority over all the kingdoms of the earth. The reign of misrule is to end when He takes the scepter, and all the crowns are given to Him. "A name written, that no man knew, but he himself" depicts His essential glory as the eternal Son, concerning which He declared that "no man knoweth the Son, but the Father" (Matthew 11:27). The mystery of His glorious person is beyond all human understanding. We rightly sing, "The Father only Thy blest name / Of Son can comprehend."

In Isaiah 63 we are told that His garments are to be reddened with the blood of His enemies. But the robe dipped in blood with which He is here seen clothed—like the rams' skins, dyed red, in the tabernacle—is the sign of His consecration unto death. It is His own blood that is here in view, the price of our redemption.

It is noteworthy that He is said to have three names. One, we have already seen, is beyond man's comprehension. The second name is "The Word of God." We know what is involved in that: for it is as the Word became flesh that He has revealed God to us. That Word was spoken in time, of which we read: "In the beginning was the Word, and the Word was with God, and the Word was God. The same was in the beginning with God" (John 1:1-2). Here we have eternity of being, one substance with the Father, but distinct personality—true deity, and eternal Sonship. This was the Word unspoken, but when the Son became incarnate, God spoke in Him. So we read, "No man hath seen God at any time; the only begotten Son, which is in the bosom of the Father, he hath declared Him," or, "told Him out." This is just a little of what is involved in this second glorious name.

In order not to break the connection we might look now at the third name or title that He bears. In verse 16 we are told that "He hath on his vesture and on his thigh a name written, King of kings, and Lord of lords." This is His official title, and it belongs to Him as Son of man, the rightful heir of all things. Earth would not recognize His claims when He was here the first time. In derision they crowned Him with thorns and gave Him a cross instead of a throne. But God is going to reverse all this soon. He is to "be exalted and extolled, and be very high" (Isaiah 52:13). All the kingdoms of earth are to be His and He will rule the nations with the iron rod of un-swerving justice.

It will be noticed, then, that in these three names we have illus-trated first, our Lord's dignity as the eternal Son; second, His incar-nation—the Word become flesh; and lastly, His second advent to reign as King of kings and Lord of lords.

The armies in Heaven who follow Him comprise (1) the church, which we have just seen as the bride; (2) the saints of former dis-pensations; and (3) the tribulation saints who had been slain un-der the beast and the antichrist. All ride forth with Him, their now triumphant Lord, when He comes to take His great power and reign.

The sharp sword that proceeds from His mouth is His word. This we have already seen in the first chapter. We remember His warn-ing to the church in Pergamos, that if there were no repentance He would fight against them with the sword of His mouth (2:16).

We are told that He treads the winepress of the wrath of God. The winepress is the figure of unsparing judgment. This we have also become familiar with in chapter 14. In Isaiah 63:1-6 we have a remarkable passage that bears on what we have here.

> Who is this that cometh from Edom, with dyed garments from Bozrah? This that is glorious in his apparel, travelling in the greatness of his strength? I that speak in righteousness, mighty to save. Wherefore art thou red in thine apparel, and thy garments like him that treadeth in the winevat? I have trodden the winepress alone; and of the people there was none with me: for I will tread them in mine anger, and trample them in my fury; and their blood shall be sprinkled upon my garments, and I will stain all my raiment. For the day of vengeance is in mine heart, and the year of my redeemed is come. And I looked, and there was none to help; and I wondered that there was none to uphold: therefore mine own arm brought salvation unto me; and my fury, it upheld me. And I will tread down the people in mine anger, and make them drunk in my fury, and I will bring down their strength to the earth.

This marvelous prophecy had a partial fulfillment in judgments
meted out to Israel's foes in the past. It will have its complete fulfillment when the Lord comes the second time to tread the winepress
of wrath and to destroy all who are His own and His people's foes,
as depicted in the last part of our chapter.

The Great Supper of God (Revelation 19:17-21)

From verse 17 to the end we have a graphic portrayal by the
master-artist of the closing scene of judgment—the great supper of
God. It is not exactly "the supper of the great God." The adjective
has become transposed in the King James version and is made to
qualify God Himself. Any critical version will show it should rather
qualify the supper. John saw an angel standing in the sun, for the
source of light which seemed to be blotted out under the bowls of
wrath is now seen resplendent in glory. The angel summoned the
birds that fly in the midst of Heaven to feast on the flesh of the great
ones of earth and their vast armies who are seen gathering together
for the Armageddon conflict.

The beast is seen marshalling his hosts with his blasphemous
ally and satellite, the false prophet—that is, the antichrist. The kings
of the earth, with all their hordes, are hurrying to the fray. They all
combine in one last desperate effort to make successful war against
the Lord Jesus Christ and everything that is of God. But like the
hosts of Sennacherib of old, they are palsied and stricken by the
blast of His mouth. Their armies become food for the birds of prey.
It is an awful picture—the climax of man's audacious resistance to
God. It is also a picture that may fill the heart with gladness as it
tells of the end of unrighteous rule on this planet and the ushering in
of the golden age for which all nations have sighed.

Note that two men are taken alive. They are the two arch-con-
spirators who have appeared so often in the book of Revelation—
the beast and the false prophet. They are the civil and religious leaders of the last league of nations, which will be Satan-inspired in its
origin and Satan-directed until its doom. These two men are "cast
alive into a lake of fire burning with brimstone," (20) where a thousand years later they are still said to be "suffering the vengeance of

eternal fire" (Jude 1:7). Incidentally this proves that the lake of fire is not annihilation and it is not purgatorial. It neither annihilates nor purifies these two fallen foes of God and man after a thousand years under judgment.

In the Old Testament we read of two men who went to Heaven without passing through death. Enoch and Elijah were translated that they should not see death. And here, before we come to the close of the New Testament, we have two men brought before us who are cast into Hell-fire without undergoing physical death. Their awful doom is for the warning of all who turn away from Him that speaks from Heaven. God's indignation is soon to fall on all who refuse the message of His grace.

Lamb of God, when Thou in glory
Shalt to this sad earth return,
All Thy foes shall quake before Thee,
All that now despise Thee, mourn;
Then shall we, at Thine appearing,
With Thee in Thy kingdom reign:
Thine the praise and Thine the glory,
Lamb of God, for sinners slain.

And now as I close, I would seek solemnly to impress on each of my readers that you may have a part in one or the other of these two suppers which we have been considering. If saved, I know you will have a place at the marriage supper of the Lamb; for every blood-redeemed one of this dispensation will be there. Not one will be missing because our blessed Lord, in grace, became the Lamb of God to die for your sins on the cross. You will share in that scene of bliss with Him. But you who refuse His grace, what will you do when the things of which we have been speaking take place? You may be among those deceived by Satan, accepting the leadership of the beast and believing the claims of the antichrist. In that case you would have part in "the great supper of God!" May God draw you to Himself now. Resist not the pleadings of the Holy Spirit, but flee at once for refuge to Him who said, "Him that cometh to me I will in no wise cast out" (John 6:37).

CHAPTER TWENTY
THE MILLENNIUM AND THE GREAT WHITE THRONE

It is often said by those who object to the doctrine of an earthly millennium, that the term itself is not found in the Bible. They insist that neither in the Old nor in the New Testaments do we ever read of a millennium. They argue from this that the teaching is manmade, not derived from the Word of God. We might reply that the mere fact that a certain term is not used in Scripture does not necessarily prove that the doctrine for which the term stands is not taught there. The word *trinity* is not found in the Bible, but all sound Christians admit the doctrine of three persons in one God. The word *substitution* is not there either; but it is written, "He was wounded for our transgressions" (Isaiah 53:5), and that is substitution. Where will you find the terms, *eternal sonship*, *deity*, *fall of man*, *depravity*, *incarnation*, *impeccability* (as applied to Christ), and many more of similar character? Certainly not on the pages of our English Bibles. But all these terms mentioned stand for great truths unmistakably taught in the Book and are a vital part of the teaching of Christianity. So the mere omission of a title or name of a doctrine does not prove the absence of the doctrine itself, nor does it prove that it is manmade.

However, we are not shut up to reasoning of this kind in regard to the *millennium*. The word in question is the Latin equivalent of an expression that is found six times in the chapter that now demands our attention. It simply means a "thousand years"; just as a *century* means "one hundred years," or a *jubilee* indicates the expiration of fifty years.

A millennium then is a time-period. It does not necessarily carry with it any thought of perfection or happiness, nor of an era of displayed divine government. Almost six millenniums have elapsed since God put man on this globe. There is another millennium and a fraction yet to run before the course of time is finished. That last thousand years is the period that we are now to consider. I trust to show that it is the predicted kingdom age of the prophets and the "dispensation of the fulness of times" of the New Testament (Ephesians 1:10). It is not only in what some have called an obscure passage in the Revelation that we read of this "good time coming." It is taught everywhere in Scripture.

The Binding of Satan (Revelation 20:1-3)

The binding of the arch-foe of God and man, is the first notable event of this reign of righteousness (1-3). Without attempting to explain all the symbols here used, it is enough to say that the passage very definitely indicates that there is a coming time when men will no longer be deceived and led astray by the great tempter. Ever since his victory over our first parents in Eden, this tempter has been the persistent and malignant foe of mankind. By his wiles untold millions have been defrauded of their birthright privileges. If men sin during the millennium it will not be on account of having been deceived. It will be simply because of self-will and the yielding to the lusts of their own hearts. For we need to remember that the kingdom age is not to be a dispensation of sinlessness. There will be some, even in that blessed time, who will dare to act in defiance of the will of God but they will quickly be dealt with in deserved judgment. Such cases, I take it, will be very exceptional, but Scripture makes it plain that there will be offenses even when God's King reigns over the earth.

The First Resurrection (Revelation 20:4-6)

In the present dispensation of grace, those who will live godly in Christ Jesus suffer persecution; righteousness suffers. But in the millennium righteousness will reign. "A king shall reign in righteousness" (Isaiah 32:1). In the eternal state, which follows the millennium, righteousness will *dwell*. It will be at home, and every adverse thing will be forever banished from the new heavens and the new earth.

Daniel prophesied of the time coming when "the saints ... shall possess the kingdom" (7:18). The words of Revelation 20:4 agree with this: "And I saw thrones, and they sat upon them, and judgment was given unto them: and I saw the souls of them that were beheaded for the witness of Jesus, and for the word of God, and which had not worshipped the beast ... and they lived and reigned with Christ a thousand years." We have here, if I understand the passage correctly, the last cohort of the first resurrection. Our Lord Himself, the saints raised at the rapture of the church, and the witnessing remnant that were slain and raised up in the seventieth week of Daniel all share in the "administration of the fullness of the seasons." This is how the late William Kelly translated the expression rendered in our Bibles "the dispensation of the fullness of times" (Ephesians 1:10). These saints appear in glory with the Lord. But we are not to understand that either He or they are to return to earth to live. Their relationship to the earth will be, I presume, very much like that of the angels in the patriarchal dispensation. They will be able to appear and disappear at will and exercise a benevolent oversight on behalf of those who live in this world. "Unto the angels hath he not put into subjection the world to come, whereof we speak" (Hebrews 2:5). That world will be subjected to the Son of man, and all who have shared with Him in His rejection will be associated with Him. These are the throne-sitters first mentioned. With them will be the rest of the tribulation saints, who will suffer death rather than deny their God in the awful days of antichrist's ascendancy. Their rapture will be when the Lord appears for the establishment of the kingdom.

"But the rest of the dead, lived not again until the thousand years were finished. This is the first resurrection" (Revelation 20:5). This does not militate against the teaching already advanced. The first cohort of the first resurrection will be summoned from their graves prior to the tribulation period and the second in the midst of that time of trouble. We have here a summary. All of these classes together make up the first resurrection—the resurrection of life, which is thus distinguished from the resurrection of judgment. Between these two will elapse the entire millennial age. The unsaved will remain in their graves until the heavens and the earth pass away. Their souls in Hades (erroneously rendered "hell" in some versions, but really the state between death and resurrection) and their bodies in the grave, they await the day of judgment at the end of time.

"Blessed and holy is he that hath part in the first resurrection: on such the second death hath no power, but they shall be priests of God and of Christ, and shall reign with him a *thousand years*" (6, italics added). This is the kingdom described in such glowing terms by Isaiah. Throughout his entire prophecy he saw, through faith's telescope, the glorious time when Israel and Judah will be one people in their own land. They will be restored in soul to God and dwell in peace every man under his own vine and fig tree. The glory of the Lord will cover the earth as the waters cover the sea. He wrote how even nature itself would respond to Messiah's rule. The wilderness and the solitary place will be glad for it, and the desert will rejoice and blossom as the rose. The animal creation too will be delivered from the curse. They will not hurt nor destroy in all God's holy mountain. The lion will eat straw like the ox. The lamb will lie down with the lion, and "a little child shall lead them" (Isaiah 11:6). All nations will then ask the way to Zion, and Jerusalem will become the metropolis, not only of a rejuvenated Palestine, but of the whole earth.

Jeremiah takes up the same happy strain. He foresaw the God of Israel sending "fishers" out into the sea of the nations, fishing out His people no matter where they may be hidden and bringing them back to the land of their fathers. He saw the city built again and inhabited by a peaceful, happy nation under the reign of the righteous Branch whom God has promised to raise up unto David. "In his days Judah shall be saved, and Israel shall dwell safely: and this is his name whereby he shall be called, the Lord our righteousness" (Jeremiah 23:6). Then they will no longer need to "teach every man his neighbour, and every man his brother, saying, Know the Lord: for all shall know [Him], from the least to the greatest" (Hebrews 8:11).

Ezekiel added to the wondrous story and told of the Spirit being poured out from on high. He described the service of the regenerated Israel, a priestly nation through whom the law of God goes out to all the lands of the nations. He depicted the millennial temple and even told us how the land is to be divided among the tribes. Ezekiel does not close his remarkable book until he can say, "The name of the city from that day shall be, [Jehovah-Shammah] The Lord is there" (Ezekiel 48:35).

All the visions of Daniel's companion apocalypse conclude with the bringing in of the fifth universal kingdom. This he told us is the kingdom of the Son of man, which is to displace every other and is to stand forever. This is the Stone cut out without hands that falls on the feet of the Gentile image and grinds it to powder. Then it becomes a great mountain and fills the whole earth. This is the kingdom conferred on the Son of man by the Ancient of days. Then the bodies of the beasts (symbolizing the four great empires that have borne rule over all the civilized earth) will be cast into the burning flame.

Hosea showed how Messiah would come in lowly grace, but rejected by Israel, He would go and return to His place until they acknowledged their sin. When they seek His face He will return to restore their souls and to ransom them from the power of the grave. He will bring in everlasting righteousness and make them a blessing to all nations.

Joel saw the great tribulation in all its intensity, and the glory that will follow. He predicted the outpouring of the Spirit, not on Israel only, but on all flesh.

Amos prophesied of the gathering again of the outcasts of Israel and their resettlement in their land under Jehovah's perfect rule.

Obadiah, who wrote the shortest of all the prophecies, though he wrote chiefly of judgment on Edom, declared triumphantly, "The kingdom shall be the Lord's" (1:21).

Only Jonah seems to have no reference to that day of Jehovah's power. Yet we may learn through him how wonderfully God will confirm the testimony of Hebrew missionaries in the beginning of the kingdom age, as they go forth to spread the gospel among those who have not heard His fame, nor seen His glory.

But Micah joined with Isaiah in describing the time when "the mountain of the house of the LORD shall be established in the top of the mountains, and…people shall flow unto it," when "the law shall go forth of Zion, and the word of the Lord from Jerusalem." Then the nations "shall beat their swords into plowshares, and their spears into pruninghooks:…neither shall they learn war any more" (Micah 4:1-3).

Nahum predicted the judgments that will befall the enemies of Jehovah in the day of His preparation. Habakkuk, standing on his watchtower, saw the coming King bringing in the glory.

Zephaniah and Haggai pointed onwards to the restoration of Israel, and through Israel the blessing of the whole world. The Lord their God will be enthroned in the midst of them, and they will serve Him with one consent.

Zechariah, the prophet of glory, gave minute details not touched on by any other. He even told of the provision to be made for children's playgrounds in the restored capital of Palestine, for he wrote, "The broad places of the city shall be full of boys and girls, playing in the broad places thereof" (Zechariah 8:5, literal rendering). He saw every spot in Jerusalem holy to the Lord, and all nations wending their way there from year to year to keep the feast of tabernacles.

Malachi completed the series and announced the soon-coming of the King, heralded by the prophet Elijah. He will tread down the wicked and sit as a refiner of silver, to purify the sons of Levi (Malachi 3:1-3). He will make His name great from the rising of the sun to the going down of the same.

Thus "to him give all the prophets witness" (Acts 10:43), that through His name remission of sins is now to be proclaimed among all nations. They also testify that He is to reign in righteousness over all the world when He comes the second time to claim the inheritance which is His by divine decree as Son and heir of all things. Then all the earth will rejoice for the eyes of the blind will be opened, the tongue of the dumb will sing, and the lame man will leap as the deer. Sorrow and sighing will flee away, and the Lord alone will be exalted for a thousand glorious years!

Satan's Final Attack (Revelation 20:7-10)

These verses record the amazing anticlimax to the story of human life on this earth. Who but God could have foreseen such an ending? It shows us the incorrigible evil of the heart of man if left to himself. While Satan is shut up in the abyss, there will be many born into the world whose obedience to the King will only be feigned. Their hearts will not be in it. When the devil is loosed for a little season at the end of the millennium, he finds a host of these ready to do his bidding and to join him in the last great rebellion against Omnipotence.

It is the old story of Satanic hatred to God and man's frailty told out again, but this time under the most favorable circumstances for man. Therefore his sin is absolutely inexcusable. Tested in *the garden of delight* man broke through the only prohibition laid on him. Tested under *conscience*, corruption and violence filled the earth, and the world had to be cleared by the deluge. Tested under the restraining influence of divinely appointed *government*, man went into idolatry, thus turning his back on his Creator. Tested under *law*, he cast off all restraint and crucified the Lord of glory. Tested under *grace*, in this present dispensation of the Holy Spirit, man has shown himself utterly unable to appreciate such mercy, has rejected the gospel, and has gone ever deeper into sin. Tested under *the personal reign of the Lord Jesus Christ* for a thousand years, some will be ready to listen to the voice of the tempter. For he will ascend from the pit of the abyss bent on one last defiant effort to thwart the purpose of God. It is a melancholy history indeed and emphasizes the truth that the heart of man is incurably evil. "The carnal mind…is not subject to the law of God, neither indeed can be" (Romans 8:7); therefore the need, in all ages, of a second birth through the Word and the Spirit of God.

The apostle Peter wrote, "The heavens and the earth which are now, are kept in store, reserved unto fire against the day of judgment" (2 Peter 3:7). This pent-up fire breaking forth from the heavens will destroy the hosts of Satan's dupes, and will purify the very globe itself, as once before it was cleansed by water. This closes the course of time and introduces the unending ages of eternity, during which the devil will be confined in the great prison-house of the lost who have resisted God's mercy and spurned His grace. What an end for him who was once "the anointed cherub" that covered the throne of God, but whose heart was lifted up because of his beauty. Thus falling through pride, he became the most accursed creature in all the universe of God! Our Lord told us that the devil "abode not in the truth" (John 8:44). He is the prince of all apostates. Apostasy has ever been the great sin into which he has malignantly sought to lead the human race.

The Great White Throne (Revelation 20:11-15)

The judgment of the great white throne is the final scene before the new heavens and the new earth are introduced. It is, as a careful study makes exceedingly clear, not "the general judgment" at the end of the world, as many have supposed. It is the judgment of the wicked who, during Christ's reign of a thousand years, have been left in the realms of the dead. The righteous who share in heavenly glory are to be revealed, as we have seen, at the judgment seat of Christ. There they will be rewarded according to their service while in this world. The living nations will be summoned to appear before the Son of man when He comes in His glory at the beginning of the millennium (Matthew 25). The wicked dead are to be raised at the end of that reign of righteousness and dealt with according to their works. The condemnation now is that men reject the Lord Jesus Christ who has made full atonement for sin in order that all may be freed from wrath through Him. But if He is rejected finally, of very necessity men must face the penalty of sin themselves.

Solemn indeed is the description of that last great assize. The august throne-occupant, we know from other Scriptures, will be none other than our Lord Jesus Christ. "The Father judgeth no man, but hath committed all judgment unto the Son: that all men should honour the Son, even as they honour the Father" (John 5:22-23). He who once hung on Calvary's cross is to be the judge of living and dead. We have already been largely occupied with the first aspect of the judgment. Now it is the doom of the wicked dead that is engaging our attention.

When the throne is set, the heavens and the earth, as we now know them, shrink away, as though the material universe were awed by the face of Him who summons the dead to their accounting. What a sea of faces will appear before Him in that solemn hour of tremendous import! All the lost of all the ages; all who preferred their sins to His salvation; all who procrastinated until for them the door of mercy was closed; all who spurned His grace and in self-will chose the way "that seemeth right unto a man" but was in truth "the way of death" (Proverbs 14:12)—all such are to be summoned to stand before that inexorably righteous throne. No condoning of sin then; no palliating or excusing in that day. The judgment of God will be according to truth, and every circumstance will be taken into account. Nothing will be overlooked. Therefore some will be beaten with many stripes and some with few, according to the measure of light given and rejected. "Shall not the judge of all the earth do right?" (Genesis 18:25) And there will be no appeal from His decisions, for His is the supreme court of the universe. "What a magnificent conception," exclaims Thomas Carlyle, "is that of a last judgment! A righting of all the wrongs of the ages." And, I may add, the tracing back of every evil act to its source, and the placing of responsibility for every offense against the moral law, where it belongs.

None will be great enough to escape that court session, none too insignificant to be overlooked. The dead, small and great, will be there. Even though their bodies had been buried for centuries, even millenniums in the depths of the sea, they will come forth at His bidding, who when He speaks will not be denied. Death, the grave which has claimed what was mortal of man, his body, will give up its prey. Hades, the world unseen, will surrender the undying spirits and souls of the lost. Man—body, soul, and spirit reunited—will stand trembling before that judgment bar. The books of record will be opened. Memory will respond to every charge. The Word of God too will be opened there, for Jesus declared that Moses' words and His words should judge men in the last day. And the book of life too will be unfolded there. Many in that vast throng had taken it for granted their names were in that book because perhaps they had been listed on the roll of some church or religious society. Let them search and look. It will bear witness against them. The Lamb has not inscribed their name in that book. "And whosoever was not found written in the book [will be] cast into the lake of fire" (Revelation 20:15).

Will any be saved who stand before the great white throne? Not one, if we read the account correctly, for death and hades are to be "emptied into the lake of fire." All the lost, whose spirits and bodies they have held in confinement so long, will be emptied out into the pit of woe. And, says God's Word, "This is the second death" (Revelation 20:14). Death is the separation of body and spirit, we are told in James 2:26. The second death is the final separation of the lost from the God who created man. Like living planets which, possessed of will, have swung out of their orbits, they dash off into the outer darkness never to find their way back to that great central sun.

The lake of fire is the symbol of immeasurable sorrow, of eternal torment. It is a divine picture intended to make the soul of the sinner shrink with dread as he contemplates the end of those who obey not the gospel. It is human character made permanent, abiding in eternal sin and therefore under the wrath of God forever. Not until Judas Iscariot and John the beloved who wrote this book clasp hands in heavenly glory, will the woes of the wicked come to an end. As to Judas, the Master he betrayed has declared, "good were it for that man if he had never been born" (Mark 14:21). Were there salvation ahead at last, even after ages of suffering, as another has strikingly pointed out, even Judas might well thank God that he had ever been permitted to live. But over the portals of the lost is inscribed, "Abandon hope, ye who enter here."

Now is the acceptable time. Now a gracious Savior waits to catch the first breathing of repentance and answers the feeblest cry of faith. Trifle not with His mercy, hope not for some vague second chance, but close with Christ now. Know for a certainty that you will have no part in the doom pronounced at the great white throne. For the Lord Himself has said, "Verily, verily, I say unto you, He that heareth my word, and believeth on him that sent me, hath everlasting life, and shall not come into [judgment]; but is passed from death unto life" (John 5:24).

CHAPTER TWENTY-ONE
CLOSING SCENES

(PART ONE)

In regard to the first division of Revelation 21 it is important to note that prophecy does not properly relate to the eternal state. It is particularly occupied with this earth up to and including the millennium. Only occasionally do we have any reference in the prophetic scriptures to the unending ages that are to follow afterwards.

Eternal Issues (Revelation 21:1-8)

"And I saw a new heaven and a new earth: for the first heaven and the first earth were passed away; and there was no more sea" (1). This verse reminds us of Isaiah's prophecy, "For, behold, I create new heavens and a new earth: and the former shall not be remembered, nor come into mind" (Isaiah 65:17); and "For as the new heavens and the new earth, which I will make, shall remain before me, saith the lord, so shall your seed and your name remain" (Isaiah 66:22). The two chapters from which these verses are quoted have to do with the millennium. But I believe we have in Revelation 21:1 faith's telescope looking toward the unchanging and unchangeable future condition that will abide forever. I have no doubt it is to these promises that the apostle Peter referred in his second Epistle. After describing the destruction by fire of the heavens and the earth that now are, he said, "Nevertheless we, according to his promise, look for new heavens and a new earth, wherein dwelleth righteousness" (2 Peter 3:13). This then is the glorious consummation to which the opening verses of Revelation 21 introduce us.

The most marvelous object of that unending condition, next to the blessed Lord Himself, will be the church, which has been redeemed to God by the precious blood of His Son. For, observe the bridal condition does not cease at the close of the millennium: "And I John saw the holy city, new Jerusalem, coming down from God out of heaven, prepared as a bride adorned for her husband." A thousand years of the reign of righteousness will have rolled by before the fulfillment of this verse, and still the holy city is seen in all the freshness and loveliness of an adorned bride.

And this happy state will abide forever, for verses 3 and 4 describe a scene of blissful communion that is never terminated. The passage is beautiful in its simplicity, and comment would only seem to be like an attempt to paint the rose. How longingly must every believing heart look forward to that glorious day.

A voice from the throne cries, "Behold, I make all things new." And John is again commanded to write and assured that "these words are true and faithful" (5). The voice then exclaims solemnly "It is done. I am Alpha and Omega, the beginning and the end" (6). It is the proclamation that all the ways of God have found their final issue in the full glory of His blessed Son, who is the first and the last.

In verse 8 we are told of those who will never enter the holy city and who will have no part in the bright glories depicted above. But before giving the awful list the Lord graciously extends another gospel invitation. He wants all to whom these words come to know that there is mercy if they will only avail themselves of it. "I will give unto him," He says, "that is athirst of the fountain of the water of life freely" (6). And He follows this with a word of encouragement to the overcomer: "He that overcometh shall inherit all things; and I will be his God, and he shall be my son" (7). The world may bid for us now, and the treacherous flesh within may seek to act in concert with that world and its god, wooing our souls from Christ. But with the glorious promises of this book before us, we must long to rise above the power of present things. In the energy of the Holy Spirit we can overcome the world by faith, in view of what Christ is preparing for those who love Him.

How gladly would we believe that not one soul of man will fail of the joy that is kept in store for those who know Christ. But alas, sin has made this impossible. So this part of our chapter closes with the tremendously solemn announcement that "the fearful, and unbelieving, and the abominable, and murderers, and whoremongers, and sorcerers, and idolaters, and all liars, shall have their part in the lake which burneth with fire and brimstone: which is the second death" (8). The list includes not only those who are generally viewed as discreditable sinners, but the cowardly and the unbelieving. The cowardly were fearful of confessing Christ, perhaps because of the sneers of professed friends, or the consequences of turning from the world. The unbelieving refused to credit the testimony God had given and to rest their souls on the work of Christ. These both are linked up with the unclean and unholy of all classes. Inasmuch as "all have sinned, and come short of the glory of God," there can be no difference in their final doom if Christ is rejected. Though, as already noticed in the last chapter, every transgression and disobedience will receive its just recompense of reward.

The City of God (Revelation 21:9-17)

Beginning with the ninth verse we have a marvelous description of the new Jerusalem. Note that this comes at the conclusion of the prophetic outline. It is a kind of appendix or supplementary description. Just as one of the seven angels that had the seven bowls full of the seven last plagues gave to John a vision of Babylon the great (17–18), so here one of the same angels now bids him come and view the bride, the Lamb's wife. Carrying him away in the Spirit to a great and high mountain, the angel shows him that great city, the holy Jerusalem, descending out of Heaven from God. Babylon was both a city and a woman—both a great system and a company of people professing to be in bridal relation with the Lamb. So here the holy Jerusalem is both a city and a woman. The city is the bride as well as the home of the saints; just as we speak of Rome when we mean the church that has her seat there, as well as the city where she sits.

By this great city descending out of Heaven from God, I understand then the diffusion of heavenly principles over all this earth during the millennium by the heavenly saint. It is through His saints that the Lord is going to claim His inheritance. We may learn in this symbolic description of the city, the great guiding principles that will prevail in that coming age, and which are full of instruction for us at the present time. The city has the glory of God, and her light is described as "like unto a stone most precious, even like a jasper stone, clear as crystal" (11). The church is to be the vessel for displaying the glory of God throughout that age of righteousness and indeed, as verse 2 has already informed us, throughout all the ages to come. The "wall great and high" speaks of separation, a divine principle that runs throughout the Word of God from the time that sin entered to the close. A wall is for protection too. The separation of God's people is not an arbitrary principle to their discomfort, as some seem to think; it is clearly for their blessing, protecting from the evil without.

Though the wall is great and high, there are twelve gates, the number of administrative completeness. The gate itself, you will remember, is in Scripture the place of judgment. So the thought would seem to be that we have here righteousness reigning and provision made for entrance and exit, holy and happy liberty in accord with the holiness of God's nature. At the gates are twelve angels, divine messengers. On the gates are written the names of the twelve tribes of the children of Israel. In the millennium, government is to be maintained, as we have already seen, through God's earthly people being restored to their own land and to unbroken fellowship with the Lord. Thus the heavens will respond to God's earthly people, Jezreel (the seed of God), in a way that means blessing for all the world. Three gates on each of the four sides of the city illustrate the universality of the divine government thus fully revealed.

The wall, we are told, had twelve foundations and in them the names of the twelve apostles of the Lamb. This agrees strikingly with our Lord's promise to the twelve that, inasmuch as they had followed Him in His rejection, when the day of the earth's regeneration comes they will sit on twelve thrones, judging the twelve tribes of Israel (Matthew 19:28). Just as in Ephesians 2 the church is pictured as a holy temple, built on the foundation of the apostles and prophets, so here the holy city rests on the chosen messengers. They are to be the representatives of that authority in the age to come.

The angel who talked with John, measured the city with a golden rod. The dimensions are given in verses 16-17: "And the city lieth foursquare." The length being as large as the breadth, and this, in each instance, is twelve thousand furlongs. The wall itself is one hundred and forty-four cubits high. We are told that the length, the breadth, and the height of the city are equal. It has been suggested from this that the city is a cube, which may indeed be. But I frankly confess that I find the symbolism in that case exceedingly difficult to visualize before the mind's eye. I rather think of that holy city as the mountain of God, a vast pyramid resting on a foursquare base. It is twelve thousand furlongs each way and rises to a height as great as its length and breadth. The throne of God and of the Lamb is the very apex of it. From the throne flows the river of the water of life, winding about the mountain and through the middle of the one street of gold. But whether we think of a cube or a pyramid, the thought is the same: it is a city of absolute perfection. Twelve, the number of governmental completeness, is seen everywhere. Who can attempt to depict it any more clearly than the verses themselves describe it. It is a city whose wall is of jasper—the glory of God; built of pure gold, like unto clear glass—the divine glory maintained by righteousness.

The foundations of the wall are garnished with all manner of precious stones, corresponding to the stones seen in the breastplate of the high priest (Exodus 28:15-21). These stones tell of the particular and peculiar preciousness that each believer has in the eyes of the Lord.

The twelve gates are twelve pearls, every gate of one pearl. Each entrance way reminds us of that one pearl of great price. Our Lord, the heavenly merchantman, sold all that He had to buy the church. For though He was rich, yet He became poor that He might make it His own forever.

The street of pure gold reminds us that our feet will stand on the righteousness of God. In His justice we will stand and walk forever. It is not mere mercy that is the ground of our salvation, but God's glory has been fully and righteously maintained in the work of Calvary's cross. Therefore He is faithful and just in receiving all who trust His Son.

On earth the church is pictured as a holy temple unto the Lord. In that day there will be no temple seen, for the Lord God Almighty

and the Lamb are the temple (22). Nearness to God will character-
ize every saint. None will be shut out. Our Lord said, "Thou hast
loved them as thou hast loved me" (John 17:23). So we can sing
even now,

> So near, so very near to God,
> I could not nearer be;
> For in the person of His Son,
> I am as near as He.

When we get home there will be no separating veil and there will
be no outer court beyond which we dare not come. We will all be at
home with God and the Lamb forevermore. That city will have no
need of created light-bearers, such as sun and moon to shine in it.
These lights are for this world, not for that which is to come. The
glory of God will be the light displayed everywhere, and the Lamb
Himself will be the lamp. For the rendering, "the Lamb is the light"
hardly conveys the full thought. The glory of God is the light, and
the Lamb is the One on whom that glory is centralized. He is the
lamp from which it all shines. The glory of God in the face of Christ
Jesus is our light even now. It is a light that has pierced our darkened hearts, and we will enjoy that light eternally in the home of the
saints above. The nations who are spared to enter the millennial
kingdom will walk in its light. All earth's rulers will bring their
glory and honor to that throne city and light their tapers at that celestial fire.

The gates, we are told, will not be shut at all by day, and night
will be unknown there (25). I do not dwell on this now, for we have
the same expression repeated in the next chapter. In that city of
holiness and blessing, no unclean thing will ever enter in to defile.
No deceiving serpent will enter into that paradise of God, nor any
who display kinship with Satan, the father of lies. Only those who
are written in the Lamb's book of life; those who have judged themselves in the presence of God; those who have put their trust in Him
who shed His precious blood for our sins on that cross of shame
may rest assured that in His book their names are written even now.
Their names will be displayed there in the holy city.

CHAPTER TWENTY-TWO
CLOSING SCENES
(PART TWO)

The first five verses of Revelation 22 continue the detailed symbolic description of the holy Jerusalem, which will be ruling over the earth during the millennium.

The River of Life (Revelation 22:1-6)

In this section we read of a pure river. David sang of a river, the streams of which will make glad the city of God. This river is the Holy Spirit's testimony to the glory of Christ. It proceeds from the throne of God and of the Lamb, for the Holy Spirit proceeds from the Father and the Son. Anyone who has tasted of that refreshing stream on earth longs to drink fully of its living stream throughout the unending day!

When man sinned in the garden on earth, God drove him out. He set the cherubim with a flaming sword to guard the way to the tree of life, lest he should eat and live forever. But that sword of flame has been sheathed in the heart of the Lord Jesus Christ Himself. And now the blessed truth is made known that He who died and rose again is that tree of life. The leaves of this tree will be for the healing of the nations during Messiah's glorious reign. The fruit of it will be for the refreshment and gladness of His redeemed saints, as they gather by that river of joy. There the curse will be unknown, for the throne of God and of the Lamb will be established in unquestioned authority. His servants will find delight in ever serving Him who, in the hour of their deepest need, served them so faithfully. They will not serve as hirelings, not seeing the Master's face, but with holy gladness in His presence. They will behold the light

of His countenance, and His name will be stamped on their foreheads.

The wonderful description of the heavenly Jerusalem closes with
verse 5: "There shall be no night there; and they need no candle,
neither light of the sun; for the Lord God giveth them light: and
they shall reign for ever and ever." Oh, the nights of darkness and
of anguish many of God's beloved people have known in this poor
world! The night is the time of mystery, the time of suffering, and
of unfulfilled desire. The day will bring the glad fruition of all our
hopes. In the full blessing of that untreated light we will reign in
light through the ages of ages—at home in the city of God.

The Divine Epilogue (Revelation 22:7-21)

The closing verses need not detain us long. They are so plain, so
simple, that they require little comment, if any. Yet they are so in-
tensely solemn, we must not pass them lightly by, but desire that
each added message might sink in deeper into our hearts. This divine epilogue consists mostly of practical messages from the glorified Lord to all those to whom this book may come in the course of
time.

The sixth verse links us again with the opening of the book. "He
said unto me, These sayings are faithful and true: and the Lord God
of the holy prophets sent his angel to show unto his servants the
things which must shortly be done." How soon may all be fulfilled
that we have been studying. Three times the Lord spoke announc-
ing His near return. In verse 7 He said, "Behold, I come quickly:
blessed is he that keepeth the sayings of the prophecy of this book."
In verse 12, "And, behold, I come quickly; and my reward is with
me, to give every man according as his work shall be." And again,
in verse 20, the last words sent down to us by our Lord from Heaven
before the canon of Scripture was closed, was this: "He which
testifieth these things saith, Surely I come quickly." To this John,
as representing all the saints, replied, "Amen. Even so, come, Lord
Jesus."

We can scarcely wonder that a second time the beloved apostle,
overwhelmed by the abundance of the revelation given to him, fell

down to worship before the feet of the angel who showed him these things. As on the previous occasion, he is forbidden to do so. The angel declared he is a fellow-servant both of John and of his brethren the prophets and of us if we are among those who keep the sayings of this book. "Worship God," he commanded. In worshiping our Lord Jesus Christ we worship God: "For in him dwelleth all the fulness of the Godhead bodily" (Colossians 2:9).

Daniel's prophecy closes with the admonition, "Go thy way, Daniel: for the words are closed up and sealed till the time of the end" (Daniel 12:9). In a former verse, the word to him was, "But thou, O Daniel, shut up the words, and seal the book, even to the time of the end" (12:4). But to John the angel said, "Seal not the sayings of the prophecy of this book: for the time is at hand" (10).

In the eleventh verse we have set before us the great truth that science itself demonstrates equally with the Word of God, namely that character tends to permanence. "He that is unjust, let him be unjust still: and he which is filthy, let him be filthy still: and he that is righteous, let him be righteous still: and he that is holy, let him be holy still." It is a divine emphasis on the solemn truth that as a man is found in that coming day, so he will remain for all eternity. In this world God is calling men to repent. Here and now, He waits to renew, by divine grace, those who commit themselves to Him. But in the eternal world there will be no power that has not been in exercise here to make the unjust righteous or the filthy clean.

The fourteenth verse is translated differently in the Revised version, and that in accordance with the best manuscripts. It is thus: "Blessed are they that wash their robes, that they may have right to the tree of life, and may enter in through the gates into the city." The promise rests on no legal grounds. It is not *doing* that gives one title to that home of the saints. It is only the precious blood of Christ, by which the acts of the saints (however well intentioned) must be washed, that fits any for entrance there. Outside forevermore will be the false, apostate teachers, designated as dogs, with those dealing with evil spirits, the unclean, and all murderers and idolaters, and whosoever loves and practices lying (15). They will be outside because they would not prepare to enter inside while God was offering mercy through His Son's atoning work.

It is noteworthy that when the blessed Lord introduced Himself by His personal name and declared His official title in connection with Israel and His special title in connection with the church, the Spirit and the bride alike are aroused to send up the invitation shout "Come." We read, "I Jesus have sent mine angel to testify unto you these things in the churches. I am the root and the offspring of David" (16). He is the *root* of David because David sprang from Him—David's Creator and Lord, who called him to guide His people Israel. And He is the *offspring* of David, for as man He was born from a daughter of David. And He is "the bright and morning star."

Immediately the Spirit and the bride respond saying, "Come." It is an invitation to Him to return to shine forth and gather His own to Himself. And all that hear are urged to join in this cry, "Come." To all those who do not yet know Him, the gospel invitation goes forth for the last time in view of His near return: "Let him that is athirst come. And whosoever will, let him take the water of life freely" (17).

In verses 18-19 in unmistakable solemnity, the glorified Lord Himself testified to every man that hears the words of the prophecy of this book.

> If any man shall add unto these things, God shall add unto him the plagues that are written in this book: And if any man shall take away from the words of the book of this prophecy, God shall take away his part out of the book of life, and out of the holy city, and from the things which are written in this book.

Oh, how unspeakably awful must be the fate of those who reject this testimony and reject its message. Better far, never to have been born than thus to refuse the Word of the living God.

Surely every believing heart can join with the apostle in the prayer, "Even so, come, Lord Jesus." But while we wait for His return, we would still seek to make known the message of His grace to a guilty world.

And so, with the apostolic benediction, this book and the entire canon of Scripture come to a close: "The grace of our Lord Jesus Christ be with you all. Amen."

AUTHOR BIOGRAPHY

HENRY ALLAN IRONSIDE, one of this century's greatest preachers, was born in Toronto, Canada, on October 14, 1876. He lived his life by faith; his needs at crucial moments were met in the most remarkable ways.

Though his classes stopped with grammar school, his fondness for reading and an incredibly retentive memory put learning to use. His scholarship was well recognized in academic circles with Wheaton College awarding an honorary Litt.D. in 1930 and Bob Jones University an honorary D.D. in 1942. Dr. Ironside was also appointed to the boards of numerous Bible institutes, seminaries, and Christian organizations.

"HAI" lived to preach and he did so widely throughout the United States and abroad. E. Schuyler English, in his biography of Ironside, revealed that during 1948, the year HAI was 72, and in spite of failing eyesight, he "gave 569 addresses, besides participating in many other ways." In his eighteen years at Chicago's Moody Memorial Church, his only pastorate, every Sunday but two had at least one profession of faith in Christ.

H. A. Ironside went to be with the Lord on January 15, 1951. Throughout his ministry, he authored expositions on 51 books of the Bible and through the great clarity of his messages led hundreds of thousands, worldwide, to a knowledge of God's Word. His words are as fresh and meaningful today as when first preached.

The official biography of Dr. Ironside, *H. A. Ironside: Ordained of the Lord*, is available from the publisher.

THE WRITTEN MINISTRY OF
H. A. IRONSIDE

Expositions

Joshua	Acts
Ezra	Romans
Nehemiah	1 & 2 Corinthians
Esther	Galatians
Psalms (1-41 only)	Ephesians
Proverbs	Philippians
Song of Solomon	Colossians
Isaiah	1 & 2 Thessalonians
Jeremiah	1 & 2 Timothy
Lamentations	Titus
Ezekiel	Philemon
Daniel	Hebrews
The Minor Prophets	James
Matthew	1 & 2 Peter
Mark	1,2, & 3 John
Luke	Jude
John	Revelation

Doctrinal Works

Baptism	Letters to a Roman Catholic
Death and Afterward	Priest
Eternal Security of the Believer	The Levitical Offerings
Holiness: The False and	Not Wrath But Rapture
the True	Wrongly Dividing the Word
The Holy Trinity	of Truth

Historical Works

The Four Hundred Silent Years
A Historical Sketch of the Brethren Movement

Other works by the author are brought back into print from time to time. All of this material is available from your local Christian bookstore or from the publisher.

LOIZEAUX

A Heritage of Ministry . . .

Paul and Timothy Loizeaux began their printing and publishing activities in the farming community of Vinton, Iowa, in 1876. Their tools were rudimentary: a hand press, several fonts of loose type, ink, and a small supply of paper. There was certainly no dream of a thriving commercial enterprise. It was merely the means of supplying the literature needs for their own ministries, with the hope that the Lord would grant a wider circulation. It wasn't a business; it was a ministry.

Our Foundation Is the Word of God

We stand without embarrassment on the great fundamentals of the faith: the inspiration and authority of Scripture, the deity and spotless humanity of our Lord Jesus Christ, His atoning sacrifice and resurrection, the indwelling of the Holy Spirit, the unity of the church, the second coming of the Lord, and the eternal destinies of the saved and lost.

Our Mission Is to Help People Understand God's Word

We are not in the entertainment business. We only publish books and computer software we believe will be of genuine help to God's people, both through the faithful exposition of Scripture and practical application of its principles to contemporary need.

Faithfulness to the Word and consistency in what we publish have been hallmarks of Loizeaux through four generations. And that means when you see the name Loizeaux on the outside, you can trust what is on the inside. That is our promise to the Lord…and to you.

If Paul and Timothy were to visit us today they would still recognize the work they began in 1876. Because some very important things haven't changed at all…this is still a ministry.